101 BIBLE CROSSWORDS

VOLUME 2

Puzzles Created by
Evelyn M. Boyington
Mary Ann Sherman
David K. Shortess
Sarah Lagerquist Simmons
Marijane G. Troyer
Tonya Vilhauer

BARBOUR
PUBLISHING

ISBN 1-59310-884-2

Crosswords were made using licensed Crossword Weaver software (www.crosswordweaver.com).

Published by Barbour Publishing, Inc., P.O. Box 719, Uhrichsville, Ohio 44683
www.barbourbooks.com

Our mission is to publish and distribute inspirational products offering exceptional value and biblical encouragement to the masses.

Member of the
Evangelical Christian
Publishers Association

Printed in the United States of America.

5 4 3 2

In memory of
Evelyn Boyington

1

ACROSS

1 "_____ them in pieces, as for the pot" (Micah 3:3)
5 "The words of _____, the son of Jakeh" (Proverbs 30:1)
9 "Of _____ the family of Arelites" (Numbers 26:17)
10 What Miriam was, once
12 The Lord God "_____ upon the high places of the earth" (Amos 4:13 NKJV)
13 Tuft of corn silk
15 Hebrew month
16 Once Barbra's costar
18 Good king of Judah
19 "And _____ lifted up his eyes, and beheld all the plain" (Genesis 13:10)
20 "Out of the half tribe of Manasseh; _____ with her suburbs" (1 Chronicles 6:70)
21 "But Moses _____ from the face of Pharaoh" (Exodus 2:15)
22 Prepare to pray
24 Where Phenice was (Acts 27:12)
25 Mosaic _____
26 Digit
27 Make smooth
31 Make payment for
35 Relax
36 Camino _____
38 "The _____ cannot leave his father" (Genesis 44:22)
39 "A bishop then must be. . ._____ to teach" (1 Timothy 3:2)
40 "The Lord himself shall give you a _____" (Isaiah 7:14)
41 Real or recorded
42 "Neither repented of their. . ._____" (Revelation 9:21)
44 _____ image
46 Eagle's nest
47 "A rough valley, which is neither _____ nor sown" (Deuteronomy 21:4)
48 Before noon, briefly
49 Author Harper and family

DOWN

1 Bring into being
2 "_____, O LORD when I cry" (Psalm 27:7)
3 "Thy counsels of _____ are faithfulness and truth" (Isaiah 25:1)
4 "The name of the first is _____. . . where there is gold" (Genesis 2:11)
5 What Abram built at Shechem
6 Equipment
7 FedEx competitor
8 Garage event, really
9 Caleb's son (1 Chronicles 2:18)
11 Video game button
12 "Should a man full of _____ be justified" (Job 11:2)
14 "Ye _____ men with burdens grievous" (Luke 11:46)
17 NY player
20 "_____! for that day is great" (Jeremiah 30:7)
21 "_____ not thyself because of evil men" (Proverbs 24:19)
23 Or _____ (part of a threat)
24 "One of the seraphims. . .having a live _____ in his hand" (Isaiah 6:6)
27 Turf fuel
28 Binea's son (1 Chronicles 8:37)
29 "I _____ all thy precepts" (Psalm 119:128)
30 "I cannot dig; to _____ I am ashamed" (Luke 16:3)
32 Biblical mount
33 "Ye shall be _____ the Priests of the LORD" (Isaiah 61:6)
34 "The land of Nod, on the east of _____"(Genesis 4:16)
36 "The glory of the LORD is _____ upon thee" (Isaiah 60:1)
37 _____ Gabriel
40 "Grievous words _____ up anger" (Proverbs 15:1)
41 "The spirit _____ him and he fell" (Mark 9:20)
43 To and _____
45 Feminine name

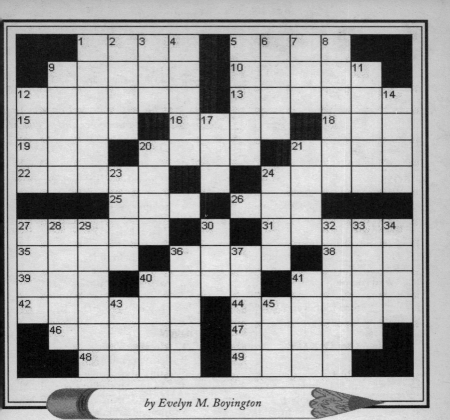

by Evelyn M. Boyington

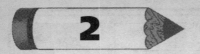

2

A Joyful Scriptural Repetitio

This is the day the LORD has mad
let us rejoice and be glad in

PSALM 118:24 N

ACROSS

1 Parts of minutes (abbr.)
5 "Then _____ you, father, send Lazarus" (Luke 16:27 NIV) (2 words)
9 List parts
14 Molecular constituent
15 "Did _____ serve with thee for Rachel?" (Genesis 29:25) (2 words)
16 Word commonly found in the Psalms
17 _____ time (not ever) (2 words)
18 Kind of tradition
19 Old saw
20 Beginning of **QUOTE** (Philippians 4:4 NIV)
22 Flow's partner
24 Word with wife or way
25 Ft. Worth school (abbr.)
26 "As _____ the east is from the west" (Psalm 103:12) (2 words)
28 **QUOTE**, part 2 (4 words)
35 Rocky hill
36 Gaddi's father (Numbers 13:11)
37 Old copier, briefly
38 "No man taketh it from me, but _____ it down of myself" (John 10:18) (2 words)
40 "M*A*S*H" persona
43 Corn or oat
44 Savants
46 Seth's sire
48 Sib
49 **QUOTE**, part 3 (5 words)
53 Steals a glimpse
54 Elizabeth II's title, for short
55 Exclamation of success
58 Carpet surface
59 End of **QUOTE**
63 "And all men _____ in their hearts of John" (Luke 3:15)
65 German song

67 "Thou art all fair, my love; there is no _____ in thee" (Song of Solomon 4:7)
68 "The labour of the _____ shall fai (Habakkuk 3:17)
69 Fancy pitcher
70 Nicholas, for one
71 More reasonable
72 Kind of fountain
73 "With sore boils from the _____ his foot" (Job 2:7)

DOWN

1 Moselle feeder
2 Sermon ending
3 And or but, briefly
4 "And Jacob said to Rebekah. . .I am a _____ man" (Genesis 27:11)
5 Immunization material
6 Make numb
7 Zeta follower
8 "Is there no balm in _____" (Jeremiah 8:22)
9 "There _____ in Gilead" (Old spiritual hymn) (3 words)
10 Hall of Famer Williams
11 "The children of _____" (Ezra 2:7
12 "_____ from the east came" (Matthew 2:1 NIV)
13 "The love of God is _____ abroad in our hearts" (Romans 5:5)
21 Finishes a cake
23 Swimsuit top
26 Robinson's Man and Detective Joe
27 "The man of God said, Where fell it?. . .and the iron did _____" (2 Kings 6:6)
28 "_____; be not afraid" (John 6:20 (3 words)
29 "Against such there is _____" (Galatians 5:23) (2 words)

by David K. Shortess

30 _____-comedy
31 Sweet ending?
32 Shapeless pond dweller (var.)
33 Beginning of A.D. (2 words)
34 Athenian legislator
39 Bark
41 Despot Amin
42 Bishop's seat
45 Slim
47 Ma Kettle portrayer, to her friends
50 "Hurt not the earth, neither the
_____" (Revelation 7:3)
51 "A word fitly spoken is like _____
of gold" (Proverbs 25:11)
52 Specters
55 Old Testament minor prophet
56 Island dance
57 A _____ apple (2 words)
59 "A bruised _____ shall he not
break" (Isaiah 42:3)

60 _____ facto
61 "Then flew one of the seraphims. . .a
live _____ in his hand" (Isaiah 6:6)
62 To be, in Paris
64 Actress Arden
66 _____ Jima

3

ACROSS

1 Carnival employees
6 Botch
10 Village in the lowlands of Judah (Joshua 15:34)
11 Jacob's twin
13 Toy for most ages
14 Impart
15 Part of polite request
18 "He _____ his countenance steadfastly" (2 Kings 8:11)
20 Gain
22 Peleg's father (Genesis 10:25)
24 Benjamin's son (Genesis 46:21)
25 Transmit
26 _____ bene
27 View
28 "_____ slayeth the silly one" (Job 5:2)
29 Nuisance
31 "Light is _____ for the righteous" (Psalm 97:11)
33 Jonah was in the _____ belly (Jonah 2:1)
35 David's captain (1 Chronicles 11:42)
38 Haman's son (Esther 9:7)
40 "In the _____ he built castles and towers" (2 Chronicles 27:4)
41 "I will make my covenant between me and _____" (Genesis 17:2)
42 "Over Edom will I cast out my _____" (Psalm 60:8)
43 Word to dog
44 B & B, for one
46 Spin
47 Strange
48 City where multitudes of Gog are to be buried (Ezekiel 39:16)
52 Old Testament prophet (abbr.)
53 Meshullam's father (Nehemiah 3:6)
55 Ethiopian province (abbr.)
56 "In _____ was there a voice heard" (Matthew 2:18)
57 Elkanah's wife (1 Samuel 1)
58 "I am the rose of _____" (Song of Solomon 2:1)

DOWN

1 Archers
2 "He hath the _____ of David" (Revelation 3:7)
3 Seth's son (Genesis 5:6)
4 Comedienne Martha
5 "And thy rod, wherewith thou _____ the river" (Exodus 17:5)
6 "The Cretians are. . .evil beasts, slo_____" (Titus 1:12)
7 "As he saith also in _____ I will call them" (Romans 9:25)
8 "By faith he sojourned in the _____ of promise" (Hebrews 11:9)
9 Shem's son (1 Chronicles 1:17)
12 Gusty
16 "Having _____ in his flesh the enmity" (Ephesians 2:15)
17 Also
19 "In _____ beginning God" (Genesis 1:1)
20 Cyst
21 "Boasters, _____ of evil things" (Romans 1:30)
23 Italian painter of late 1400s
25 "When thou _____ him out" (Deuteronomy 15:13)
30 Calculated guess (abbr.)
32 "The LORD is a man of _____" (Exodus 15:3)
33 "And sounded, and found it twenty _____" (Acts 27:28)
34 Rate
36 Jonathan's brother (1 Samuel 14:49)
37 Joseph's wife (Genesis 41:45)
39 Elkanah's son (1 Chronicles 6:25)
40 "Send unto Babylon _____, that shall fan her" (Jeremiah 51:2)
45 Land where Cain dwelt (Genesis 4:16)
48 Wading bird (arch.)
49 "Were forbidden of the Holy Ghost to preach the word in _____" (Acts 16:6)
50 Father of Saul's concubine (2 Samuel 3:7)

by Sarah Lagerquist Simmons

51 City formerly known as Hamath
53 Big ___
54 Laughing sound

4

ACROSS

1 Prostitute who hid spies (Joshua 2)
5 Animal David killed (1 Samuel 17:35–37)
8 "_____ ye therefore, and teach all nations" (Matthew 28:19)
11 Greek letter
13 He penned many Psalms
15 D.C. quadrant
16 Raw mineral
17 Horse's command (var.)
18 He wrestled with God (Genesis 32:24)
21 "Incline thine ear unto _____" (Psalm 102:2)
22 Baking pit
24 Sooner state (abbr.)
25 Mighty man of David (1 Kings 1:8)
27 Reed instrument
29 His face shone after meeting God (Exodus 34:29)
30 His weapon was a jawbone (Judges 15:16)
32 "And it came to pass _____ midnight" (Ruth 3:8)
33 "These are unclean for you: the weasel, the _____" (Leviticus 11:29 NIV)
34 "Here comes. . .a chariot with a _____ of horses" (Isaiah 21:9 NIV)
36 "There was not a man left in _____ or Beth-el" (Joshua 8:17)
37 Blood factor
38 Death notice (abbr.)
39 "Whose shoes I _____ not worthy to bear" (Matthew 3:11)
40 "_____ anger was kindled against Balaam" (Numbers 24:10)
43 "Let _____ build up the wall of Jerusalem" (Nehemiah 2:17)
46 Evil women
49 "They bring thee a _____ heifer without spot" (Numbers 19:2)
51 "_____ all that is in thine heart" (1 Samuel 14:7)
52 NE Canadian province (abbr.)
53 "The LORD _____ with favor on Abel" (Genesis 4:4 NIV)
54 Popular
55 "Shall play on the hole of the _____ (Isaiah 11:8)
57 Printer's measure
59 Governmental county subdivision (abbr.)
60 Encore (Fr.)
62 Great _____, biblically speaking
63 "The portion of their _____" (Psalm 11:6)
65 Discretion
66 Reference info (abbr.)
67 "Give me children, or _____ I die" (Genesis 30:1)
70 "_____ off the gold rings" (Exodus 32:2 NASB)
72 Oriental tea (var.)
73 He was buried near Hebron (Genesis 25:7–10)
74 Midwest state (abbr.)

DOWN

2 "Abimelech took an _____ in his hand" (Judges 9:48)
3 Daddy (Aramaic)
4 Exist
5 Short retort
6 Year of our Lord (abbr.)
7 Sin is like a filthy _____ (Isaiah 64:6)
8 He asked God for a sign (Judges 6:36–38)
9 Curious
10 Noah's son (Genesis 9:18)

by Marijane G. Troyer

12 "King Rehoboam _____ counsel with the old men" (2 Chronicles 10:6)
14 Vigor
15 Issachar's son (Genesis 46:13)
18 "He executed the _____ of the LORD" (Deuteronomy 33:21)
19 "For which of you. . .counteth the _____" (Luke 14:28)
20 "On the two stones the way a _____ cutter engraves a seal" (Exodus 28:11 NIV)
23 Lot's son (Genesis 19:36–37)
25 "Take me. . .a _____ of three years old" (Genesis 15:9)
26 His name means "laughter"
28 "Of the oaks of Bashan have they made thine _____" (Ezekiel 27:6)
30 Prophet who challenged Saul
31 "Cakes. . .and wafers unleavened anointed with _____" (Exodus 29:2)

35 Apiece (abbr.)
41 Baby goat (Isaiah 11:6)
42 She favored Jacob (var.)
44 Narrow opening
45 Esau and Nimrod
46 Brother of Benjamin
47 Atomic number 30 (abbr.)
48 Small portion (John 13:26)
49 First name in country music
50 Royal decree
51 German article
56 Dad, in other words
58 Greek letter
61 What Jacob made Esau (NIV)
64 By means of
65 Hot or cold beverage
68 Musical scale note
69 Quieting sound
71 American tree sloth

5

ACROSS
1 Shammai's brother (1 Chronicles 2:28)
5 Feminine nickname
9 Lawyers' livelihood
14 Addition column
15 Solomon's grandson (Matthew 1:7)
16 Naomi's daughter-in-law
17 "Talmai, the children of _____" (Joshua 15:14)
18 Window part
19 Lift up
20 Good (colloq.)
21 City beside Adam (Joshua 3:16)
23 Perfect score, to some
24 "And _____, which were dukes" (Joshua 13:21)
25 Obtain
26 Luxury car, for short
29 "Whose _____ was the sea" (Nahum 3:8)
32 Exclamation
35 Gad's son (Genesis 46:16)
37 Ripen
38 Duke of Edom (Genesis 36:43)
39 Feminine name
40 House of _____, which reported contentions (1 Corinthians 1:11)
42 "And _____ shall offer gifts" (Psalm 72:10)
43 Sugary finishes?
44 Dine
45 Ezra's son (1 Chronicles 4:17)
46 Resting place
47 Also known as Dorcas (Acts 9:36)
50 Gershwin
51 Owns
52 Spats
53 Pet
56 _____ Hill, in Athens
57 Be pushy
60 Not these
61 Marshes
62 San _____, CA
63 Jahdai's son (1 Chronicles 2:47)
64 In the past
65 "The curse upon Mount _____" (Deuteronomy 11:29)
66 Ashur's wife (1 Chronicles 4:5)
67 Busy ones
68 Musical sign

DOWN
1 "Now _____ was over all the host of Israel" (2 Samuel 20:23)
2 "And there was one _____, a prophetess" (Luke 2:36)
3 _____ Sea
4 Question
5 Sweet melon
6 Eliab's son (Numbers 16:1)
7 Mosaic member?
8 Stop
9 Brassy one?
10 Jether's son (1 Chronicles 7:38)
11 Barbecue bar
12 Comfort
13 "Samuel took a stone and set it between Mizpeh and _____" (1 Samuel 7:12)
21 Jeduthun's son (1 Chronicles 25:3)
22 Concur
26 Esau's brother
27 Jesus ____ from the tomb
28 "Whether he have _____ a son" (Exodus 21:31)
30 Raphu's son (Numbers 13:9)
31 Earlier than the present time
32 Gad's son (Genesis 46:16)
33 "Placed them in Halah and in _____ (2 Kings 17:6)
34 "Look from the top of _____" (Song of Solomon 4:8)
36 "_____ Boot" (honored German film)
38 "A rose _____ rose" (2 words)
40 Discontinue
41 Minor prophet (abbr.)
45 _____ of life
47 "Spreadeth abroad her wings, _____ them" (Deuteronomy 32:11

by Tonya Vilhauer

48 Daze
49 Belmont beauties
51 Gomer's husband
53 First Christian martyr (abbr., var.)
54 Biblical pronoun
55 Turn over
56 "_____; God hath numbered thy
   kingdom, and finished it"
   (Daniel 5:26)
57 Dressing gown
58 "Nevertheless _____ heart was
   perfect" (1 Kings 15:14)
59 Liquefy
61 Watch pocket
62 Major prophet (abbr.)

6

ACROSS

1 "If thou canst _____, all things are possible" (Mark 9:23)
7 "He took the seven loaves, and _____ thanks" (Mark 8:6)
8 Despondent
10 Donned
12 Low dam
14 "Members should have the same _____ one for another" (1 Corinthians 12:25)
15 Greek letter
17 "His raiment [was] white as _____" (Matthew 28:3)
19 Number of sons of Sarah
20 "_____ the son of Meshullam" (1 Chronicles 9:7)
22 Father of Hophni and Phinehas
23 Part of the Bible (abbr.)
24 "The _____ is past, the summer is ended" (Jeremiah 8:20)
26 Conjunction (Fr.)
27 Minister (abbr.)
28 Age
29 Judah's firstborn (Genesis 38:6)
31 Heal
34 Preposition (Sp.)
35 Aegean or Adriatic
37 Parable of the _____ (also known as Sower)
38 Affirmative
39 "She became a pillar of _____" (Genesis 19:26)
41 Where Cain dwelt (Genesis 4:16)
42 "Rulers of fifties, and rulers of _____" (Exodus 18:21)
43 "I will _____ bread from heaven for you" (Exodus 16:4)
45 Pad décor?
46 Understands
48 Ready cash
49 "_____ the word with joy" (Luke 8:13)

DOWN

1 "And all _____ him witness" (Luke 4:22)
2 "The serpent beguiled _____" (2 Corinthians 11:3)
3 Article (Fr.)
4 Redactor (abbr.)
5 "_____, and pay unto the LORD your God" (Psalm 76:11)
6 Farm denizens
7 Tipper _____
9 "Doth he not leave the ninety and _____, and goeth" (Matthew 18:12)
10 "The LORD is my shepherd, I shall not _____" (Psalm 23:1)
11 "Work out your own _____ with fear and trembling" (Philippians 2:12)
13 Rhett, to Clark
14 "Whosoever shall _____ that Jesus is the Son of God" (1 John 4:15)
15 Pitch
16 Little (suffix)
18 "Do not bear false _____" (Luke 18:20)
20 What Jesus does
21 Consumers
24 "Every woman shall borrow of _____ neighbor" (Exodus 3:22)
25 Kind of hold
30 "Wilt thou _____ it up in three days" (John 2:20)
32 "The _____ of man is Lord" (Matthew 12:8)
33 _____ gold
34 "Thou shalt _____ me thrice" (Matthew 26:34)
36 Exclamation of regret
38 Cry out
40 Row
42 Mosaic piece
44 Born (Fr.)
45 Fifty-four, to Livy
47 Where Furman U. is (abbr.)
48 Note on musical scale

by Evelyn M. Boyington

Celestial Signs of the End Times

*[In] those days shall the sun be darkened,
and the moon shall not give her light,
and the stars shall fall from heaven.*

MATTHEW 24:29

ACROSS

1 "And God _____ every thing that he had made" (Genesis 1:31)
4 Jonah follower
9 "The word is _____ thee, even in thy mouth" (Romans 10:8)
13 Asian nursemaid
15 Greek market
16 Referring to (2 words)
17 "As the _____ among thorns" (Song of Solomon 2:2)
18 Cold cream maker
19 Ivan or Peter
20 "God _____ his work which he had made" (Genesis 2:2)
22 "Go and walk through the land, and _____ it" (Joshua 18:8)
24 **CELESTIAL SIGN** (Joel 2:31) (3 words)
27 "Am I _____, or a whale" (Job 7:12) (2 words)
28 University of Oregon locale
31 Little (suffix)
34 Upbeat
36 "I _____ to those whose sin does not lead to death" (1 John 5:16 NIV)
37 **CELESTIAL SIGN** (Amos 8:9) (5 words)
41 Middle Eastern chieftain (var.)
42 Shop with ready-to-serve foods
43 They give TLC
44 Noted lean and fat noneaters
46 Iris locale
48 **CELESTIAL SIGN** (Revelation 8:10) (3 words)
54 Mascara applier
56 Set of steps over a fence
57 Cross or neuron
58 Legume
61 Dutch cheese
62 "_____ are for kids"
63 Swelling from excess fluids
64 San _____, city in northern Italy
65 Unit of time (abbr.)
66 Four-door model, usually
67 "Water _____ round about the altar" (1 Kings 18:35)

DOWN

1 "And Melchizedek king of _____ brought forth" (Genesis 14:18)
2 Kind of organic acid
3 Ralph _____ Emerson
4 "As the men started on their way to _____ out the land" (Joshua 18:8 NIV)
5 "Because _____ to my Father" (John 16:10) (2 words)
6 Tenant-owned apartment, for short
7 Arabic unit of dry measure
8 Bother
9 Four-fifths of the atmosphere
10 "It's cold out here. . . . Why don't you go _____ a while?" (2 words)
11 Kind of bag
12 "And he said, Behold, I am _____, Lord" (Acts 9:10)
14 Serengeti laugher
21 Game player
23 Royal attendants
25 "And they _____ no candle, neither light of the sun" (Revelation 22:5)
26 Source of poi
29 It's a gas
30 European sea eagles
31 "To maintain good works for necessary _____" (Titus 3:14)
32 "A little leaven leaveneth the whole _____" (Galatians 5:9)
33 Peppy
35 Not away from (abbr.)
38 Transmission

by David K. Shortess

39 Neither positive nor negative (abbr.)
40 Thomas _____ Edison
45 Apple and soy
47 "_____ the Fall," Miller play
49 Hebrew letter (var.)
50 "And came and _____ them into the pot of pottage" (2 Kings 4:39)
51 Duck known for its down
52 Alpaca's cousin
53 Detroit dud
54 Medics (abbr.)
55 Time long ago (poet.)
59 Grandma (Ger.)
60 Sure's rival

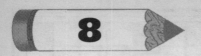

8

ACROSS

1 Barbara _____ Geddes
4 Not right
6 Medicinal plant
11 "Thee have I _____ righteous" (Genesis 7:1)
13 Continent
15 Omega, for short
17 Scourge
19 "King David did _____ unto the LORD" (2 Samuel 8:11)
21 Louis XV, to Louis Pasteur
22 Cut down
23 Language of early Bibles
24 Samuel's firstborn son (1 Chronicles 6:28)
27 Resurrection Sunday
28 "Fulfilling the _____ of the flesh" (Ephesians 2:3)
29 Haunt to some
31 Two lengths of a pool
32 Droll
35 City in Simeon's inheritance (Joshua 19:8)
38 Span
41 "He that _____ his life for my sake" (Matthew 10:39)
43 "Their conscience _____ with a hot iron" (1 Timothy 4:2)
44 German article
45 "Whose wife shall _____ be of them" (Mark 12:23)
46 Stories
47 _____ is more
49 Mizraim's son (Genesis 10:13)
51 "They opened their mouth wide against me, and said _____" (Psalm 35:21)
53 Absorbed with, as a topic
54 Youth
55 Give a nickname
56 "Of the tribe of _____ were sealed twelve thousand" (Revelation 7:6)
57 City of Zebulon (Joshua 19:15)
59 To and _____
60 Tebah's mother (Genesis 22:24)
61 Bean curd
62 Query
63 "My speech shall distill as the _____" (Deuteronomy 32:2)
64 Fib

DOWN

2 "Was spoken by _____ the prophet" (Matthew 4:14)
3 Limb
4 "Hear, O Israel: The LORD our God is _____ LORD" (Deuteronomy 6:4)
5 Dim
6 Abet's assistant
7 Pins
8 "In a portion of the lawgiver, was he _____" (Deuteronomy 33:21)
9 All
10 When crocuses may come (abbr.)
12 "So I went, and hid it by _____ as the LORD commanded" (Jeremiah 13:5)
14 _____ system
16 Lion's _____
18 "Thy law do I _____" (Psalm 119:163)
20 Tiger, for one
22 "Yielding fruit after _____ kind" (Genesis 1:11)
25 Missionary with Paul
26 "The land of Zebulon, and the land of _____" (Matthew 4:15)
28 Cote _____ (Gold Coast)
30 "Lend him sufficient for his _____" (Deuteronomy 15:8)
32 Stubborn
33 "The angel of God spoke unto me in a _____" (Genesis 31:11)
34 Sun _____
36 "Being _____ from the commonwealth of Israel, and strangers" (Ephesians 2:12)
37 Godzilla, and others
39 "And he was afraid, and said, How _____ is this place" (Genesis 28:17)

by Sarah Lagerquist Simmons

40 Talmai king of _____
   (2 Samuel 3:3)
42 Bavai's father (Nehemiah 3:18)
44 "What then? Art thou _____"
   (John 1:21)
48 Delilah lived in this valley
   (Judges 16:4)
50 Elon's daughter (Genesis 36:2)
52 "Give a dog _____" (2 words)
58 Why's cohort

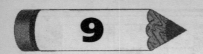

9

ACROSS

1 Abraham's hometown
3 Ground bud
7 "There shall come a _____ out of Jacob" (Numbers 24:17)
11 Solidified lava (abbr.)
13 Death investigator
15 "If I _____ the locusts to devour the land" (2 Chronicles 7:13)
17 Concerning
18 God (Lat.)
19 Given to Eve
20 School organization (abbr.)
21 Musical abbreviation (abbr.)
22 "O, _____ . . .thou that killest the prophets" (Matthew 23:37)
25 Aquatic mammal
27 "Stand in the _____ before me" (Ezekiel 22:30)
28 "His hands are as gold _____ set with the beryl" (Song of Solomon 5:14)
32 Tear's partner
33 "Israel is a scattered _____" (Jeremiah 50:17)
35 "Render therefore to all their _____" (Romans 13:7)
36 "My moisture is turned into the _____ of summer" (Psalm 32:4)
37 Tribal people settling in Joppa (pl.)
39 Gershwin
40 Magician who opposed Moses (2 Timothy 3:8)
44 Shuthelah's son's family member (Numbers 26:36)
48 Place of Napoleon's exile
49 "Then Joseph commanded to fill their _____ with corn" (Genesis 42:25)
50 Garden flower
51 "And if ye shall say, What shall _____ the seventh year?" (Leviticus 25:20) (2 words)
53 "Be thou diligent to know the _____ of thy flocks" (Proverbs 27:23)
54 Soldier's award (abbr.)

55 "A wicked man is _____" (Proverbs 13:5)
57 _____ Elyon, meaning "God Most High"
59 Celebrity-filled magazine
60 H.S. requirement, usually
61 "When saw we thee an hungred, or _____" (Matthew 25:44)
64 "Whose shoe's latchet I am not worthy to _____" (John 1:27)
68 Electrical unit (abbr.)
69 Donkey (Sp.)
70 Corner

DOWN

1 _____-Berkeley (abbr.)
2 "Just as he was speaking, the _____ crowed" (Luke 22:60 NIV)
3 Not yet in stock (abbr.)
4 "_____ whose wings thou art come to trust" (Ruth 2:12)
5 Unsavory look
6 "For we _____ nothing into this world" (1 Timothy 6:7)
7 "He shall cause the house to be _____ within round about" (Leviticus 14:41)
8 "They _____ not, neither do they spin" (Matthew 6:28)
9 Fossil resin
10 Old German money (abbr.)
11 "Go to the _____, thou sluggard" (Proverbs 6:6)
12 Ohio college town
14 Atomic number 104 (abbr.)
16 News service (abbr.)
21 Political columnist Maureen
22 New name for Gideon (Judges 6:32)
23 College fraternity (abbr.)
24 One of a nomadic tribe that sold Joseph
26 Path for Confucian followers
29 "Down to the grove of _____ trees" (Song of Solomon 6:11 NIV)
30 Equine command
31 Military draft organization (abbr.)

by Marijane G. Troyer

33 "Thy _____ shall be iron and brass" (Deuteronomy 33:25)
34 "_____ of clean and unclean animals" (Genesis 7:8 NIV)
38 Powerful D.C. lobby
40 _____ for Jesus (messianic group)
41 Descendant of Jonathan (1 Chronicles 8:36)
42 British military honor (abbr.)
43 Valley of _____ (1 Chronicles 18:12 NIV)
44 Barely survives (2 words)
45 Golden years' account (abbr.)
46 Is a faithful steward
47 Compass direction
52 Travel packages
53 Facial expression
56 General organization (abbr.)
58 Pituitary hormone (abbr.)
60 River to the Adriatic

61 "Seeing I _____ a great people" (Joshua 17:14)
62 Grant Wood's state (abbr.)
63 Via
65 Movie type (abbr.)
66 Seventh-century British language (abbr.)
67 _____ Cid

10

ACROSS

1 Babylonian god (Isaiah 46:1)
5 Old Testament book
9 Poke
12 By oneself
14 Secure
15 Canine command
16 Underground members?
17 "Shalt remain by the stone _____" (1 Samuel 20:19)
18 Israelite leader (Nehemiah 10:26)
19 Omega, for short
20 "The caravans of _____ look for water" (Job 6:19 NIV)
22 Accuse
23 Military branch
24 Compared to
26 Island near Paul's shipwreck (Acts 27:7)
28 Stopover during Hebrews' wandering (Deuteronomy 10:6)
31 "And Moses _____ all the words" (Exodus 24:4)
32 "Then shall the _____ be ashamed" (Micah 3:7)
33 Debtor's declaration (abbr.)
35 "They made upon the _____ of the robe pomegranates" (Exodus 39:24)
36 "Where the birds make their _____" (Psalm 104:17)
37 Micaiah's father (2 Chronicles 18:7)
38 "_____, though I walk through the valley" (Psalm 23:4)
39 One of the cliffs near Philistine outpost (1 Samuel 14:4)
40 Ner's son (1 Samuel 14:50)
41 "Thou. . .art come unto a people which thou _____" (Ruth 2:11)
43 Electrical unit
44 "According to all that her mother in law _____ her" (Ruth 3:6)
45 Double this for deficiency disease
46 "Jair died, and was buried in _____" (Judges 10:5)
49 Powder room (Sp.)
50 Kind of bear
53 Mideast gulf
54 Podiatric problem
56 Famous
58 Extremely
59 Jesse's father (Ruth 4:22)
60 Trap
61 In the style of (suffix)
62 Mistress
63 Instrument (suffix)

DOWN

1 "And his _____ shall be called Wonderful" (Isaiah 9:6)
2 North Carolina college
3 Fearless
4 Single
5 Adversary
6 "Jonathan; Peleth, and _____" (1 Chronicles 2:33)
7 "Wheat and _____ were not smitten" (Exodus 9:32)
8 "_____ power is given unto me" (Matthew 28:18)
9 Simon's father (John 1:42)
10 "_____, and Shema, and Moladah" (Joshua 15:26)
11 Nota _____
13 Property
15 "Is not _____ as Carchemish?" (Isaiah 10:9)
21 Adam's rib?
22 Hurdles
23 New Jersey _____ (pro team)
24 "Hast broken the _____ of the ungodly" (Psalm 3:7)
25 "Restore all that was _____" (2 Kings 8:6)
26 Brook
27 Citizenship Paul claimed
28 "The sin which doth so easily _____" (Hebrews 12:1)
29 Lotan's sister (Genesis 36:22)
30 Became a recluse, with "up"
31 How come
32 Feel in one's bones
34 Former Mideast initials

by Tonya Vilhauer

36 Lack
37 Name meaning "Hebrew"
39 What the ugly duckling became
40 "_____ rod that budded" (Hebrews 9:4)
42 "For a present horns of ivory and _____" (Ezekiel 27:15)
43 Swampy area
45 Toss about
46 Den
47 Summer coolers
48 Only
49 "It _____ worms, and stank" (Exodus 16:20)
50 The sun, for example
51 David, after Goliath
52 First home
54 N.T. book (abbr.)
55 O.T. minor prophet (var.)
57 Canadian province (abbr.)

11

ACROSS

1 Hebrew
3 Prince of Wales, for one
5 Where Noah's ark landed
10 Men
12 "And the winepress was trodden . . .even unto the horse _____" (Revelation 14:20)
14 Meadows
17 Shemida's son (1 Chronicles 7:19)
20 "Fruit of the righteous is a _____ of life" (Proverbs 11:30)
21 Greek letter
23 "Tell ye it in _____, that Moab is spoiled" (Jeremiah 48:20)
24 Else
25 "_____ the woman saw that the tree was good" (Genesis 3:6)
26 Poetic contraction
27 Proboscis
29 _____ on parle francais
30 First
32 _____-ed column
33 "Put a _____ on it"
34 "Should be no _____ in the body" (1 Corinthians 12:25)
37 Coach Parseghian
38 "Breathed _____ his nostrils" (Genesis 2:7)
40 Huge
42 Judah's daughter-in-law (Genesis 38:6)
44 "She had made an _____ in a grove" (2 Chronicles 15:16)
47 "The tongue of the wise useth knowledge _____" (Proverbs 15:2)
49 "He _____ Pharaoh's heart" (Exodus 7:13)
51 Facts
52 What "would smell as sweet" (2 words)
53 Writer Wiesel, and others
56 Man, for one
58 Medieval serf
59 Simeon's son (Genesis 46:10)
60 Cry's partner

61 Cook's measure (abbr.)
62 Old Testament book (abbr.)
63 Coffee, to some

DOWN

2 Does not improve
3 Jephthah fled to this land (Judges 11:3)
4 Jacques, to Jeanne
5 Any
6 Man who came with Zerubbabel (Ezra 2:2)
7 Korah's son (Exodus 6:24)
8 Educated, in a way
9 Carrier to Tokyo (abbr.)
11 "For the _____ of this service. . . supplieth the want of the saints" (2 Corinthians 9:12)
13 Amalek fought with Israel here (Exodus 17:8)
15 Peoples (prefix)
16 Dionysius the _____ (Acts 17:34)
18 "I bow my _____ unto the Father of our Lord Jesus Christ" (Ephesians 3:14)
19 King of Gezer (Joshua 10:33)
22 "Just a _____"
28 King Azariah built and restored this city to Judah (2 Kings 14:22)
31 "I have been much _____ from coming to you" (Romans 15:22)
35 Corp.'s relative
36 Minor prophet
39 O.T. book (abbr.)
41 _____ the Jairite (2 Samuel 20:26)
43 Site of Mars' Hill
44 City of Zebulon (Joshua 19:15)
45 Composer Yoko
46 Bandleader Brown
48 Force of nature?
50 "Nothing runs like a _____"
54 Advocate (Suffix)
55 Start of fall (abbr.)
57 "_____ took of the fruit thereof" (Genesis 3:6)

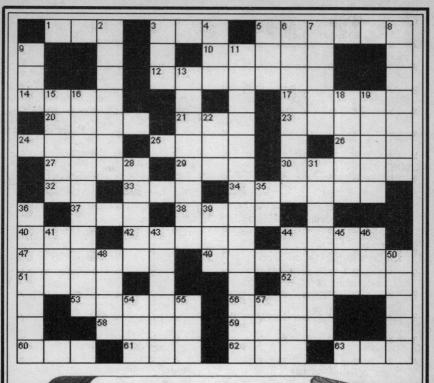

by Sarah Lagerquist Simmons

Egypt's Plagues

"Let my people go. . .or this time I will send the full force of my plagues against you.

EXODUS 9:13–14 NIV

ACROSS

1 Kilauea product
5 Greek mountain
9 "Now the Valley of Siddim was full _____ pits" (Genesis 14:10 NIV) (2 words)
14 Elliptical
15 Dudley Do-Right's girlfriend
16 "I speak as a _____ am more" (2 Corinthians 11:23) (2 words)
17 Three **PLAGUES** (Exodus 9:9, 8:21, 8:2) (3 words)
20 Have
21 Pre-Aztec Mexican tribe
22 Winglike structures
23 "Is any thing _____ hard for the LORD" (Genesis 18:14)
24 "Who will _____ to every man according to" (Romans 2:6)
26 Another **PLAGUE** (Exodus 7:17) (3 words)
32 Dancer Castle of old
33 Bells ringing
34 "For this is the _____ and the prophets" (Matthew 7:12)
37 "Then Paul stood in the midst of _____ hill" (Acts 17:22)
38 One hundredth of one liter (abbr.) (2 words)
39 Island east of Java
40 That has (suffix)
41 Nemesis
42 "And, lo, a great multitude, which no man _____ number" (Revelation 7:9)
43 Another **PLAGUE** (Exodus 12:29) (3 words)
45 Conversation (var.)
48 Born, in Bordeaux
49 1952 Winter Olympics site
50 "And did _____ showbread" (Mark 2:26) (2 words)

54 "Your lightning _____ up the world" (Psalm 77:18 NIV)
57 Three more **PLAGUES** (Exodus 10:13, 9:22, 8:17) (3 words)
60 Related on mother's side
61 Close to, in a game
62 "I watch, and _____ a sparrow alone upon the house top" (Psalm 102:7) (2 words)
63 "And gave the _____, and caused them to understand the reading" (Nehemiah 8:8)
64 Sicilian volcano
65 "_____ harm yourself! We are all here!" (Acts 16:28 NIV)

DOWN

1 Gray wolf
2 "We have four men which have _____ on them" (Acts 21:23) (2 words)
3 "Shall _____ words have an end" (Job 16:3)
4 "They are _____ gone aside" (Psalm 14:3)
5 "They went through the flood _____" (Psalm 66:6) (2 words)
6 "Go and _____ that thou hast" (Matthew 19:21)
7 Narrow opening
8 Away from the wind
9 "And the publican, standing afar _____" (Luke 18:13)
10 "Looking _____ hasting unto the coming of the day of God" (2 Peter 3:12) (2 words)
11 "To prostitution, _____ wine and new" (Hosea 4:11 NIV) (2 words)
12 Pond organisms
13 Stair part
18 Candy or toy

by David K. Shortess

19 "And the heavens shall be rolled together as a _____" (Isaiah 34:4)
23 Addition column
25 Greek dawn goddess
26 Hoarfrost
27 Persia, today
28 Like grass (Fr.)
29 "The watchman _____ the gate for him" (John 10:3 NIV)
30 "John Brown's Body" poet
31 On the _____
34 Praise
35 "If I give _____ possess to the poor" (1 Corinthians 13:3 NIV) (2 words)
36 "For _____ is the gate" (Matthew 7:13)
38 K-Mart competitor
39 "A _____ of him shall not be broken" (John 19:36)
41 Personal profile, for short

42 Angler's basket
43 Disparages
44 "And they put _____ purple robe" (John 19:2) (3 words)
45 Distributes, with *out*
46 "This _____ of them" (Mark 14:69) (2 words)
47 Alaska Highway, once
51 "_____ forgive our debtors" (Matthew 6:12) (2 words)
52 "And God saw _____ it was good" (Genesis 1:10)
53 Small mountain lake
54 VIP transporter
55 "_____ do all things through Christ" (Philippians 4:13) (2 words)
56 "We should not _____ the Lord" (1 Corinthians 10:9 NIV)
58 "Ye shall not _____ me" (Luke 13:35)
59 Boy

13

ACROSS

1 Influence
5 Put in a safe place
8 Shammai's brother (1 Chronicles 2:32)
12 Shakespearean traitor
13 Exist
14 General Bradley, to friends
15 "The _____ of my heart are enlarged" (Psalm 25:17)
17 Antitoxins
18 "_____ them about thy neck" (Proverbs 6:21)
19 "He _____ the doors of heaven" (Psalm 78:23)
21 "If thy _____ eye offend thee" (Matthew 5:29)
24 Hit with, as a fine
25 Crude metals
26 "Thy truth _____ unto the clouds" (Psalm 108:4)
30 Cooking utensil
31 "Draw you before the judgment _____" (James 2:6)
32 _____ Lanka
33 "Ye have us for an _____" (Philippians 3:17)
35 Has _____ (former great)
36 "They compassed me about like _____" (Psalm 118:12)
37 "Be ye not unequally _____ together with unbelievers" (2 Corinthians 6:14)
38 Reputation
41 Encountered
42 "Isaac blessed Jacob and _____" (Hebrews 11:20)
43 "Let _____ grow instead of wheat" (Job 31:40)
48 African despot
49 "Give _____, O my people, to my law" (Psalm 78:1)
50 Blood or finish
51 Combine
52 Salon request
53 First home

DOWN

1 Pose
2 Philistine activity
3 Time past
4 "Even the _____ shall faint and be weary" (Isaiah 40:30)
5 Burr's longtime costar
6 Wrath
7 Barren
8 "Israel loved _____ more than all his children" (Genesis 37:3)
9 "Let all the people say, _____" (Psalm 106:48)
10 Challenge
11 Canaanite king (Numbers 21:1)
16 Memory measure, to IBM
20 Cold weather boots
21 Lasso
22 "He hath. . .cut the bars of _____ in sunder" (Psalm 107:16)
23 Understands
24 "Thou art worthy to take the book and to open the _____" (Revelation 5:9)
26 Sought forgiveness
27 Where Isaac named a well (Genesis 26:20)
28 _____ of Life
29 Sight or quarters
31 Small merganser
34 "That ye may _____ in hope" (Romans 15:13)
35 "Every _____ shall be filled with wine" (Jeremiah 13:12)
37 Affirmative
38 Paper quantity
39 Short story by Saki
40 "I will fasten him as a _____ in a sure place" (Isaiah 22:23)
41 Fen
44 Secretariat's supper
45 Cover
46 Compass point
47 Elected official (abbr.)

by *Evelyn M. Boyington*

14

ACROSS

1 All (comb. form)
4 Elements
9 Legal eagles (abbr.)
12 "Adam was first formed, then _____" (1 Timothy 2:13)
13 Now (Sp.)
14 Eastern state university (abbr.)
15 Humble
16 Hailed
17 Jacob's son
18 "There was not a man to _____ the ground" (Genesis 2:5)
20 "The Lord shall hiss. . .for the _____ that is in the land of Assyria" (Isaiah 7:18)
21 Solomon, for one
22 Tinted
24 Librarian's mantra (pl.)
25 Oath
27 Greek letter
28 "Cornelius, a centurion of the band called the _____ band" (Acts 10:1)
29 Also known as Cephas
31 "Concerning the fiery _____" (1 Peter 4:12)
34 "All the world should be _____" (Luke 2:1)
36 "The words of Job are _____" (Job 31:40)
38 Millinery
39 Tiny
41 Head over heels
42 "By grace ye _____ saved" (Ephesians 2:5)
43 "I commend unto you _____ our sister" (Romans 16:1)
45 Eur. lang.
46 "They _____ in the dry places like a river" (Psalm 105:41)
47 Hilton, for one
48 Person or thing (suffix)
49 First _____
50 Arlene, Roald, and others
51 Sixties' organization (abbr.)

DOWN

1 Fur
2 Stay away from
3 Afresh
4 Handle clumsily
5 Ahaziah's father (1 Kings 22:49)
6 Fido's friend
7 "The _____ yielding fruit" (Genesis 1:12)
8 Blue
9 Jacob's offspring
10 Pulls along
11 _____ qua non
19 High priests, tribally
21 Radiant
23 Paid attention to, with on
24 Time _____
26 Combat
27 "He brought me up also out of an horrible _____" (Psalm 40:2)
29 _____ the Arbite (2 Samuel 23:35)
30 Prolong
32 Sayings
33 Myth
34 "Son of Abraham, which was the son of _____" (Luke 3:34)
35 "Day nor night _____ sleep" (Ecclesiastes 8:16)
37 "To quench all the fiery _____" (Ephesians 6:16)
39 Cowboy's command
40 Watch maker
43 Degree of difficulty? (abbr.)
44 Chicago rails

by Tonya Vilhauer

15

ACROSS
1 Yad _____, Jerusalem Holocaust memorial
4 Bane
9 A while back
11 "The _____ of the ox shall be quit" (Exodus 21:28)
13 "Salute _____ my kinsman" (Romans 16:11)
16 Solomon built this fortification (1 Kings 11:27)
17 Deli sub
18 "And _____ walked with God: and he was not" (Genesis 5:24)
20 Widow of _____ (Luke 7:11)
21 Old Testament prophet (abbr.)
22 "Treacherous _____ have dealt treacherously" (Isaiah 24:16)
24 Superlative suffix
26 "Eat, and _____ forever" (Genesis 3:22)
27 "Take, _____: this is my body" (Mark 14:22)
29 People destroyed by Esau's descendants (Deuteronomy 2:12, 22)
30 Samuel's mentor
33 "An _____ for every man" (Exodus 16:16)
35 Pad
36 "From the _____ of thy wood" (Deuteronomy 29:11)
37 Swaddle
38 "I will give unto thee the _____ of the kingdom" (Matthew 16:19)
39 Haggi's brother (Genesis 46:16)
41 Loot
42 O. T. book
45 "They _____ knowledge" (Proverbs 1:29)
48 Susi's son (Numbers 13:11)
49 Change or pail
50 Eleazar was _____ son (Exodus 6:25)
52 The _____ Spoonful, 70s group
55 Sturdy canine, for short
56 _____ paper
57 N. T. book (abbr.)
58 "The _____ that is called Patmos" (Revelation 1:9)
59 _____ Row

DOWN
2 Caress
3 Chief
4 Pride
5 New Testament book (abbr.)
6 Pigs
7 "Then shall there _____ and deliverance arise" (Esther 4:14)
8 Press
10 "There was not among the children of Israel a _____ person than he" (1 Samuel 9:2)
12 Belonging to Hophni's father
13 King of Judah (abbr.)
14 "_____ I saw Elba"
15 "I am _____ both to the Greeks and to the Barbarians" (Romans 1:14)
17 "He that _____ him out a sepulcher on high" (Isaiah 22:16)
19 "If now I _____ found favour in thy sight" (Genesis 18:3)
23 May be more
25 Chief priest (Ezra 8:24)
28 "Look now _____ heaven" (Genesis 15:5)
31 Short poem or song (arch.)
32 "That which groweth of _____ own accord" (Leviticus 25:5)
34 "_____ is broken in pieces; her idols are humiliated" (Jeremiah 50:2 NKJV)
37 "The _____ of heaven were opened" (Genesis 7:11)
40 Poacher's targets?
43 City of Judah (Joshua 15:32)
44 Hurry
45 Exclamation, to Henri
46 "He set my feet on ___" (Psalm 40:2 NIV) (2 words)

by Sarah Lagerquist Simmons

47 _____ Gate, in Jerusalem
51 Dauphin's dad (Fr.)
53 LVI divided by VIII
54 Third party (abbr.)

Paul's First Missionary Journey

"Set apart for me Barnabas and Saul. . . ."
So. . .they placed their hands on them and sent them off.

ACTS 13:2–3 NIV

ACROSS

1 Blue Grotto locale
6 Clinton's Attorney General
10 One-time Iranian head
14 Fatty acid
15 Teen follower?
16 Lacquered metalware
17 **CITY** visited by Paul (Acts 13:13)
18 Mrs. Nick Charles
19 MP's target
20 "For _____ a little while" (Psalm 37:10)
21 Corporal or Sergeant (abbr.)
23 Another **CITY** (Acts 13:51)
25 City in southern Turkey
27 "The _____ cannot leave his father" (Genesis 44:22)
28 Another **CITY** (Acts 13:6)
31 "And _____ of heaven shall fall" (Mark 13:25) (2 words)
36 Elevator man
37 Head, in France
39 Subject
40 D-Day craft
41 Another **CITY** (Acts 13:5)
43 "He is of _____; ask him" (John 9:23)
44 "And _____ they sufficed them not" (Judges 21:14) (2 words)
46 Alack's cohort
47 Elvis Presley's middle name
48 Deli meat
50 Another **CITY** (Acts 14:6)
52 Stimpy's pal
53 "What thou seest, write in _____" (Revelation 1:11) (2 words)
55 Another **CITY** (Acts 13:14)
59 "Be not wise in thine _____ eyes" (Proverbs 3:7)
60 "Ye shall not _____ of it" (Genesis 3:3)

63 "Which things the angels desire to _____ into" (1 Peter 1:12)
64 Learn, with of
66 Another **CITY** (Acts 14:6)
68 "That they may be one, even _____ are one" (John 17:22) (2 words)
69 "They have not known the Father _____" (John 16:3 NIV) (2 words)
70 Columnist Goodman
71 Benign cysts
72 "He went into the synagogue. . .and stood up for to _____" (Luke 4:16)
73 Cambodian currency (pl.)

DOWN

1 "This is the _____ of the letter that they sent unto him" (Ezra 4:11)
2 On the sheltered side
3 Bright-eyed and bushy-tailed
4 Semi, to some
5 "_____ all things through Christ which strengtheneth me" (Philippians 4:13) (3 words)
6 Talked a lot (2 words)
7 Kind of trip
8 Salathiel's father (Luke 3:27)
9 "As if a man had enquired at the _____ of God" (2 Samuel 16:23)
10 "To _____ minister in the name of the LORD" (Deuteronomy 18:5) (2 words)
11 "Consider _____ love thy precepts" (Psalm 119:159) (2 words)
12 Baseball's Moises or Felipe
13 At the _____
22 "Let him first _____ stone at her" (John 8:7) (2 words)
24 Drying ovens
25 Words of delight
26 Another **CITY** (Acts 14:25)
28 Coral reef builder

by David K. Shortess

29 "For the king had ___ a navy"
   (1 Kings 10:22) (2 words)
30 PA univ., familiarly, and frontier fort
32 Blood (prefix)
33 "He went up into a mountain
   _____ to pray" (Matthew 14:23)
34 _____ mortis
35 La Scala interlude
38 Craggy faced cowboy actor Jack
41 "Be not wroth very _____ LORD"
   (Isaiah 64:9) (2 words)
42 "Exalt him that _____, and abase
   him that is high" (Ezekiel 21:26)
   (2 words)
45 "If someone _____ you on one
   cheek" (Luke 6:29 NIV)
47 "Or if he _____ a fish, will he give"
   (Matthew 7:10)
49 "Which hope we have as an _____
   of the soul" (Hebrews 6:19)

51 Far off
54 Made numb
55 "Are _____ unto themselves"
   (Romans 2:14) (2 words)
56 Win by a _____
57 "Out of the _____ of Bethlehem"
   (John 7:42)
58 "Then said I, _____ am I; send me"
   (Isaiah 6:8)
60 Perry's creator
61 "Where is _____ thy brother"
   (Gen. 4:9)
62 "I will not destroy it for _____
   sake" (Genesis 18:32)
65 "Seeing I _____ stranger"
   (Ruth 2:10) (2 words)
67 Hophni's father (1 Samuel 4:4)

17

ACROSS

1 Iron (abbr.)
3 Father of human race
7 Outdoor theater or restaurant
12 Hannah's priest
14 Insistent
16 Midwestern state (abbr.)
17 "Bind this _____ of scarlet thread in the window" (Joshua 2:18)
19 "She let them down by a _____ through the window" (Joshua 2:15)
20 Presage
22 Jacob's devious uncle
24 Make bigger (abbr.)
25 Stiff
26 "The _____ death has no power over them" (Revelation 20:6 NIV)
28 Cell for biomedical research
30 Substitute for pitcher at bat (abbr.)
31 Presidential command when Congress is not in session (abbr.)
32 Sodium (abbr.)
33 Memo abbr.
35 Is there
37 "Became mighty _____. . .of old" (Genesis 6:4)
38 _____ Lewis (initials)
39 "She hath none _____ comfort her" (Lamentations 1:2)
40 Row
42 Prepare for publication
43 College degree (abbr.)
44 "When thou seest the _____. . . shouldest be driven to worship" (Deuteronomy 4:19)
45 One Stooge
46 _____ carte
47 Arm bone
49 "As a _____ is full of birds" (Jeremiah 5:27)
51 Financial officer (abbr.)
53 Composer Anderson
55 Author of Pentateuch
56 Plants new lawn
57 Hawaiian food

58 "_____ me, and deliver me from the hand of strange children" (Psalm 144:11)
59 Antiviral drug for autoimmune infections (abbr.)
61 "Vashti. . .hath not done wrong to the king _____" (Esther 1:16)
63 Teachers' org.
65 Positive
67 "___ tu, Brute"
68 "Falleth to the Chaldeans that _____ you" (Jeremiah 21:9)
71 Salt (Fr.)
72 "And _____ ox also shall they divide" (Exodus 21:35) (2 words)
73 "God made them _____ and female" (Mark 10:6)
74 Highest degree in ministry (abbr.)

DOWN

1 "Cain was very wroth, and his countenance _____" (Genesis 4:5)
2 "There appeared. . .Moses and _____ talking with him" (Matthew 17:3)
4 Lawyer for the state (abbr.)
5 Marketing piece
6 Ancient kingdom north of Greece
7 "Rescue. . .my _____ from the lions" (Psalm 35:17)
8 Circular (abbr.)
9 "_____ maketh no matter to me" (Galatians 2:6)
10 Where New Delhi is capital
11 "Have I _____ of mad men" (1 Samuel 21:15)
13 "My children are with me _____" (Luke 11:7) (2 words)
15 Day of the week (abbr.)
18 "Let _____ esteem other better than themselves" (Philippians 2:3)
20 Caskets
21 Eye
23 "Let _____ joyful voice come therein" (Job 3:7)

by Marijane G. Troyer

25 Amount of moisture in the air (abbr.)
27 "For a camel to go through a _____ eye" (Luke 18:25)
29 Widow who lost two sons in Moab
34 "And when _____ failed in the land of Egypt" (Genesis 47:15)
36 Way (Chinese)
37 "They will look at their _____ crops" (Jeremiah 12:13 MSG)
38 "God _____ the light Day, and the darkness. . .Night" (Genesis 1:5)
39 Pronoun (Fr.)
41 Pull back in disgust
43 Government department (abbr.)
44 Precious, bloodred stone (Exodus 28:17)
48 "These women had. . .cared for his _____" (Mark 15:41 NIV)

50 "Raiment was white _____ the light" (Matthew 17:2)
51 Singer _____ Lopez
52 "_____ me from the hand of the mighty" (Job 6:23)
54 Bone
55 "And the ark rested in the seventh _____" (Genesis 8:4)
57 "My tongue is like the pen of a skillful _____" (Psalm 45:1 NLT)
60 Trapper's treasure
62 Irish Breakfast, for one
64 _____ Khan
66 "His eyes shall be _____ with wine" (Genesis 49:12)
68 "The genealogy is not to _____ reckoned" (1 Chronicles 5:1)
69 Plains state (abbr.)
70 _____ Shaddai, name for God

18

ACROSS
1 Next
6 Baseball stat.
8 Soft drink
12 Tell
13 "Ye have _____ with untempered mortar" (Ezekiel 13:14)
15 Poison
16 Noticed
17 Perjure
18 Joab's "armourbearer" (1 Chronicles 11:39)
21 Aid for indigent
23 Gap
24 "Where thou _____, will I die" (Ruth 1:17)
26 Groovy
27 Blockade
29 Brazil, for one
30 Angelic accoutrement
31 "Open thou my _____" (Psalm 51:15)
34 Benefit
36 "Whose wife shall _____ be" (Mark 12:23)
37 "As. . .sharpens _____" (Proverbs 27:17 NKJV)
38 Korean, for example
39 Bat
41 Living in (suffix)
42 _____ de mer
43 "Stop right there" (2 words)
46 Bon _____, Comet competitor
47 _____ Valley near Los Angeles
50 Scratch
53 Of the chest cavity
55 Remit
56 Liquid measure equaling about six pints (Exodus 29:40)
57 Hebrew month
58 Hew
59 Place in Judah where Saul numbered his forces (1 Samuel 15:4)

DOWN
2 Citizen
3 Number of commandments
4 Esau's father-in-law (Genesis 26:3
5 Town of Benjamin north of Jerusalem (Joshua 18:25)
6 "The head of Samaria is _____ son" (Isaiah 7:9)
7 Fancy
8 "Father. . .remove this _____ fro me" (Luke 22:42)
9 Kimono sash
10 Onionlike vegetables
11 Put together
14 Theatrical gesture
15 Filthy
17 "The world _____ and fadeth away" (Isaiah 24:4)
19 Nun's son (Deuteronomy 32:44)
20 Man who came with Zerubbabel (Ezra 2:2)
22 In awe of
25 Joseph's grandchild (Numbers 1:1(
28 _____ Heights, in Middle East
32 One of twelve disciples
33 "The Lord _____ a mark upon Cain" (Genesis 4:15)
35 Where Ibid. is found (abbr.)
40 Earful?
42 Jesus' earthly mother
44 Den dweller
45 Sarah's son
48 Coin
49 Here, en Paris
50 "He _____ on the ground and made clay" (John 9:6)
51 Walking stick
52 Chedorlaomer was king of _____ (Genesis 14:1)
54 Adam and Eve _____ from God (Genesis 3:8)

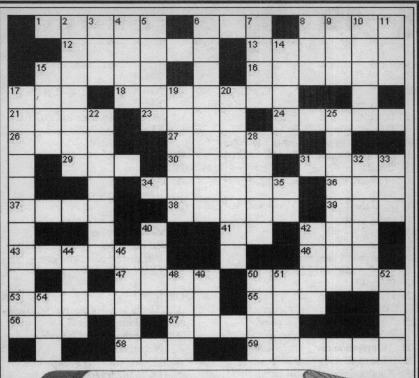

by Sarah Lagerquist Simmons

19

ACROSS

1 Time period
5 Inactive
9 Bosc and Anjou
14 "Of _____, the family of the Oznites" (Numbers 26:16)
15 Cruel
16 Seaweed, for example
17 Save
18 "Till thou hast _____ the very last mite" (Luke 12:59)
19 Morsel
20 Sin
21 "Merchants received the linen _____ at a price" (1 Kings 10:28)
22 Singed
23 Harbor
24 "With a strong ____" (Jeremiah 21:5)
25 "_____ they shall flee away" (Nahum 2:8)
28 Ammihud's son (1 Chronicles 9:4)
31 Type of tie
34 Korah's father (Exodus 6:21)
36 "For every one that _____ shall be cut off" (Zechariah 5:3)
39 "And _____ lived after he begat Peleg" (Genesis 11:17)
40 Pots' partners
42 Lave
43 "I am Alpha and Omega, the first and the _____" (Revelation 1:11)
44 "And _____ did that which was right" (1 Kings 15:11)
45 _____ Colonies, in Iowa
46 "Neither shall ye touch it, lest ye _____" (Genesis 3:3)
47 "With the _____ and deacons" (Philippians 1:1)
50 Strike
51 "Purim after the name of _____" (Esther 9:26)
52 Appeal
53 "Stingeth like an _____" (Proverbs 23:32)
56 "The gods of Hamath, and of _____" (2 Kings 18:34)
58 "Man will _____ thee at the law" (Matthew 5:40)
61 Abram's wife (Genesis 11:29)
62 "Shebam, and Nebo, and _____" (Numbers 32:3)
63 Holler
64 Location
65 Despicable
66 "The province of ____" (Daniel 8:2)
67 "They _____ fig leaves together" (Genesis 3:7)
68 "Gold, and silver, ivory, and _____ and peacocks" (1 Kings 10:22)
69 "Sell that ye have, and give _____" (Luke 12:33)

DOWN

1 "The _____ of my transgressions" (Lamentations 1:14)
2 Son of the ruler of Mizpah (Nehemiah 3:19)
3 "_____ with her suburbs" (1 Chronicles 6:70)
4 Tombstone initials
5 "I may _____ unto you some spiritual gift" (Romans 1:11)
6 "Seven years of _____ began to come" (Genesis 41:54)
7 "I have _____ still and been quiet" (Job 3:13)
8 Omega, briefly
9 "The _____ reeds by the brooks" (Isaiah 19:7)
10 Bathsheba's father (2 Samuel 11:3)
11 End of *teen*
12 "They which run in a _____ run all" (1 Corinthians 9:24)
13 Ranking, as in tennis
21 "Be clean, and change _____ garments" (Genesis 35:2)
22 International org. started in 1865 (abbr.)
25 Submit
26 Naarai's father (1 Chronicles 11:37)
27 "_____ are the generations of Noah" (Genesis 6:9)

by Tonya Vilhauer

29 "The children of _____" (Ezra 2:50)
30 "That which groweth of _____ own accord" (Leviticus 25:5)
31 "And from _____ and from Berothai" (2 Samuel 8:8)
32 Shemaiah's first son (1 Chronicles 26:7)
33 "Barley harvest and of _____ harvest" (Ruth 2:23)
35 "Thou _____ cursed above all cattle" (Genesis 3:14) (sing.)
37 "I know both how to be _____" (Philippians 4:12)
38 Old Testament book (abbr.)
40 Team of two
41 "They laded their _____ with the corn" (Genesis 42:26)
47 "We are _____ with him by baptism" (Romans 6:4)
48 "Instructing those that _____ themselves" (2 Timothy 2:25)

49 Geometric surfaces
51 "Grace be unto you, and _____, from him" (Revelation 1:4)
53 "Poison of _____ is under their lips" (Romans 3:13)
54 Roy's "pard"
55 "Let us _____ near with a true heart" (Hebrews 10:22)
56 "And he said, _____, Father" (Mark 14:36)
57 "I _____ where I sowed not" (Matthew 25:26)
58 "That no man might buy or _____" (Revelation 13:17)
59 Jehush and Eliphelet's brother (1 Chronicles 8:39)
60 "Under oaks and poplars and _____" (Hosea 4:13)
63 "_____, let God be true" (Romans 3:4)

Bethlehem's Visitor

*And thou Bethlehem,
out of thee shall come a Govern
that shall rule my people Isra*

MATTHEW 2

ACROSS

1 Brig occupant
5 "Who passing through the valley of _____ make it a well" (Psalm 84:6)
9 "If he arrives _____ will come with him to see you" (Hebrews 13:23 NIV) (2 words)
14 Puerto _____
15 Maj. Hoople's favorite expression
16 "But the _____ are the children of the wicked one" (Matthew 13:38)
17 U.S. island occupied by Japan during WWII
18 Goulash
19 Bathsheba's first husband (2 Samuel 11:3)
20 **VISITORS** (Luke 2:15) (2 words)
23 "Yet we did _____ him stricken" (Isaiah 53:4)
24 Mr. Charles
25 O.T. book (abbr.)
28 Scale notes
29 Deteriorate
32 "Praise thy _____ Zion" (Psalm 147:12) (2 words)
33 City from which David took "exceeding much brass" (2 Samuel 8:8)
34 Corolla component
35 More **VISITORS** (Luke 2:4–7) (3 words)
40 "You are worried and _____ about many things" (Luke 10:41 NIV)
41 "The Philistines gathered _____ Dammim" (2 Samuel 23:9 NIV) (2 words)
42 Mend, as a sock
43 Open, as a flag
45 Weasel
48 Golfer Ernie
49 Menlo Park monogram
50 Electrical unit
52 More **VISITORS** (Matthew 2:1–11) (3 words)
55 Stockpile
58 Mariner who discovered Cape of Good Hope
59 Bye-bye
60 "Whom shall _____" (Psalm 27:1) (2 words)
61 Sea eagle
62 Land west of Nod (Genesis 4:16)
63 In accord (2 words)
64 "But in _____ and in truth" (1 John 3:18)
65 "And Jacob _____ his clothes" (Genesis 37:34)

DOWN

1 Top drawer
2 "Compassed about _____ great a cloud of witnesses" (Hebrews 12:1) (2 words)
3 Musical groups
4 Despicable person
5 "Behold now _____, which I mad with thee" (Job 40:15)
6 "I had rebuilt the wall and not _____ was left in it" (Nehemiah 6:1 NIV) (2 words)
7 Not "plastic"
8 Stick like glue
9 "_____ to show thyself approved unto God" (2 Timothy 2:15)
10 "Wherein shall go no galley with _____" (Isaiah 33:21)
11 "Give light to my eyes, _____ will sleep in death" (Psalm 13:3 NIV) (2 words)
12 Education assn.
13 Like –*like*

by David K. Shortess

21 What Jesus did at Lazarus's tomb (2 words)
22 "They _____ the ship aground" (Acts 27:41)
25 "But he answered her _____ word" (Matthew 15:23) (2 words)
26 "The twelfth month, which is the month _____" (Esther 3:13)
27 "Sacrifice, _____, acceptable unto God" (Romans 12:1)
30 British rule in India
31 Quiverful
32 Rubies, for example
33 Has _____, kin of also ran
34 "In _____ and hymns and spiritual songs" (Colossians 3:16)
35 Revelation preceder
36 Iridescent gem
37 Belonging to Lithuania and Estonia, once (abbr.)
38 Former cabinet secretary Udall, to his friends

39 "His hand is still _____" (Isaiah 10:4 NIV)
43 Egypt and Syria, once (abbr.)
44 Required
45 Created again
46 "The ten horns which thou sawest _____ kings" (Revelation 17:12) (2 words)
47 Apartment dweller, often
49 "And God said, Let _____ be light" (Genesis 1:3)
51 Andrew's brother
52 Comparison word
53 Ireland, formerly
54 "And your moon will _____ no more" (Isaiah 60:20 NIV)
55 Mole's milieu? (abbr.)
56 Exchange student organization (abbr.)
57 Company bigwig (abbr.)

21

ACROSS

1 Feminine name
4 "They lavish gold. . .and _____ a goldsmith" (Isaiah 46:6)
8 Word in carol title
11 Meat cut
13 Where Adam met Eve
14 "How long _____ ye slack to go" (Joshua 18:3)
15 New Testament prophetess
16 "These six _____ of barley gave he me" (Ruth 3:17)
18 Appear
19 Sign of infection
20 "Thou shalt not _____ the Lord thy God" (Matthew 4:7)
24 "Let the _____ bring forth the living creatures" (Genesis 1:24)
28 Mr. Rogers
30 Bible language (abbr.)
32 Poetic contraction
33 Donkey
34 Chooses
36 Gold (Fr.)
37 Greek letter
38 "To proclaim the acceptable _____ of the LORD" (Isaiah 61:2)
39 Dutch city
40 What Matthew collected
43 "Learn his ways and get a _____ to thy soul" (Proverbs 22:25)
45 "Go to the _____, thou sluggard" (Proverbs 6:6)
47 Minor prophet
50 Feeds
55 Only
56 "And _____ did that which was right" (1 Kings 15:11)
57 "My mercy will I _____ for him for evermore" (Psalm 89:28)
58 Child or ladder
59 Weekday (abbr.)
60 Whirlpool
61 Spicy

DOWN

1 Exclamation
2 "There is _____ like me in all the earth" (Exodus 9:14)
3 Number of rams sacrificed upon Ezra's arrival in Jerusalem (Ezra 8:35)
4 Haw's partner
5 Chemical suffix
6 "They shall _____ the whirlwind" (Hosea 8:7)
7 Follow
8 Upset
9 Raw metal
10 Cable sports network (abbr.)
12 Cite
17 NATO member (abbr.)
21 "A _____ of God came unto me" (Judges 13:6)
22 "_____ one for another" (James 5:16)
23 Subdues
25 "The LORD _____ the soul of his servants" (Psalm 34:22)
26 Walked
27 "He said, _____ am I, my son" (Genesis 22:7)
28 Extremely attentive
29 Greek mountain
31 "What _____ ye by these stones" (Joshua 4:6)
35 Mrs., in Madrid
41 Consume
42 Devilish disguise?
44 Offering options
46 "An ass _____, and a colt with her" (Matthew 21:2)
48 Popular cookie
49 Fall time (abbr.)
50 "They _____ it, and so they marveled" (Psalm 48:5)
51 Employ
52 "When ye fast be not. . .of a _____ countenance" (Matthew 6:16)
53 Masculine name
54 Caleb, for one

by Evelyn M. Boyington

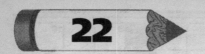

22

Miracles of Jesus

Jesus said to them
"I have shown you many great miracles from the Father."

ACROSS

1 Separate
6 Miss or Mrs.
9 Last word in the Bible (Revelation 22:21)
13 Abraham's first wife (Gen. 17:15)
14 "But thou shalt give _____ now" (1 Samuel 2:16) (2 words)
16 Jacob's third son (Exodus 1:2)
17 "We are true men; we _____ spies" (Genesis 42:31) (2 words)
18 _____ Valley, CA
19 Chemical suffix (pl.)
20 **MIRACLE** (John 12:1) (2 words)
23 Organic compound
24 Shows or does (suffix)
25 He may save a lot
29 "For my yoke is _____" (Matthew 11:30)
31 Police charity (abbr.)
34 Bus or potent preceder
35 Psyche parts
36 Put one foot in front of the other
37 **MIRACLE** (Matthew 14:15–21) (3 words)
40 S-shaped moldings
41 Attention-getting word
42 "_____ of a Thousand Days"
43 Prof's lab helpers
44 Italian noble house
46 Took a turn in the lineup
48 Popular sandwich, briefly
49 Vessels (abbr.)
51 **MIRACLE** (Matthew 8:16) (3 words)
57 "They will _____ on wings like eagles" (Isaiah 40:31 NIV)
58 "Blessed are the _____ in spirit" (Matthew 5:3)
59 Get used to
61 Go bad, as fruit

62 Fairytale monster
63 "And, behold, Joseph was _____ the pit" (Genesis 37:29) (2 words)
64 Flying fish-eaters
65 "Calling on the _____ of the Lord" (Acts 22:16)
66 Long lock

DOWN

1 "Like _____ father pitieth his children" (Psalm 103:13) (2 words)
2 Catherine _____, last wife of Henry VIII
3 Kind of code
4 "Yet they _____ have not spoken to them" (Jeremiah 23:21) (2 words)
5 "But what things were gain. . . _____ counted loss" (Philippians 3:7) (2 words)
6 Mess up
7 **MIRACLE** (Mark 4:37–39) (3 words)
8 "A trap _____ him by the heel" (Job 18:9 NIV)
9 "Be on guard! Be _____! You do not know when" (Mark 13:33 NIV)
10 Beanery item
11 First lady, and others
12 Serbian city
15 NYC museum
21 Direction from Tucson to Santa Fe (abbr.)
22 How or where
25 "And who will _____ us" (Isaiah 6:8) (2 words)
26 "I am Alpha and _____" (Revelation 1:8)
27 South American range
28 "The Lord is the strength of my _____" (Psalm 27:1)
30 Tennis great

31 Sow

32 C'est une _____ idee

33 "And all these things shall be _____ unto you" (Luke 12:31)

35 "Will ___ the flesh of bulls" (Psalm 50:13) (2 words)

36 Test taken by HS sophs (abbr.)

38 "Or to which of my creditors did _____ you" (Isaiah 50:1 NIV) (2 words)

39 Old European game with three players and forty cards

45 "Who enter Dagon's temple at Ashdod _____ the threshold" (1 Samuel 5:5 NIV) (2 words)

47 Agree to

48 "Nor gather into _____" (Matthew 6:26)

50 Number of Noah's sons

51 "What, could ye not watch with me one _____" (Matthew 26:40)

52 "And all who _____ their living from the sea" (Revelation 18:17 NIV)

53 "Whom are you pursuing? A dead _____ flea" (1 Samuel 24:14 NIV) (2 words)

54 "So neither _____ my brethren, nor my servants" (Nehemiah 4:23) (2 words)

55 Like a kitten

56 Actor Kristofferson

57 Part of the names of many Quebec towns (abbr.)

60 Printers' measures

ACROSS

1 Hawaii (pl.)
6 Ishmael's son (Genesis 25:14)
11 Attorney
12 Bury
14 Top _____
16 King of Assyria (Isaiah 20:1)
18 "Ye know neither the _____ nor the hour" (Matthew 25:13)
19 Dine
21 Book of the Pentateuch (abbr.)
22 Ax
24 "To day shalt thou be with me in _____" (Luke 23:43)
27 Lot's aunt
29 Nod, to Fido
30 A distance
31 Cut
33 "God created he _____" (Genesis 1:27)
35 Reed
36 Ahiam's father (1 Chronicles 11:35)
38 "Which come to you in _____ clothing" (Matthew 7:15)
41 Naomi's new name (Ruth 1:20)
42 "Jabal; he was the father of such as dwell in _____" (Genesis 4:20)
43 American _____ (college course, briefly)
45 Pointy end
46 Wild
47 Hananiah's son (1 Chronicles 3:21)
49 "I _____ no pleasant bread" (Daniel 10:3)
50 Shobal's son (Genesis 36:23)
51 Whom Abram wed
52 Mail

DOWN

2 "Judge between the _____ and the revenger" (Numbers 35:24)
3 Criminal, for one
4 "Thy _____ and thy she goats" (Genesis 31:38)
5 Vermont product
6 Spouse (abbr.)
7 Tear
8 "There are. . .voices in the world, and none of them is without _____" (1 Corinthians 14:10)
9 Stir
10 Curious
13 Join
15 Survivor of Jericho (Joshua 6:17)
17 King of the Amalekites (1 Samuel 15:8)
20 Foot, to some
23 "He that _____ his father and chaseth away his mother" (Proverbs 19:26)
25 Uncooked
26 Capital city of the Northern Kingdom of Israel
28 Stringed instruments
32 Existed
33 Noah's son
34 Lost
35 "Their _____ exercised to discern both good and evil" (Hebrews 5:14)
37 Benjamin's son (1 Chronicles 8:2)
39 Cook leftovers
40 _____ marker, highway sign
43 "When he came unto _____, the Philistines shouted" (Judges 15:14)
44 Pats
47 Old Testament book (abbr.)
48 "God is _____ judge" (Psalm 75:7)

by Sarah Lagerquist Simmons

ACROSS

1 Government org. in which most have vested interest
4 "Regem, and Jotham, and _____" (1 Chronicles 2:47)
10 Bonkers
14 Thing to pass
15 Resist
16 "Er and _____ died in the land of Canaan" (Numbers 26:19)
17 Jether's son (1 Chronicles 7:38)
18 "The children of Sisera, the children of _____" (Ezra 2:53)
19 Common fear
20 Valley or ravine in Middle East
22 "Mispereth, Bigvai, _____" (Nehemiah 7:7)
24 Old Testament book (abbr.)
25 Scandinavian carrier (abbr.)
28 "Whose soever sins ye _____, they are remitted unto them" (John 20:23)
30 Chuza's wife (Luke 8:3)
33 "_____, come forth" (John 11:43)
37 David was a king of _____ (see 1 Chronicles 22:8)
38 "And I was as a _____ man that openeth not his mouth" (Psalm 38:13)
40 "The sons of Reuel; _____, and Zerah" (Genesis 36:13)
41 "There was one _____, a prophetess" (Luke 2:36)
43 Ruth's love
45 Palti's father (Numbers 13:9)
46 "How long shall this man be a _____ unto us" (Exodus 10:7)
48 "Who shall _____ him up" (Numbers 24:9)
50 Aside from
51 Jehu's father (1 Kings 16:1)
53 "Machnadebai, _____, Sharai" (Ezra 10:40)
55 "And Zimri begot _____" (1 Chronicles 8:36)
57 Time past

58 Book of creation (abbr.)
61 Actress Ward
63 Church areas
68 Comply
70 "And the coast turneth to _____" (Joshua 19:29)
73 "Thou shouldest make thy _____ as high as the eagle" (Jeremiah 49:16)
74 Troubled breath
75 "Johanan, and Dalaiah, and _____" (1 Chronicles 3:24)
76 European dictator
77 Kitchen shapes
78 "He made narrowed _____ round about" (1 Kings 6:6)
79 More than pat

DOWN

1 British playwright
2 "Through faith also _____ herself received strength" (Hebrews 11:11)
3 "And they came to the threshingfloor of _____" (Genesis 50:10)
4 Received
5 New Testament book (abbr.)
6 Unit of measure equivalent to 9 inches
7 "An _____ of barley seed" (Leviticus 27:16)
8 Jonathan's father (Ezra 10:15)
9 "The king was merry with wine, he commanded _____" (Esther 1:10)
10 "And tempted _____ in the desert" (Psalm 106:14)
11 Israelite leader (Nehemiah 10:26)
12 _____ du Nord, in Paris
13 Egyptian symbol of life
21 Amoz's prophet son (abbr.)
23 "From the hill _____" (Psalm 42:6)
26 Also
27 Give the cold shoulder
29 "They departed from _____" (Numbers 33:27)

by Tonya Vilhauer

30 "The son of _____, which was the son of Joseph" (Luke 3:24)

31 "The threshingfloor of _____ the Jebusite" (2 Chronicles 3:1)

32 Minor prophet

34 "Nohah the fourth, and _____ the fifth" (1 Chronicles 8:2)

35 "Of the sons also of Bigvai; _____" (Ezra 8:14)

36 Have nothing to do with

37 Purify

39 "To the moles and to the _____" (Isaiah 2:20)

42 Aminadab's father (Matthew 1:4)

44 "The Nethinims: the children of _____" (Nehemiah 7:46)

47 Cainan's father (Genesis 5:9)

49 Tease

52 "Amram, and _____, Hebron, and Uzziel" (Numbers 3:19)

54 Offspring

56 By oneself

58 "If an ox _____ a man or a woman" (Exodus 21:28)

59 "The curse upon mount _____" (Deuteronomy 11:29)

60 Dickens's "Little" woman

62 "Nevertheless _____ heart was perfect" (1 Kings 15:14)

64 "The _____ are a people not strong" (Proverbs 30:25)

65 "The keepers of the walls took away my _____" (Song of Solomon 5:7)

66 Como _____? (Sp. greeting)

67 F-_____ (photography term)

69 Affirmative

71 "Go to the _____, thou sluggard" (Proverbs 6:6)

72 Not hers

25

ACROSS

1 "The _____ is my Shepherd" (Psalm 32:1)
5 "My grace is _____" (2 Corinthians 12:9)
12 River on Polish border
13 Avoid
14 Year of our Lord (abbr.)
15 French coal-mining region
18 NHL team (abbr.)
19 "The LORD wrought a great _____ that day" (2 Samuel 23:10)
20 Letter abbr.
21 Place (O.E.)
23 Jackie's second
25 "The righteous shall flourish like the palm _____" (Psalm 92:12)
27 Midwest state (abbr.)
28 "Saul, and the archers _____ him" (1 Samuel 31:3)
29 "Joseph's _____ brethren went down to buy corn" (Genesis 42:3)
31 German article
32 Gospel author
34 Prophet who rebuked David
36 Protected product symbol
37 "The words of king _____" (Proverbs 31:1)
41 _____ generis
43 "He will laugh at the _____ of the innocent" (Job 9:23)
46 "Give me children, _____ else I die" (Genesis 30:1)
47 "Who is lord over _____" (Psalm 12:4)
48 Sunny state (abbr.)
49 "Pulse to eat, and water to _____" (Daniel 1:12)
52 Cabinet secretary's domain (abbr.)
53 Where children learn Bible lessons (abbr.)
54 Med. provider
55 Peter or Bridget
56 Coach Parseghian
57 Civil War general
58 Book after Nahum (abbr.)
61 Direction (abbr.)
63 Eye part
65 Nonprescription med. (abbr.)
67 Eastern university (abbr.)
68 "No galley with _____ will ride them" (Isaiah 33:21 NIV)
70 "As a thread of _____ is broken" (Judges 16:9)
71 Eras
73 "Be lord over thy _____" (Genesis 27:29)
74 "Jesus. . .withdrew to _____ places and prayed" (Luke 5:16 NIV)

DOWN

1 "And makes himself rich with _____" (Habakkuk 2:6 NASB)
2 "The _____ number. . .is to be redeemed" (Numbers 3:48)
3 Concerning
4 Ancient Celtic priest
5 "May he. . .be. . .a _____ of your old age" (Ruth 4:15 NASB)
6 "Where is the _____ of the oppressor?" (Isaiah 51:13)
7 Town celebration (abbr.)
8 _____ League
9 "For. . .barley was in the _____" (Exodus 9:31)
10 Home of Fargo (abbr.)
11 Taunts
16 Artery
17 First name of "Exodus" hero
19 King Xerxes' queen
20 "Go to thy fathers in _____" (Genesis 15:15)
22 Down for the count (abbr.)
24 "The _____ of the LORD. . .will perform this" (Isaiah 9:7)
26 Address abbr., for some
29 Weekday (abbr.)
30 Compass direction
32 "Even so, come, Lord _____" (Revelation 22:20)
33 Southwest state (abbr.)
35 Russian ruler

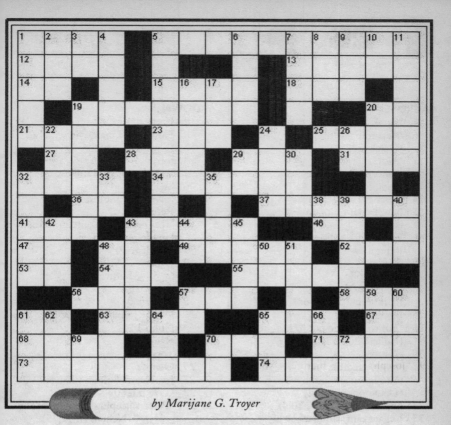

38 "Show Me" state (abbr.)
39 David had him killed
40 "And God said, _____ there be
   light" (Genesis 1:3)
42 Naval ship's abbr.
43 Absalom killed to avenge her
   (2 Samuel 13:14, 28)
44 Part of a personality
45 Tree of _____ (Genesis 2:9)
48 Savior
50 "Thou shalt have _____ portion"
   (Ezra 4:16)
51 "Mine heart shall be _____ unto
   you" (1 Chronicles 12:17)
57 Place of the seal (abbr., Lat.)
59 Adam's son
60 "Perhaps he is deep in thought, or
   _____" (1 Kings 18:27 NIV)
61 "Will a man _____ God?"
   (Malachi 3:8)

62 "They used. . ._____ for mortar"
   (Genesis 11:3 NIV)
64 You (Ger.)
65 Says who?
66 "I _____ do all things"
   (Philippians 4:13)
69 Indian coin (abbr.)
70 Home of NFL Titans (abbr.)
72 "We bring good things to life"
   company (abbr.)

by Marijane G. Troyer

26

ACROSS

1 "Look out!"
6 "According as thou _____ me" (Genesis 27:19)
11 "As. . .sharpens _____" (Proverbs 27:17 NIV)
12 Comply
14 Issachar's son (Genesis 46:13)
15 Number of holes on some golf courses
16 Those with a discount (abbr.)
19 Benign cyst
20 Sandra _____ O'Connor
21 Good (colloq.)
23 _____ of America (Minnesota attraction)
25 Now's partner
26 "For we wrestle not _____ flesh" (Ephesians 6:12)
30 Chastises
33 "Every creditor that _____ought unto his neighbour" (Deuteronomy 15:2)
34 Javan's son (Genesis 10:4)
35 Legal exam, familiarly
36 Can
37 Get ready
40 Hagar, and others (var.)
44 "And the _____ in their mount Seir" (Genesis 14:6)
45 "The moving of my lips should _____ your grief" (Job 16:5)
46 So be it
47 Shuthelah's son (Numbers 26:36)
48 Cerise, for one
49 However (var.)
51 Question
54 _____ Khan
55 Jezebel's god
56 Flesh and _____
58 Part of the action
59 Minor prophet
60 Shrines
61 "He _____ him down cedars" (Isaiah 44:14)

DOWN

2 Irony
3 How pretty maids sit, with "all in" (2 words)
4 Job
5 Ahira's father (Numbers 1:15)
6 Shackle
7 Solomon's grandson (Matthew 1:7)
8 Refuse
9 "It is better. . .to enter into the kingdom of God with one _____" (Mark 9:47)
10 Dreary
13 _____-Barnea
17 Anger
18 Maligned
21 Where John was baptizing (John 1:28)
22 Range
24 Top
25 Owns
27 Jeroboam's father (1 Kings 11:26)
28 Gaze intently
29 "Porters keeping the ward at the _____" (Nehemiah 12:25)
30 Part of the northern border of Judah's land (Joshua 15:6)
31 "Moses and _____ talking with him" (Matthew 17:3)
32 Bands
37 Twin son of Judah and Tamar (Genesis 38:29)
38 Paul was a citizen of _____
39 Peg
41 "Stand in _____ and sin not" (Psalm 4:4)
42 "His king shall be higher than _____" (Numbers 24:7)
43 Governing body
49 Iowa town off U.S. 30
50 Hirsute one has plenty
52 A few
53 Understand
55 Louisville Slugger, for one
57 Direction from Minneapolis to Chicago

by Sarah Lagerquist Simmons

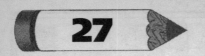

27

Miracles in Danie

[God] rescues and he saves; he performs sign
and wonders in the heavens and on the earth

DANIEL 6:27 NI

ACROSS

1 "There is no ___ discerning and wise as you" (Genesis 41:39 NIV) (2 words)
6 Hearty's cohort
10 "For, lo, the winter is _____" (Song of Solomon 2:11)
14 Summer TV fare, often
15 Indigo plant
16 He was red all over (Genesis 25:25)
17 Where God intervened to save Daniel's friends (Daniel 3:20–28) (3 words)
20 "But Jonathan was very _____ of David" (1 Samuel 19:1 NIV)
21 "And he will make her wilderness like _____" (Isaiah 51:3)
22 "Even Assyria has joined them ____ strength to the descendants of Lot" (Psalm 83:8 NIV) (2 words)
25 "Thou hast not _____ unto men, but unto God" (Acts 5:4)
26 Haw's opposite
29 In the distance
30 Accumulate
32 "Without _____ of brightness?" (Amos 5:20 NIV) (2 words)
33 "_____ a girl"
34 Oaf
35 "And in an hour that he is not _____ of" (Matthew 24:50)
36 Where God intervened to save Daniel (Daniel 6:16) (3 words)
40 Took a turn (2 words)
42 "Whither have ye made a _____ to day" (1 Samuel 27:10)
43 "And _____ soul sin" (Leviticus 5:1) (2 words)
46 "_____ I trying to please men?" (Galatians 1:10 NIV) (2 words)
47 "Be self-controlled and _____" (1 Peter 5:8 NIV)
49 "And _____ hour he is not aware" (Luke 12:46) (2 words)

50 "Nor standeth in the _____ of sinners" (Psalm 1:1)
51 Made it home?
52 Go back
54 Bath powder
55 "The _____ came to Jesus by night" (John 3:2)
56 What God wrote on the wall (Daniel 5:25 NIV) (3 words)
63 Where Esfahan is
64 "Go and _____ potter's earthen bottle" (Jeremiah 19:1) (2 words)
65 "Such knowledge _____ wonderful for me" (Psalm 139:6) (2 words)
66 Prohibitionists
67 Land of Seir (Genesis 32:3)
68 Depends on

DOWN

1 Table scrap
2 Ezra follower (abbr.)
3 "And how long will it be _____ they believe me" (Numbers 14:11)
4 "That the Son of man must _____ many things" (Mark 8:31)
5 Leek relative
6 "It is _____ for thee to kick agains the pricks" (Acts 26:14)
7 "And see if there be _____ wicked way in me" (Psalm 139:24)
8 "The _____ more than meat" (Luke 12:23) (2 words)
9 Slips away from
10 Quaker William
11 Jehoshaphat's father (1 Kings 15:24)
12 Biological pouch
13 Calendar abbreviation
18 "I will bring to an _____ the groaning she caused" (Isaiah 21:2 NIV) (2 words)
19 "By the way of the _____ sea" (Numbers 14:25)
22 _____ chi

by David K. Shortess

23 "This do ye, as _____ as ye drink it" (1 Corinthians 11:25)
24 "And I will raise him up at the _____" (John 6:40) (2 words)
25 "I have _____ to no purpose" (Isaiah 49:4 NIV)
26 Monument rock
27 Give _____ to
28 Pink, at times
31 Pronoun (Fr.)
32 "But my heart standeth in _____ of thy word" (Psalm 119:161)
34 Game, _____, match
35 "Can _____ one cubit unto his stature" (Matthew 6:27)
37 Father of Canaan (Gen. 9:18)
38 "_____ standeth in the way of sinners" (Psalm 1:1)
39 Official under Darius (Daniel 6:1 NIV)
40 "Consider the lilies of the field, _____ they grow" (Matthew 6:28)

41 Jether's son (1 Chronicles 7:38)
44 "Be not _____ from me" (Psalm 38:21)
45 Sluggard's teacher? (Proverbs 6:6)
47 Maintain
48 "Dogs came and _____ his sores" (Luke 16:21)
49 Opposed to
51 "And he _____ down among the ashes" (Job 2:8)
53 Certain correspondence
54 Perfect scores, to some
55 Close forcefully
56 Naval officer (abbr.)
57 "They do alway _____ in their heart" (Hebrews 3:10)
58 "I tell you, _____: but, except ye repent" (Luke 13:3)
59 Ike's command (abbr.)
60 R.R. depot
61 It may be charged?
62 Phone book listings (abbr.)

28

ACROSS

1 "The cloud the garment. . .thick darkness a _____ for it" (Job 38:9)
11 Chaste
12 Press
14 Remedy
15 "Give _____, O my people, to my law" (Psalm 78:1)
18 "On the hole of the _____" (Isaiah 11:8)
19 Undergraduate degree (abbr.)
20 "If any man will _____ thee" (Matthew 5:40)
22 Robert E., and others
24 Smooth transition
25 Touchy
26 "By the threshingfloor of _____" (1 Chronicles 21:15)
28 "And Joseph said. . .God will surely _____ you" (Genesis 50:24)
29 "_____ of the brooks of Gaash" (2 Samuel 23:30)
30 "The _____ also dwelt in Seir" (Deuteronomy 2:12)
31 Jacob's new name
34 Pontius _____
37 Prophets
40 Sum
41 Proportion
42 Cut costs, with "down"
44 "Didst thou not _____ me" (Genesis 12:18)
45 "He planteth an _____, and the rain doth nourish it" (Isaiah 44:14)
46 Owns
47 Hot _____
49 He did not side with Adonijah (1 Kings 1:8)
50 "The fourth river is _____" (Genesis 2:14)
52 New York Mets' great Tommy
53 Jacob's wife
54 "A man. . .seeketh and _____ with all wisdom" (Proverbs 18:1)

DOWN

2 Germane
3 "In the plain of _____" (Daniel 3:1)
4 Sheath
5 Jumped
6 Halo
7 Diving bird
8 _____ fide
9 Hill builder
10 "And he erected there an altar, and called it _____" (Genesis 33:20)
13 "A sacrifice to God for a _____ savour" (Ephesians 5:2)
16 Aircraft (Prefix, var.)
17 "A voice of the LORD that _____ recompence to his enemies" (Isaiah 66:6)
20 Kinsman saluted by Paul (Romans 16:21)
21 _____ and the Thummim (Exodus 28:30)
23 Not glad
25 Title for Winston Churchill
27 "Adam gave _____ to all cattle" (Genesis 2:20)
28 Become ill
32 "Fill the waters in the _____" (Genesis 1:22)
33 Exist
35 Abraham's nephew
36 Tall one?
38 Yad _____, Jerusalem Holocaust memorial
39 Proclaim
42 "Rock, _____, scissors"
43 Adored, with "on"
46 Gigantic
48 Cope with
50 Consume
51 "_____ shall be called Woman" (Genesis 2:23)

by Sarah Lagerquist Simmons

ACROSS

1 Rebound
6 "The inhabitants of _____ gather themselves to flee" (Isaiah 10:31)
11 Gypsy
14 "Johanan, and Dalaiah, and _____" (1 Chronicles 3:24)
15 "And _____ thereon a great heap of stones" (Joshua 8:29)
16 Master (Sp.)
17 Musical sounds
18 "The children of _____" (Ezra 2:50)
19 Part of HRH
20 "He _____ Abram" (Genesis 12:16)
22 Statue
24 "The appointed barley and the _____" (Isaiah 28:25)
25 "And _____, and Ramah, and Hazor" (Joshua 19:36)
26 "Out of _____ came down governors" (Judges 5:14)
30 Grandmother of Esau
32 Correspond
33 Shimei's father (1 Kings 2:8)
34 _____ Minor
38 Debris
39 Sheresh's son (1 Chronicles 7:16)
40 Remainder
41 "_____ was a great man among the Anakims" (Joshua 14:15)
42 Chemical suffix (pl.)
43 "The children of _____, the children of Darkon" (Nehemiah 7:58)
44 King who was once a shepherd
46 Cruised
47 "And from thence unto _____" (Acts 21:1)
50 Addition total
51 "Henoch, and _____, and Eldaah" (1 Chronicles 1:33)
52 "In _____ were twelve fountains of water" (Numbers 33:9)
54 Shirt maker
58 Church Paul wrote (abbr.)
59 Atone
61 "By the river of _____" (Daniel 8:2)
62 "And Adam called his wife's name _____" (Genesis 3:20)
63 Retaliate
64 Go into the sunset?
65 Saw _____
66 Part of TLC
67 Mound

DOWN

1 Actress Blanchett
2 Soon (arch.)
3 Go on and on
4 Unique person
5 Agonies
6 Grind
7 Comfort
8 Tie up
9 Prophet son of Amoz (abbr.)
10 "Children of _____, the children of Harsha" (Ezra 2:52)
11 Shema's son (1 Chronicles 2:44)
12 "I am Alpha and _____" (Revelation 22:13)
13 Plain of _____, where Abram entered Canaan (Genesis 12:6)
21 Atmosphere
23 "_____ the Netophathite" (2 Samuel 23:28)
25 Ancient Syria, biblically
26 "Call me not Naomi, call me _____" (Ruth 1:20)
27 Jakeh's son (Proverbs 30:1)
28 Baby's bed
29 Ruler of the half part of Keilah (Nehemiah 3:18)
30 Nadab's son who died without children (1 Chronicles 2:30)
31 Coach Parseghian, and others
33 "Jahziel, and _____, and Jezer" (1 Chronicles 7:13)
35 Barrier
36 Sea key

by Tonya Vilhauer

37 "And they came to the threshingfloor of _____" (Genesis 50:10)
42 Actress Gabor
43 Congestion
45 Where the ark came to rest
46 July, for example
47 American Motors model
48 Over
49 Spent
50 Blockade
52 "The land is as the garden of _____" (Joel 2:3)
53 Loan
54 Issue
55 Jai _____
56 Execute perfectly (colloq.)
57 Cultivate
60 First lady

30

ACROSS

1 "Come not _____ your wives" (Exodus 19:15)
3 Sulk
6 "There was a _____ round about the throne" (Revelation 4:3)
11 "Also he sent forth a _____ from him" (Genesis 8:8)
13 Master or sir (Hindi)
14 "Follow _____" (Matthew 4:19 NIV)
15 Irish island
16 Printer's measure
17 "I pray thee, _____ and eat of my venison" (Genesis 27:19)
18 "And Lamech took unto him _____ wives" (Genesis 4:19)
19 _____ de mer
20 Noah's son
22 Rapid marching style (abbr.)
23 "_____ kindness unto my master Abraham" (Genesis 24:12)
26 Lake above Ohio
28 Prophet who anointed Saul
31 "Who will make me a _____" (Job 24:25)
33 Where fall foliage is beautiful in U.S. (abbr.)
35 "Behold, thou art _____, my love" (Song of Solomon 4:1)
36 "The LORD _____ me to the house of my master's brethren" (Genesis 24:27)
37 _____ Shaddai
38 Where there was no room
39 Mark aimed at in curling
40 Bills all paid (abbr.)
41 Do alone
42 "She gave _____ of the tree" (Genesis 3:12)
43 Conjunction (Fr.)
44 Talk aimlessly
46 By virtue of office (Lat., Abbr.)
47 Society of Jesus (abbr.)
49 Regional telephone co. (abbr.)
52 Dear _____
53 Local law (abbr.)
54 Crazy ones (colloq.)
57 Acreage
59 Alas (Ger.)
61 Hidden valuables
62 Numeral (Sp.)
63 American revolutionary Allen
65 "Roaring lions _____ their prey" (Psalm 22:13 NIV)
67 Asian country (abbr.)
68 "But the dove found _____ rest" (Genesis 8:9)
69 Continent (abbr.)
71 Also
72 Broadcast
74 Travel abbr.
75 Noah's son
76 "_____ evil and cultivate good" (1 Peter 3:11 MSG)
77 Quieting sound

DOWN

1 First man and his designees (Genesis 2:20) (2 words)
2 Complete body of Jewish law
3 "They that handle the _____ of the writer" (Judges 5:14)
4 "Neither shall ye _____ enchantment" (Leviticus 19:26)
5 Hats
6 "_____ up and walk" (Acts 3:6)
7 Belonging to king of Gerar (Genesis 20)
8 Southwestern state (abbr.)
9 "It is _____ that I give her to thee" (Genesis 29:19)
10 "Make thee an ark of gopher _____" (Genesis 6:14)
12 Low areas (arch.)
21 Hydrochloric acid (abbr.)
22 Day (Sp.)
24 Flying females in WWII (abbr.)
25 "A calm disposition _____ intemperate rage" (Ecclesiastes 10:4 MSG)
27 "And I will _____ you out of their bondage" (Exodus 6:6)

by Marijane G. Troyer

29 Spouse
30 "And _____ the lamp of God went out" (1 Samuel 3:3)
32 "I. . .do bring a _____ of waters" (Genesis 6:17)
34 Compass direction (abbr.)
36 Lake, in Lyon (Fr.)
37 Forget me nots?
41 Wide river valley
45 Where Joshua sent his men after Jericho (Joshua 7:2)
47 "Get away!"
48 He was seduced by Potiphar's wife
50 Sky description, perhaps
51 NE state (abbr.)
55 When close game is played, maybe (abbr.)
56 Fissile rock
58 Romans' wraps
60 Book division (abbr.)

63 Beige shade
64 Ham's father
66 In a _____ (going nowhere)
69 Garden State (abbr.)
70 Two-year college degree (abbr.)
73 Popular

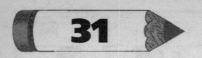

31

A Godly Light

The people walking in darkness have seen a great light;
on those living in the land of the shadow of death a light has dawned.

ISAIAH 9:2 NIV

ACROSS

1 Sign gas
5 Certain packages (abbr.)
9 Penne, for one
14 Fairytale bad guy
15 Pledge
16 Spicy stews
17 Significant periods
18 _____ cava
19 Card or mat
20 "And God said, _____"
   (Genesis 1:3) (4 words)
23 Jeanne d'Arc, e.g.
24 Northwest Pennsylvania county
25 Mini _____
26 "That _____ after the dust of the
   earth" (Amos 2:7)
27 "For _____ price is far above
   rubies" (Proverbs 31:10)
28 "Silence the _____ and the
   avenger" (Psalm 8:2 NIV)
31 "I _____ and stricken in age"
   (Joshua 23:2) (2 words)
34 Bilhah's first son
   (Genesis 30:4–6)
35 Like a breezeway
36 With 52 Across: "When _____
   spoke again to the people, he
   _____" (John 8:12 NIV) (5 words)
40 He saw a plumb line
41 Barley beard
42 Radon and argon
43 Reagan, familiarly
44 So long
45 Beach acquisitions
47 Asian holiday
48 "And the famine was _____ in the
   land" (Genesis 43:1)
49 Number cruncher (abbr.)
52 See 36 Across (4 words)
57 _____ ear

DOWN

1 Christmas carols
2 Crested wader
3 Hold forth
4 "Then I said, I shall die in my
   _____" (Job 29:18)
5 Grotto
6 "He beheld the city, and wept
   _____" (Luke 19:41) (2 words)
7 Gift recipient
8 Mop a deck
9 "And Jacob took him rods of green
   _____" (Genesis 30:37)
10 Exhausted (2 words)
11 Dross
12 Dash accessory (abbr.)
13 "And upon _____ day Herod. . .
   made an oration" (Acts 12:21)
   (2 words)
21 "Lift up your _____, O ye gates"
   (Psalm 24:7)
22 "I, _____, am the LORD" (Isaiah
   43:11) (2 words)
26 Besides
27 Owned
28 One size _____ all
29 "Whether is greater, he that sitteth
   at meat, _____ that serveth" (Luke
   22:27) (2 words)

58 "And _____ not unto thine own
   understanding" (Proverbs 3:5)
59 "Whither have ye made a _____
   today" (1 Samuel 27:10)
60 Military goof
61 "And there was one _____, a
   prophetess" (Luke 2:36)
62 Aussie pal
63 Rich cake
64 Duds
65 Scraped by, with "out"

by David K. Shortess

30 Espies
31 "Some cakes and _____ of honey"
   (1 Kings 14:3 NIV) (2 words)
32 Office note
33 "So thou, _____ of man"
   (Ezekiel 33:7) (2 words)
34 "He will silence her noisy _____"
   (Jeremiah 51:55 NIV)
35 Medical test for men (abbr.)
37 "Many will _____ me in that day"
   (Matthew 7:22) (2 words)
38 "Standeth in _____ of thy word"
   (Psalm. 119:161)
39 Former VP Spiro
44 "If ye _____ men, let one of your
   brethren be bound" (Genesis 42:19)
   (2 words)
45 "Haman was come. . ._____
   Mordecai on the gallows"
   (Esther 6:4) (2 words)

46 Game sites
47 Grand _____ auto
48 Office aide, briefly
49 Kick the bucket
50 Home _____
51 "These things shall be _____ unto
   you" (Matthew 6:33)
52 Itemize
53 "I will _____ wise cast out"
   (John 6:37) (2 words)
54 Snarl (arch.)
55 Not bubbly
56 "Because they have not known the
   Father _____" (John 16:3 NIV)
   (2 words)

32

ACROSS

1 "Eloi, Eloi, _____ sabachthani?" (Mark 15:34)
5 Obligation
9 Playwright Henrik
14 "And _____ lived after he begat Peleg" (Genesis 11:17)
15 Always
16 Take care of (2 words)
17 Hebrew month
18 "Their fathers shall they _____ away with them" (Leviticus 26:39)
19 Actor Ed
20 Pathetic
22 Characteristics
24 "For the wine press is full, the _____ overflow" (Joel 3:13 NKJV)
25 Diamonds (colloq.)
26 "Remembering mine affliction and my _____" (Lamentations 3:19)
29 Good (colloq.)
31 "And _____ went out before the men of Shechem" (Judges 9:39)
35 Apart
36 James's brother (Jude 1:1)
37 "The son of _____, which was the son of Nagge" (Luke 3:25)
38 "Man will _____ thee at the law" (Matthew 5:40)
39 Masters
40 _____ of man (Jesus)
41 Rescue
43 Columnist Landers, and others
44 Gem
46 Hushim's father (1 Chronicles 7:12)
47 "I _____ down under his shadow with great delight" (Song of Solomon 2:3)
48 Handbags
49 Agency (abbr.)
51 "Arsenic and Old _____"
52 Admission
55 Mortified
59 "Fine linen, and coral, and _____" (Ezekiel 27:16)
60 Paddles

62 "Calcol, and _____: five of them" (1 Chronicles 2:6)
63 Separate
64 Coax
65 "The tower of _____" (Genesis 35:21)
66 "Some _____ fell by the way side" (Matthew 13:4)
67 "Not _____ unto men, but unto God" (Acts 5:4)
68 Lease

DOWN

1 Take the plunge
2 Kish's father (2 Chronicles 29:12)
3 Protein source
4 Attained, with "at"
5 "Turn away the _____ from the faith" (Acts 13:8)
6 "_____ have compassed me about" (Psalm 40:12)
7 Son of (Heb.)
8 Fixed weight allowance
9 Abraham's son
10 "The Chaldeans that _____ you" (Jeremiah 21:9)
11 Forwarded
12 Hot times in Tours (Fr.)
13 Scandinavian country (abbr.)
21 Transportation fee
23 Doesn't walk
26 Word in spirituals
27 "Imnah, and _____, and Ishuai" (1 Chronicles 7:30)
28 Colander
29 Like some toast
30 Does arithmetic
32 "Met with us at _____" (Acts 20:14)
33 By oneself
34 Boundaries
36 Simon's father (John 1:42)
39 Doesn't expire
42 Built
44 Certain
45 "And the _____ of grapes" (Amos 9:13)

by Tonya Vilhauer

48 Got a C, at least
50 Prophets
51 Immense
52 Shammah's father (2 Samuel 23:11)
53 "A _____, and a stone lay upon it" (John 11:38)
54 "Vexed his righteous _____" (2 Peter 2:8)
56 "And there _____ him a booth" (Jonah 4:5)
57 "Shuthelah: of _____, the family" (Numbers 26:36)
58 Arrow
59 "They laded their _____ with the corn" (Genesis 42:26)
61 First name of "Exodus" hero

33

ACROSS

1 Man whose sons were David's heroes (2 Samuel 23:32)
7 Most evil
12 _____-ho
13 "We which are _____ and remain unto the coming" (1 Thessalonians 4:15)
14 "Deliver thee from the snare of the _____" (Psalm 91:3)
15 Some at San Quentin
17 Old Testament book (abbr.)
18 In three ways (comb. form)
19 He rode Traveler
20 Greek letter
22 Hophni and Phinehas were _____ sons (1 Samuel 4:16–17)
24 Era
26 "Beguiled you in the matter of _____" (Numbers 25:18)
27 Levite during David's time who was a seer (2 Chronicles 29:30)
29 There are (Sp.)
30 "Israel did eat _____ forty years" (Exodus 16:35)
31 "Of the tribe of Benjamin, an _____. . .a Pharisee" (Philippians 3:5)
33 Reclined
34 "Neither be ye _____as were some of them" (1 Corinthians 10:7)
35 Transformation
38 Judged
42 Amana, for one
43 Computer memory unit
45 Put away
46 Sighing exclamation
47 Attention
48 Deer, biblically
49 Blow
50 Pispah's brother (1 Chronicles 7:38)
52 "That which groweth of _____ own accord" (Leviticus 25:5)
55 Busy one
56 "Let me escape _____. . .and my soul shall live" (Genesis 19:20)
58 "His eyes are like the _____ of the morning" (Job 41:18)
60 Early
61 Deal
62 "Thou shalt break the _____ thereof" (Ezekiel 23:34)
63 Disciple whom Paul greets (Romans 16:14)

DOWN

2 Ahisamach's son (Exodus 31:6)
3 Baste
4 Cease
5 "The LORD shall reign forever and _____" (Exodus 15:18)
6 Baruch's father (Jeremiah 32:12)
7 Dale
8 First name of 70s tennis star
9 Magazine known for its photography
10 Mother of all living (Genesis 3:20)
11 Snake
14 Not real
16 "The sun _____ upon the water" (2 Kings 3:22)
17 "Unto the tower of _____ they sanctified it" (Nehemiah 3:1)
21 Mehujael's father (Genesis 4:18)
23 "Give me also _____ of water" (Joshua 15:19)
25 "I have given order to the churches of _____" (1 Corinthians 16:1)
26 "Every one that _____ among them that are numbered" (Exodus 30:14)
28 "Way of the slothful man is as a _____ of thorns" (Proverbs 15:19)
30 Prince of Persia and Media under Ahasuerus (Esther 1:14)
32 Sorrow
33 What Edom means
35 "He disappointeth the devices of the _____" (Job 5:12)
36 Assyrian area where Israelites were taken by Sargon (2 Kings 17:6)
37 Maaseiah's father (Nehemiah 3:23)

by Sarah Lagerquist Simmons

39 Ruth, originally
40 "And be it indeed that I have
   _____" (Job 19:4)
41 Hate
43 Chef James, and others
44 Testeth
50 Hushim's father (1 Chronicles 7:12)
51 "_____ in the audience of the
   people" (Exodus 24:7)
53 Hiram was king of _____
   (2 Samuel 5:11)
54 Oracle
57 _____ Robe, Lloyd C. Douglas
   novel
59 Old Testament book (abbr.)

34

ACROSS

1 He ruled over almost a billion people for more than 25 years
3 Low-ranked naval officer (abbr.)
6 "And I saw as the colour of _____ as the appearance of fire" (Ezekiel 1:27)
9 Scandinavian carrier (abbr.)
11 "And ere the lamp of God went out in the _____ of the Lord" (1 Samuel 3:3)
14 He wears a mask at home
16 Southern state (abbr.)
17 Expert
19 _____ Cid
21 Feminine name
22 "Nevertheless David took the _____ of Zion" (1 Chronicles 11:5)
24 Large truck, to some
26 House or ground
28 On the summit
30 Copied
32 In the manner of
33 Parent, to some
34 Not too good or bad (abbr.)
35 "Some bread and some _____ stew" (Genesis 25:34 NIV)
38 "And there accompanied him into Asia Sopater of _____" (Acts 20:4)
40 For example (L.)
42 "You alone are to be _____" (Psalm 76:7 NIV)
44 Where children learn about God (abbr.)
45 "Slew a lion in a pit in a _____ day" (1 Chronicles 11:22)
47 "None is so fierce that _____ stir him up" (Job 41:10)
50 Musical singing note
51 "_____ what?"
52 Sandwich (abbr.)
54 "And a __ of three years old" (Genesis 15:9)
55 "Their calls will _____ through the windows" (Zephaniah 2:14 NIV)
57 Ridge

59 "The _____ shall eat and be satisfied" (Psalm 22:26)
61 Slippery ones
63 Continent (abbr.)
64 New England state (abbr.)
65 2,000 pounds
66 "And _____ the seventh day God ended his work" (Genesis 2:2)
68 Spy who brought back good report
70 Um's cousin
71 Wandering one
73 False sense, to Christians (abbr.)
74 "As the trees of lign _____" (Numbers 24:6)
75 Hebrew letter
76 "And one more thing" (abbr.)

DOWN

1 Led Hebrews to Promised Land
2 Big Ten school (abbr.)
3 See
4 "Each man _____ a sword to his side" (Exodus 32:27 NIV)
5 "I _____ the LORD" (Leviticus 22:3)
6 "_____, master! for it was borrowed" (2 Kings 6:5)
7 "Or in things too high for _____" (Psalm 131:1)
8 "For ye tithe mint and _____ and all manner of herbs" (Luke 11:42)
10 One of the twelve spies (Numbers 13:12)
12 Engineering major (abbr.)
13 Part of Costa del Sol (Sp.)
15 Emerald Isle (abbr.)
17 "But ye shall destroy their _____" (Exodus 34:13)
18 Company VIP (abbr.)
20 "Seven days shall there be no _____ found in your houses" (Exodus 12:19)
22 "She shall be _____ Woman" (Genesis 2:23)
23 Do to a shrew
25 Brit. politician, maybe

27 Wild animal's dwelling
29 Princess's nemesis, in tale
31 Rebel against
36 Location of NH and VT
37 Dosage, maybe
39 Vashti's successor
41 "And thou shalt dwell in the land of
   _____" (Genesis 45:10)
43 Women's historical organization
   (abbr.)
45 "_____ took of the fruit"
   (Genesis 3:6)
46 "Behold, I will put a fleece of
   _____" (Judges 6:37)
48 Egyptian sun god
49 Village 7 miles from Jerusalem
52 College degree (abbr.)
53 Grad student, at times (abbr.)
56 Lowest Anglo-Saxon freeman
58 19th-century evangelist

60 Asa and Ahab
62 "And he begat _____ and
   daughters" (Genesis 5:4)
63 Got rid of
65 Ceylon, for example
67 "But the dove found _____ rest for
   the sole of her foot" (Genesis 8:9)
68 Affirmative (Ger.)
69 Almost (abbr.)
72 Salem's state (abbr.)

35

ACROSS

1 "_____; Thy kingdom is divided" (Daniel 5:28)
6 "Let me do it" (2 words)
10 Cracked open
14 "Duke Timnah, duke _____" (1 Chronicles 1:51)
15 Spray weapon
16 Character on TV's "Hawaii 5-0"
17 Wear away
18 "Between blood and blood, between _____" (Deuteronomy 17:8)
19 "Belly is as wine which hath no _____" (Job 32:19)
20 "Not by the door into the _____" (John 10:1)
22 "Between Nineveh and _____" (Genesis 10:12)
23 Son of Zorobabel (Luke 3:27)
24 "Showed thee, O _____, what is good" (Micah 6:8)
25 Hymn (abbr.)
28 "_____ no man any thing" (Romans 13:8)
29 "Causeth contentions to cease, and _____ between the mighty" (Proverbs 18:18)
33 Paddles
35 "Unto him was Carshena, Shethar, _____" (Esther 1:14)
36 Helez's son (1 Chronicles 2:39)
40 "Thou art _____ in the balances" (Daniel 5:27)
41 "Said unto her, _____ cumi" (Mark 5:41)
42 "Glean _____ of corn" (Ruth 2:2)
43 "Herds that fed in Sharon was _____" (1 Chronicles 27:29)
44 New Testament book (abbr.)
47 _____ income
48 Old Testament book (abbr.)
49 "The sin which doth so easily _____" (Hebrews 12:1)
51 Remit
54 _____ nest
58 Iridescent stone
60 Glimpse
61 "Johanan, and Dalaiah, and _____" (1 Chronicles 3:24)
62 Mud
63 Fabled creature
64 Actor Jack, and others
65 "That _____ after the dust of the earth" (Amos 2:7)
66 "And unto Enoch was born _____" (Genesis 4:18)
67 Clean

DOWN

1 "And whatsoever goeth upon his _____" (Leviticus 11:27)
2 "Whom thou slewest in the valley of _____" (1 Samuel 21:9)
3 Ascend
4 "Fall into the mouth of the_____" (Nahum 3:12)
5 "Ebal, _____, and Onam" (Genesis 36:23)
6 Foist upon
7 _____ lily
8 Did well, as on an exam
9 Teachers' org.
10 Benefit
11 She slew Sisera
12 "There was one _____, a prophetess" (Luke 2:36)
13 Kind of IRA
21 Not many
22 "Pharez, Hezron, and _____" (1 Chronicles 4:1)
24 "And there _____ him a booth" (Jonah 4:5)
25 "As certain also of your own _____" (Acts 17:28)
26 Eber's father (Genesis 11:14)
27 Gad's son (Genesis 46:16)
29 "Delivered me out of the _____ of the lion" (1 Samuel 17:37)
30 _____ Frome, Wharton novel
31 Yonder
32 "For thou _____ cast me into the deep" (Jonah 2:3)

34 "For thus _____ the Lᴏʀᴅ of hosts"
(Haggai 2:6)
37 Dried grain stalks
38 Ahaziah's father (1 Kings 22:49)
39 "Bethel on the west, and _____ on
the east" (Genesis 12:8)
44 "Ye have _____ treasure together"
(James 5:3)
45 Cornerstone abbr.
46 "I have yet to speak on God's
_____" (Job 36:2)
49 "Shilshah, and Ithran, and _____"
(1 Chronicles 7:37)
50 Choir member
51 "_____ and Circumstance"
52 Capital of Western Samoa
53 "Merchants received the linen
_____ at a price"
(1 Kings 10:28)
54 Anxiety

55 "And it is a _____ thing"
(Daniel 2:11)
56 Expires
57 Platter
59 Allow
60 Greek letter

by Tonya Vilhauer

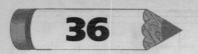

Three Monetary Lesson[s]

The three theme answers a[re]
possible titles for the three lessons cite[d]
all dealing with coi[ns]

ACROSS

1 "An _____ pleasing to the Lord" (Leviticus 1:9 NIV)
6 Transcript data (abbr.)
9 "Crying, _____, Father" (Galatians 4:6)
13 Largest Philippine island
14 "Eat not of it _____, nor sodden" (Exodus 12:9)
15 Chunk of earth
16 **LESSON 1:** When a sinner repents (Luke 15:8–10 NIV) (4 words)
19 Daily Planet reporter
20 "He _____ and worshipped him" (Mark 5:6)
21 "Men condemned to die in the _____" (1 Corinthians 4:9 NIV)
22 "How long will it be _____ they believe me" (Numbers 14:11)
23 Valley of _____ Hinnom (Joshua 18:16 NIV)
24 "Walking after their _____ lusts" (Jude 16)
25 Links gadget
26 Sure competitor?
27 _____ Mahal
30 Get soaked?
33 Obtain
34 Woody's son
35 **LESSON 2:** On the paying of taxes (Matthew 17:27 NIV) (5 words)
38 "From the lions' _____" (Song of Solomon 4:8)
39 "You may know the hope to which he _____ called you" (Ephesians 1:18 NIV)
40 Philistines' god (Judges 16:23)
41 112° 30' from N
42 "Their conscience seared with a _____ iron" (1 Timothy 4:2)
43 "_____ it is written" (Matthew 4:6)

44 "And the _____ of Carmel shall wither" (Amos 1:2)
45 Push hard
46 Mineral spring
49 "And _____ Aaron of his garments" (Numbers 20:26)
52 "A wise _____ maketh a glad father" (Proverbs 10:1)
53 _____ Street
54 **LESSON 3:** True sacrifice (Mark 12:41–44) (3 words)
57 "They _____ perverse and crooke[d] generation" (Deuteronomy 32:5) (2 words)
58 "_____ no man any thing" (Romans 13:8)
59 Esso competitor
60 Signs of spring
61 "For our _____ is come" (Lamentations 4:18)
62 "She maketh fine _____ " (Proverbs 31:24)

DOWN

1 "Cast alive into _____ of fire" (Revelation 19:20) (2 words)
2 "I will make thee _____ over man[y] things" (Matthew 25:21)
3 Earth's natural UV blocking layer
4 "It is _____ holy unto the LORD" (Exodus 30:10)
5 "Go to the _____ " (Proverbs 6:6)
6 "For in this we _____ " (2 Corinthians 5:2)
7 "The _____ as of a woman in travail" (Jeremiah 22:23)
8 Rye bristle
9 Sign of fall
10 "And he made a vail of _____ " (Exodus 36:35)
11 Former capital of West Germany

by David K. Shortess

12 "Then he shall _____ fifth part" (Leviticus 27:13) (2 words)
17 Manitoba tribe
18 Forest youngster
23 _____ there, done that
24 "And again he denied with an _____" (Matthew 26:72)
25 "Give us _____ day our daily bread" (Matthew 6:11)
26 All _____ are off
27 Math branch
28 "Sweeter _____ than honey" (Psalm 19:10)
29 Zebedee's son (Matthew 10:2)
30 Said (arch.)
31 Hits a hole-in-one
32 Musical sound
33 Pest
34 "So is good news from _____ country" (Proverbs 25:25) (2 words)
36 Where "pancake" is understood (abbr.)

37 Esau's land
42 Arizona tribe
43 "Who _____ the coals into flame" (Isaiah 54:16 NIV)
44 Natives of northern New Mexico
45 "Nevertheless the men _____ hard" (Jonah 1:13)
46 "And _____ the right hand of God" (Mark 16:19) (2 words)
47 _____ work (such as sewing)
48 "Happy Days" actor Williams
49 Pierce
50 "No _____ Street"
51 "A _____ shaken with the wind" (Matthew 11:7)
52 "That which was _____ in his heart" (Matthew 13:19)
53 "La Boheme" role
55 "A loving _____, a graceful deer" (Proverbs 5:19 NIV)
56 Last O.T. book

37

ACROSS

1 Formerly Persia
5 "Woe to _____ that is filthy and polluted" (Zephaniah 3:1)
8 Axis
12 Spire
13 Where Sargon took some captive Israelites (2 Kings 17:6)
15 "Hold the _____" (deli order)
16 Coin
17 City in Naphtali (Joshua 19:33)
18 David's grandfather
19 City between Zoreah and Zanoah (Joshua 15:33–34)
21 "Grafted contrary to _____ into a good olive tree" (Romans 11:24)
23 Quaint
24 Presidential initials
25 Court's partner
28 Actress Sandra
29 Dell models, e.g.
32 Taut
33 "Ye shall speak into the _____" (1 Corinthians 14:9)
34 Apartment, in England
35 "As a bowing wall. . .as a _____ fence" (Psalm 62:3)
37 Geometric surface
38 Addition column
39 Wail
40 Depends, with "on"
41 By
42 Greek letter
43 Slang
44 Pronoun (Fr.)
45 Slob
46 Realm
49 Having feet (pl.)
53 Twelve months
54 "That's all, _____"
56 Newspaper sect.
58 Rim
59 Perspire
60 Broccoli _____
61 "With your _____ after you" (Genesis 9:9)

62 Old Testament book (abbr.)
63 Wall Street abbr.

DOWN

1 Govt. regulatory agency
2 "Deliver thyself as a _____ from the hand of the hunter" (Proverbs 6:5)
3 New Testament prophetess
4 NJ pro team
5 Bedad's son (Genesis 36:35)
6 Shimei's father (1 Kings 4:18)
7 "A _____ caught in a thicket by his horns" (Genesis 22:13)
8 Struck, biblically
9 Fragrance by Dana
10 One who stares
11 Type
13 What Paul touched to heal the sick (Acts 19:12)
14 Block
20 Mount, to some
22 Summer drink
25 Rock
26 Also known as Cephas
27 Hill builders
28 Burrow
29 City near Dallas
30 Biblical verb
31 Jeanne d'Arc (abbr.)
33 At all
34 Tire
35 Lid
36 Ezbon's brother (1 Chronicles 7:7)
37 "They came to _____ in Pamphylia" (Acts 13:13)
40 "Thou takest up that thou _____ not down" (Luke 19:21, var.)
42 _____ favor (Sp.)
44 Stuck
45 Remaliah's son (2 Kings 15:25)
46 "Your _____ shall be opened" (Genesis 3:5)
47 Darius the _____ (Daniel 11:1)
48 Leaf
49 _____ bargain

by Sarah Lagerquist Simmons

50 Unable to decide
51 Popular Internet site
52 Brothers and sisters, for short
55 Have
57 Summer shirt

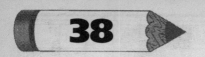

38

Jesus and the Sea

Note that of the long theme answers, only 17 Across is a direct quote from scripture. The other two, 41 and 65 Across, are not.

ACROSS

1 Georgetown jocks
6 One of two countries that claims Everest
11 "Which of you shall have. . .an ox fallen into a _____" (Luke 14:5)
14 Not hidden
15 "And if a man shall _____ pit. . . and not cover it" (Exodus 21:33) (2 words)
16 Jazz, for one
17 "And in the fourth watch of the night Jesus went unto them, _____" (Matthew 14:25) (4 words)
20 "It shall be _____ with him" (Isaiah 3:11)
21 "Praise the _____" (Psalm 115:18)
22 "He _____ his meat and eats his fill" (Isaiah 44:16 NIV)
23 David, to many
24 Forks in the road
25 Leaf attachment point
28 "_____ art thou" (Genesis 27:32)
30 "Neither could any man _____ him" (Mark 5:4)
34 Hemoglobin deficiency
37 "And his word is not _____" (1 John 1:10) (2 words)
40 Shea spectator
41 What happened when a great storm arose on the sea (Mark 4:39) (4 words)
44 NATO member (abbr.)
45 Edible plant of the genus Brassica
46 "But if thou _____ go down, go thou with. . .thy servant" (Judges 7:10) (2 words)
47 CIA operative
49 "Get up! Pick up your _____ and walk" (John 5:8 NIV)
51 "_____ John" (missive type)
52 "Barnabas they called _____" (Acts 14:12 NIV)

55 French 101 verb
58 "A young _____ and told Moses" (Numbers 11:27 NIV) (2 words)
61 _____ vera
62 "They that _____ in tears shall reap in joy" (Psalm 126:5)
65 What Peter, James, and John found in their nets (Luke 5:4–7) (5 words)
68 Vote cast
69 "In the first month, that is, the month _____" (Esther 3:7)
70 Clear the board
71 Poem of praise
72 Alamogordo's county
73 "Art thou a _____" (Acts 22:27)

DOWN

1 "Consider _____ love thy precepts" (Psalm 119:159) (2 words)
2 Track shape
3 Give a holler
4 "Take up the _____ of the covenant" (Joshua 3:6)
5 Steps on a fence
6 "He causeth the grass _____ for the cattle" (Psalm 104:14) (2 words)
7 Trendy digital accessory
8 _____-oni, Rachel's son
9 "She crieth. . .at the _____ of the city" (Proverbs 8:3)
10 California/Nevada border lake
11 "And it came to _____" (Genesis 6:1)
12 "Through thy precepts _____ understanding" (Psalm 119:104) (2 words)
13 Herbal and green
18 Than
19 "_____ of Eden," Steinbeck opus
23 Blood (prefix)
24 Habit
25 Follower of Micah

by David K. Shortess

26 "As the Lord hath called every
   _____ let him walk"
   (1 Corinthians 7:17) (2 words)
27 Transferable picture
29 "And shall _____ multitude of sins"
   (James 5:20) (2 words)
31 "And the tongue is _____, a world
   of iniquity" (James 3:6) (2 words)
32 Devilfish
33 "There is a woman that hath a
   familiar spirit at _____"
   (1 Samuel 28:7)
35 Type
36 "Seeing I _____ stranger"
   (Ruth 2:10) (2 words)
38 Most TV channels (abbr.)
39 Understand
42 "Under oaks and poplars and
   _____" (Hosea 4:13)
43 Trudge through
48 Old Testament scribe
50 "They should _____ man of him"
   (Mark 8:30) (2 words)

53 "Ye shall _____ manner of fat"
   (Leviticus 7:23) (2 words)
54 Not qualified
56 "It was _____ painful for me"
   (Psalm 73:16)
57 Direct toward
58 Minnesota clinic
59 "Ish-bosheth, who lay on _____ at
   noon" (2 Samuel 4:5) (2 words)
60 "These are a smoke in my _____"
   (Isaiah 65:5)
61 Like a wing
62 Burma neighbor, once
63 Greek mountain
64 "_____ I was a child"
   (1 Corinthians 13:11)
66 "_____ not vain repetitions"
   (Matthew 6:7)
67 "From going to and _____ in the
   earth" (Job 1:7)

39

ACROSS

1 Mountain range considered boundary between Europe and Asia
5 Riches' predecessors
9 Jeroboam's father (2 Kings 15:18)
14 Expensive perfume, such as Mary used
15 Chelub's son (1 Chronicles 27:26)
16 "Adam, Sheth, _____" (1 Chronicles 1:1)
17 Everglades critter, for short
18 Resemble
19 "To the battle at _____" (Numbers 21:33)
20 Was first
21 "Children of base men: they were _____ than the earth" (Job 30:8)
22 We should be not just hearers but _____ of the Word
23 "Of Eri, the family of the _____" (Numbers 26:16)
25 "And Simeon that was called _____" (Acts 13:1)
26 Hill builders
28 Bani's son (Ezra 10:34)
31 "_____ the Carmelite" (1 Chronicles 11:37)
34 Linger
37 "Even the city of _____ the father of Anak" (Joshua 15:13)
38 Ahithophel's son (2 Samuel 23:34)
39 "And over the fowl of the _____" (Genesis 1:26)
40 Sharar's son (2 Samuel 23:33)
41 Saw, for one
42 "_____ and Caiaphas being the high priests" (Luke 3:2)
44 Maui is one
45 "_____ builders did hew them" (1 Kings 5:18)
47 Hoover, for example
49 Hirsute
52 Cleansed
57 "Child shall play on the hole of the _____" (Isaiah 11:8)

60 "And Serug lived thirty years, and begat _____" (Genesis 11:22)
62 Complete
63 Ezra's son (1 Chronicles 4:17)
65 "Maaz, and Jamin, and _____" (1 Chronicles 2:27)
67 "As he saith also in _____" (Romans 9:25)
68 Single
69 Cush's son (Genesis 10:7)
70 Construe
71 More sunburned
72 "And _____ gave names to all cattle" (Genesis 2:20)
73 Finishes

DOWN

1 Sam, for one
2 More precious
3 "Shuni, and Ezbon, Eri, and _____" (Genesis 46:16)
4 Third World countries, mostly (abbr.)
5 Withstand
6 "Eleasah his son, _____ his son" (1 Chronicles 8:37)
7 Jade, for example
8 Hosah's son (1 Chronicles 26:10)
9 "And _____ not that any should testify of man" (John 2:25)
10 Witch of _____
11 Drill
12 "Phanuel, of the tribe of _____" (Luke 2:36)
13 "_____ is the day which the LORD hath made" (Psalm 118:24)
21 Ire
24 "And Rekem, and Irpeel, and _____" (Joshua 18:27)
27 "And the _____, and the pelican, and the gier eagle" (Leviticus 11:18)
28 Author Leon
29 "The curse upon Mount _____" (Deuteronomy 11:29)
30 Whom Jesus healed, with "the"

by Tonya Vilhauer

31 "And Ephron dwelt among the children of _____" (Genesis 23:10)
32 "_____, lama sabachthani?" (Mark 15:34)
33 "Which is Hebron, and _____" (Joshua 15:54)
35 "On the east side of _____" (Numbers 34:11)
36 "And unto Enoch was born _____" (Genesis 4:18)
37 Aram's brother (1 Chronicles 7:34)
42 Continent
43 Adage
46 Mien
48 Gullet
50 Zorobabel's son (Luke 3:27)
51 "Be ye not unequally _____ together" (2 Corinthians 6:14)
53 Lake _____ Drive, in Chicago

54 "Their _____, and their hats" (Daniel 3:21)
55 "Shuthelah his son, and Ezer, and _____" (1 Chronicles 7:21)
56 Actions
57 Partly open
58 Parlor (Sp.)
59 Till
61 Singer McEntire
64 "Thou believest that there is _____ God" (James 2:19)
66 "And a _____ of three years old" (Genesis 15:9)

40

ACROSS

1 King of Judah for 41 years
4 Split rattan
8 "The king of Israel is come out to seek a _____" (1 Samuel 26:20)
12 New Testament book (abbr.)
13 Kind of code
14 Base
15 Be a gymnast
17 "A time to cast away _____, and a time to gather" (Ecclesiastes 3:5)
19 Cuddle, in earlier days
20 Judge of Israel
21 Overweight
24 Gad's son (Genesis 46:16)
27 Pest
29 Close
31 _____ Sea
32 I _____ (name of God)
33 "We were driven up and down in _____" (Acts 27:27)
34 D.C. quadrant
35 "I will _____ you out of their bondage" (Exodus 6:6)
37 Abbey, for one
38 "Many of them. . .used curious _____" (Acts 19:19)
40 Tempest
42 "They make _____ to shed innocent blood" (Isaiah 59:7)
44 "Samuel said unto the _____, Bring the portion" (1 Samuel 9:23)
46 Situate
49 "I will _____ again unto you" (Acts 18:21)
51 More intense
52 "The words of _____, who was among the herdmen of Tekoa" (Amos 1:1)
53 Tie
55 Samuel's mentor
56 "Drink the _____ blood of the grape" (Deuteronomy 32:14)
57 "There is no _____ to them that fear him" (Psalm 34:9)
58 80 or 66 (abbr.)

DOWN

1 "Praise him for his mighty _____" (Psalm 150:2)
2 Pea _____
3 Just about
4 "Is not _____ as Carchemish" (Isaiah 10:9)
5 Is
6 Iowa's neighbor (abbr.)
7 "Take thine _____, eat, drink, and be merry" (Luke 12:19)
8 Whole wheat, for one
9 "As with the _____, so with the borrower" (Isaiah 24:2)
10 "Set seven _____ lambs of the flock by themselves" (Genesis 21:28)
11 Much of magazines
16 "They were baptized, _____ men and women" (Acts 8:12)
18 Abraham's father (Luke 3:34)
22 Disentangle
23 "_____ lived seventy years and begat Abram" (Genesis 11:26)
25 In case
26 March time
27 _____ Hill, in Athens
28 Leave out
30 Verdi opera
33 "Put on the full _____ of God" (Ephesians 6:11 NIV)
36 Luke, for one
38 Tamarisk tree
39 Grim one?
41 "An old lion; who shall _____ him up" (Genesis 49:9)
43 "She. . .had _____ all that she had" (Mark 5:26)
45 "They _____ that he had spoken the parable against them" (Mark 12:12)
47 Ancient European
48 Great Lake
49 Strike
50 Flightless bird
51 Lair
54 Kind of hospital (abbr.)

by Evelyn M. Boyington

41

ACROSS

1 Grandmother of Jesse
5 Jether's son (1 Chronicles 7:38)
8 Mordecai's nemesis
13 Region
14 "_____, TEKEL, UPHARSIN" (Daniel 5:25)
16 God's love for man (Gr.)
17 "Who will make me a _____" (Job 24:25)
18 Ellipsoidal
19 Yarns
20 Relaxes, with "up"
22 "_____ lived ninety years" (Genesis 5:9)
24 Ease
25 Descendants of a Manassite clan of Gilead (Numbers 26:32)
28 "He may _____ mercy upon you" (Jeremiah 42:12)
29 Odious
34 "_____ did that which was right in the eyes of the LORD" (1 Kings 15:11)
37 Enan's son (Numbers 1:15)
38 Issue
41 "Hast thou entered into the _____ of the sea?" (Job 38:16)
43 Squeak
44 As well
45 "I do _____ my bow in the cloud" (Genesis 9:13)
46 Asp
49 "They did _____ it with an omer" (Exodus 16:18)
51 "As a bride _____ herself with her jewels" (Isaiah 61:10)
53 Guitarist's aid, briefly
56 Grant's _____, in NYC
59 Craft
60 Senior
62 John's time on Patmos, for example
64 "Observe the month of _____" (Deuteronomy 16:1)
66 Lazy

67 Prince of Persia and Media under Ahasuerus (Esther 1:14)
68 Alike
69 Rivals
70 All
71 "The soldiers _____ him away" (Mark 15:16)
72 Chemical suffixes

DOWN

1 Abnormal breathing sound
2 Bathsheba's husband
3 Antagonize
4 Beth-gader's father (1 Chronicles 2:51)
5 Master (Sp.)
6 Worship
7 Elioenai's son (1 Chronicles 3:24)
8 Derby, for one
9 Sarai's handmaid (Galatians 4:24)
10 Gender
11 Mimics
12 "As an eagle stirreth up her _____" (Deuteronomy 32:11)
15 Uzziah rebuilt this city (2 Chronicles 26:1–2)
21 _____ Na Na, "oldies" group
23 "Joseph gathered corn as the sand of the _____" (Genesis 41:49)
26 "The fire shall _____ be burning" (Leviticus 6:13)
27 What the Magi followed
30 Naaman's brother (Genesis 46:21)
31 "Whatsoever hath _____ and scales in the waters" (Leviticus 11:9)
32 "The Pharisees began to _____ him vehemently" (Luke 11:53)
33 "That which shall befall you in the _____ days" (Genesis 49:1)
34 Belonging to NCAA's eastern conference (abbr.)
35 Holding a grudge
36 Mamre's brother (Genesis 14:13)
39 Competent
40 Got by

by Sarah Lagerquist Simmons

41 Once
42 Bard
47 "City of the priests" (1 Samuel 22:19)
48 "Came unto them to _____ in five days" (Acts 20:6)
50 "I am _____ door" (John 10:9)
52 Abigail's husband (1 Samuel 25:3)
53 Make room for? (2 words)
54 Noisy scene
55 Beg
56 "The inhabitants of the land of _____ brought water to him" (Isaiah 21:14)
57 Farm team?
58 "The _____ places thereof and the marishes" (Ezekiel 47:11)
61 "Breathed into his nostrils the breath of _____" (Genesis 2:7)

63 Dec. in NYC
65 Put to _____

"The kingdom of heaven is like a king wh
prepared a wedding banquet for his son

MATTHEW 22:2 N

ACROSS

1 "Do not stand up for _____ cause" (Ecclesiastes 8:3 NIV) (2 words)
5 Official records
9 Memorable shrine
14 "With what measure ye _____, it shall be measured to you" (Mark 4:24)
15 "A threefold _____ is not quickly broken" (Ecclesiastes 4:12)
16 "And it came to pass in the month _____" (Nehemiah 2:1)
17 "That in the _____ to come" (Ephesians 2:7)
18 Altitude (abbr.)
19 Slip by
20 Start of **QUOTE** (Song of Solomon 2:4 NIV) (4 words)
23 "_____ by Starlight," pop hit of the 40s
24 Olds model
25 IRA kin
28 **QUOTE**, part 2 (3 words)
32 Wee sizes (abbr.)
35 "And they will _____ out of his kingdom" (Matthew 13:41 NIV)
36 Leah's first son (Genesis 29:32)
37 **QUOTE**, part 3 (1 word)
39 To _____
41 "Drunk my wine with my milk: _____ friends" (Song of Solomon 5:1) (2 words)
42 "The priest is to offer _____ sin offering" (Numbers 6:11 NIV) (3 words)
45 Shem's father (Genesis 6:10)
48 Tennis shot
49 **QUOTE**, part 4 (3 words)
52 _____ Cruces, NM
53 Soap staple, once
54 "What _____ is that to you" (Luke 6:32 NIV)
58 End of **QUOTE** (4 words)
61 Over's partner
64 County or party
65 "Be as I am; for I _____ ye are" (Galatians 4:12) (2 words)
66 "From the _____ of thy wood" (Deuteronomy 29:11)
67 "And it had great _____ teeth" (Daniel 7:7)
68 "And pitched his _____ there" (Genesis 26:25)
69 "In darkness have _____ great light" (Isaiah 9:2) (2 words)
70 Aerie
71 "For my yoke is _____" (Matthew 11:30)

DOWN

1 Asian nannies
2 "When thou shalt _____ children" (Deuteronomy 4:25)
3 "While they _____ stood near them under a tree" (Genesis 18:8 NIV) (2 words)
4 Use reverse osmosis
5 Old movie film material
6 Soda pop flavor
7 "Star _____"
8 Verb modifier
9 Windflower
10 "Man shall not _____ by bread alone" (Matthew 4:4)
11 Abijam's successor (1 Kings 15:8)
12 "I am not _____, most noble Festus" (Acts 26:25)
13 "Was not arrayed like _____ of these" (Matthew 6:29)
21 "The Lord is _____ to anger" (Nahum 1:3)

by David K. Shortess

22 "Let us draw _____ with a true heart" (Hebrews 10:22)
25 Japheth's son (Genesis 10:2)
26 "David, _____ thine own house" (2 Chronicles 10:16) (2 words)
27 "As yet shall he remain _____ that day" (Isaiah 10:32) (2 words)
29 "_____ thee two tables of stone" (Exodus 34:1)
30 Minneapolis suburb
31 What, in Juarez
32 Sandbar
33 "Our fathers did eat _____ in the desert" (John 6:31)
34 Iditarod vehicles
38 _____-dee-dah
40 Large amount
43 "And I'll give you ten shekels of _____ year" (Judges 17:10 NIV) (2 words)

44 "Carried away unto these dumb idols, even _____ were led" (1 Corinthians 12:2) (2 words)
46 _____ of days
47 Not his
50 "Alexander's Ragtime Band" composer
51 Integrate
55 "She replied, _____ special favor" (Judges 1:15 NIV) (3 words)
56 "The Great" and "The Terrible"
57 Irritable
58 "They are all hot as an _____" (Hosea 7:7)
59 "I sink in deep _____" (Psalm 69:2)
60 Adam's grandson (Luke 3:38)
61 Relatives of oohs
62 Bonnet occupant?
63 "_____ no man any thing, but to love one another" (Romans 13:8)

43

ACROSS

1 "Whatsoever creepeth upon the earth, after their _____" (Genesis 8:19)
6 Throng
10 Daddy (Aramaic)
14 Sarah's son
15 Not ending
16 Seethe
17 Abishag the _____, a young virgin (1 Kings 1:3)
19 Suggestion
20 "And put _____ into the garden of Eden" (Genesis 2:15)
21 Understand
22 "Like a serpent; _____ poison is under their lips" (Psalm 140:3)
24 Line formed at the joint of two pieces of material
25 "They which are in _____ be turned away from me" (2 Timothy 1:15)
26 Grant Wood, for example
29 "The _____ of a wound cleanseth away evil" (Proverbs 20:30)
33 Brief
34 Squash, for one
35 White or bald-faced
36 "And straightway they forsook their _____" (Mark 1:18)
37 "But I _____ you. . .to go and bear fruit" (John 15:16 NIV)
38 Wheel
39 "And there was war between _____ and Baasha" (1 Kings 15:16)
40 Man of the _____
41 "Were with him from _____ of Judah" (2 Samuel 6:2)
42 Shallum's father (Nehemiah 3:12)
44 "Take of them of the captivity, even of _____" (Zechariah 6:10)
45 Turf
46 "And _____ it with the king's ring" (Esther 8:8)
47 Neoteric

50 "They _____ to and fro" (Psalm 107:27)
51 "Moses went. . .and _____ him up into the mount" (Exodus 24:18)
54 Judah's son (Genesis 38:4)
55 "The robber _____ up their substance" (Job 5:5)
58 Farm measure
59 "Trode them down with _____ over against Gibeah" (Judges 20:43)
60 Magi, for example
61 Bow
62 Colored, as Easter eggs
63 "Thou shalt rise up before the _____ head" (Leviticus 19:32)

DOWN

1 Saul's father (1 Samuel 9:3)
2 Zoheth's father (1 Chronicles 4:20)
3 "Son of Amos, which was the son of _____" (Luke 3:25)
4 Jacob's son
5 "Then thou _____ me with dreams" (Job 7:14)
6 Lotan's son (Genesis 36:22)
7 Roman poet
8 Group
9 "For where your _____ is, there" (Matthew 6:21)
10 Gideoni's son (Numbers 10:24)
11 Augur
12 Coffin
13 "They shall say in all the highways, _____" (Amos 5:16)
18 "And did all eat the same spiritual _____" (1 Corinthians 10:3)
23 Withered away
24 "Saying, _____, ye are brethren" (Acts 7:26)
25 "Departed from Dophkah, and encamped in _____" (Numbers 33:13)
26 "The children of _____" (Ezra 2:50)
27 Zorobabel's son (Luke 3:27)
28 Aggregate

by Tonya Vilhauer

29 "Made him a _____, and sat under it" (Jonah 4:5)
30 "Shuthelah his son, and Ezer, and _____" (1 Chronicles 7:21)
31 "House of Millo, which goeth down to _____" (2 Kings 12:20)
32 "Mattathias, which was the son of _____" (Luke 3:26)
34 "They were all filled with the Holy _____" (Acts 2:4)
37 "He that is to be _____ shall wash" (Leviticus 14:8)
38 Corridor
40 Former spouse of Sonny
41 "Ziph, and Telem, and _____" (Joshua 15:24)
43 Unlocked
44 Canine command
46 Nadab's son who died without children (1 Chronicles 2:30)

47 Orpah's land
48 Formerly
49 Mend
50 Destroy (Brit.)
51 Shimei's father (1 Kings 2:8)
52 "The children of _____ of Hezekiah" (Ezra 2:16)
53 "Thy rod and thy staff _____ comfort me" (Psalm 23:4)
56 "Turn again, my daughters, go your _____" (Ruth 1:12)
57 "That he _____ loveth God love his brother" (1 John 4:21)

44

ACROSS

1 Stool or stone
5 New grass
8 Chest, maybe
12 Stew
13 First woman
14 Retired, in a way
15 God
16 Stomach
17 Affection
18 Ms. Horne, and others
20 Torn apart
21 "God trieth the hearts and _____"
(Psalm 7:9)
23 Japheth's son (Genesis 10:2)
24 City of Asher (Judges 1:31)
26 "He that _____ a matter separateth
very friends" (Proverbs 17:9)
30 Buddhist sect
31 "I am _____ door" (John 10:9)
32 O.T. book (abbr.)
34 Actor Lugosi
35 Owns
36 Smooth
38 Build
39 Fee
40 Hot _____
41 Bela's son (1 Chronicles 7:7)
43 "_____, lama sabachthani?"
(Mark 15:34)
44 Being
45 _____ sequitur
46 Meek
47 Pronoun, to King James
48 Relative
49 Zerubbabel's son
(1 Chronicles 3:20)

DOWN

1 Go 9 to 5
2 More mature, maybe
3 Solo
4 _____ Lama
5 Noah's son (Luke 3:36)
6 Egg-shaped
7 Mist
8 City near Aenon where John the
Baptist baptized (John 3:23)
9 Over's partner
10 Temperature
11 Utopia
19 Nip
20 Toga
22 "Destroy all the children of _____
(Numbers 24:17)
23 "And the ___ of hell shall not
prevail" (Matthew 16:18)
25 "And Isaac came from the way of the
well _____" (Genesis 24:62)
26 Set free
27 One who is subject to law
28 "Make _____ a crown of gold"
(Exodus 25:24)
29 Joktan's son (Genesis 10:29)
30 Haman's spouse (Esther 5:10)
33 Grow
34 Consumed with troubles
37 Town on the boundary between
Zebulun and Asher (Joshua 19:27)
41 "I wrote them with _____ in the
book" (Jeremiah 36:18)
42 Where there was no room?

by Sarah Lagerquist Simmons

45

ACROSS

1 "But Noah found _____ in the eyes of the Lord" (Genesis 6:8)
5 Advanced degree (abbr.)
7 IOU, in other words
11 Fabled dwarflike creature
12 "Have I _____ of mad men" (1 Samuel 21:15)
13 Some votes
15 Hawaiian island
16 "And it is a _____ thing that the king requireth" (Daniel 2:11)
17 "For thee have I seen righteous before _____ in this generation" (Genesis 7:1)
18 O.T. time
19 Marching cadence (abbr.)
20 "And there shall come forth a rod out of the _____ of Jesse" (Isaiah 11:1)
21 Thanks (Brit.)
22 Andy Capp's wife
23 "_____, Joy of Man's Desiring"
26 "I will not be afraid what man can _____ unto me" (Psalm 56:11)
28 Proofreader's mark
30 Highway sign of years past
32 "Containing the gold _____ of manna" (Hebrews 9:4 MSG)
34 "Wake up, harp! wake up, _____" (Psalm 57:8 MSG)
35 Egg
37 Spineless one (colloq.)
39 "And Abraham was old, and well stricken in _____" (Genesis 24:1)
41 Ship's initials
42 Time long past
43 Salary _____ (pl.)
44 _____ Canals in U.S. and Canada
46 Volunteer state (abbr.)
47 Blind, in falconry
48 Chesapeake, for one (abbr.)
50 "Yea, hath God said, _____ shall not eat of every tree of the garden" (Genesis 3:1)
51 "_____ teach us to number our days" (Psalm 90:12)
52 Affirmative
55 Ocean shelf made of coral
57 "And the _____ he prepared. . .to set there the ark" (1 Kings 6:19)
60 Pine _____
62 College degree (abbr.)
63 "And fell on their faces in _____ worship" (1 Kings 18:39 MSG)
66 College plant?
68 Article (Ger.)
69 "In all places where I _____ my name" (Exodus 20:24)
71 Baking chamber
73 "And it came to pass _____ the seventh day" (2 Samuel 12:18)
75 "By man shall his blood be _____" (Genesis 9:6)
76 Greek letter
77 Weekday (abbr.)
78 "And I shall be whiter than _____" (Psalm 51:7)
79 Eugene's home? (abbr.)
80 "And thou shalt make a _____ seat of pure gold" (Exodus 25:17)

DOWN

1 "The dust will become _____" (Exodus 8:16 NIV)
2 _____ Tae Woo, South Korean president
3 Entertains
4 Time from Christ's birth (abbr.)
5 Mal de _____
6 Holy _____
8 "Neither shall thine _____ pity him" (Deuteronomy 13:8)
9 "He will not suffer thy foot to _____ moved" (Psalm 121:3)
10 What Moses brought down from Mount Sinai (pl.)
11 "For _____ so loved the world" (John 3:16)
12 "I will never blot out his _____" (Revelation 3:5 NIV)
14 Teatime treats
16 "For God had made them _____ with great joy" (Nehemiah 12:43)

by Marijane G. Troyer

17 "So that thou shalt be _____ for the sight of thine eyes" (Deuteronomy 28:34)
24 "But my God shall _____ all your need" (Philippians 4:19)
25 Abraham's homeland
27 Spread
29 "And rejoiced with great _____" (1 Kings 1:40)
30 "_____ your bread there" (Amos 7:12 NIV)
31 D.C. quadrant
33 Continent (abbr.)
36 Adult U.S. citizen, maybe
38 Actress West
40 Where Brownies bake? (abbr.)
45 Midianite priest killed by Gideon (Judges 7:25)
47 Energy or system
49 Library sect.
50 Alpine sound

51 Where Clemson U. is (abbr.)
53 French conjunction
54 Mentioned
56 "But the just shall live by his _____" (Habakkuk 2:4)
58 David's son, who coveted his half sister
59 "From following the _____ great with young" (Psalm 78:71)
61 Home on wheels (abbr.)
64 "Their calls will _____ through the windows" (Zephaniah 2:14 NIV)
65 "For the LORD. . .plentifully rewardeth the proud _____" (Psalm 31:23)
67 "Then _____ eyes shall be opened" (Genesis 3:5)
70 Byway (abbr.)
72 Prodigal son's nadir, in a word
74 _____ show
76 Augusta is its capital (abbr.)

46

Whom Will You Serve?

Serve the LORD with gladness
come before his presence with singing.

PSALM 100:2

ACROSS

1 Start of **QUOTE** (Joshua 24:15 NIV)
4 Takes a dip
9 Took on
14 Cabinet wood
15 "Their strength is _____ still" (Isaiah 30:7) (2 words)
16 Range maker
17 "We sailed to the _____ of Crete" (Acts 27:7 NIV)
18 "Like men condemned to die in the _____" (1 Corinthians 4:9 NIV)
19 Country singer Travis
20 **QUOTE**, part 2 (5 words)
23 "Kiss Me, _____"
24 Glide on water or snow
25 Inhabitant of northern Iraq
29 Rave's other half
33 "Let the young _____ arise" (2 Samuel 2:14) (2 words)
35 "_____ is this King of glory" (Psalm 24:8)
38 Call her Mara (Ruth 1:20)
41 "Most _____ Felix" (Acts 24:3)
42 **QUOTE**, part 3 (3 words)
45 "How long shall _____ with you" (Mark 9:19 NIV) (2 words)
46 "So, as much as in me _____ ready to preach" (Romans 1:15) (3 words)
47 Latin case (abbr.)
48 "Beware of the _____ of the Pharisees" (Mark 8:15)
50 Prohibitionists
52 "Woe to them that are at _____ in Zion" (Amos 6:1)
53 Row
56 *¿Cómo _____ usted?*
60 End of **QUOTE** (3 words)
65 "For who _____ save the LORD" (Psalm 18:31) (2 words)
68 "Such _____ in darkness and in the shadow of death" (Psalm 107:10) (2 words)
69 Pooh's pal
70 "And it shall be to the LORD for _____" (Isaiah 55:13) (2 words)
71 "Out of _____ the issues of life" (Proverbs 4:23) (2 words)
72 What Malchus lost, for a time
73 "_____ are trapped by evil times" (Ecclesiastes 9:12 NIV) (2 words)
74 Nostrils
75 ID number (abbr.)

DOWN

1 Moabite king (Numbers 22:4)
2 "Whoever touches thorns _____ tool of iron" (2 Samuel 23:7 NIV) (2 words)
3 Felony
4 "And I will give him the morning _____" (Revelation 2:28)
5 "And the _____ shall eat them like wool" (Isaiah 51:8)
6 "Lo, _____ four men loose" (Daniel 3:25) (2 words)
7 Biblical currency (pl.)
8 Offended, in a way (var.)
9 "Do thyself no _____: for we are all here" (Acts 16:28)
10 "That _____ how frail I am" (Psalm 39:4) (3 words)
11 Bled, like fabric
12 "World without _____. Amen" (Ephesians 3:21)
13 "Give us this _____ our daily bread" (Matthew 6:11)
21 "_____ the land of the free"
22 "Mine eye also is _____ by reason" (Job 17:7)
26 Not asked for
27 "_____ great stone unto me this day" (1 Samuel 14:33) (2 words)
28 "And Isaac _____ in Gerar" (Genesis 26:6)

by David K. Shortess

30 "Moment, in the twinkling of _____" (1 Corinthians 15:52) (2 words)

31 Minor prophet (abbr.)

32 "This _____ say, is meaningless" (Ecclesiastes 8:14 NIV) (2 words)

34 Nemesis

35 "In that, _____ we were yet sinners" (Romans 5:8)

36 Beeri's son (Hosea 1:1)

37 "Hast thou not poured me _____ milk" (Job 10:10) (2 words)

39 D.C. United is one of its teams (abbr.)

40 "She gave me of the tree, and _____ eat" (Genesis 3:12) (2 words)

43 "I may provoke to emulation. . .and might_____ of them" (Romans 11:14) (2 words)

44 "Neither shall they learn _____ any more" (Micah 4:3)

49 Conjunction

51 Salt, in Bordeaux

54 "Why do. . .the people imagine _____ thing" (Psalm 2:1) (2 words)

55 "Come. . .into a desert place, and _____ while" (Mark 6:31) (2 words)

57 One of Job's afflictions (pl.)

58 "And they passing by Mysia came down to _____" (Acts 16:8)

59 "That women _____ themselves in modest apparel" (1 Timothy 2:9)

61 Perfect place

62 Romanov despot

63 Employ

64 Summers on the Seine

65 Belonging to Midwest state (abbr.)

66 _____-cone

67 Herd of whales

47

ACROSS

1 "The _____ looks of man shall be humbled" (Isaiah 2:11)
5 Flock tenders (Luke 2:8)
13 Expert
14 "They look and _____ upon me" (Psalm 22:17)
15 "He cuts me off from the _____" (Isaiah 38:12 NKJV)
16 Crabapple
18 Ahira's father (Numbers 1:15)
19 The valley of _____ (Psalm 84:6)
20 Rules etched in stone (Exodus 34:1) (2 words)
23 "My _____ is no longer central" (Galatians 2:20 MSG)
24 Sluggard's suggested role model (Proverbs 6:6)
25 "_____! Susanna" (song)
26 Maternal bird (Luke 13:34)
28 "They came to meet us. . .on the _____ Way" (Acts 28:15 NLT)
31 "He hath given occasions of speech against _____" (Deuteronomy 22:17)
32 Samarian prophet (2 Chronicles 28:9)
34 Subway's opposite (abbr.)
35 Follows Old Testament (abbr.)
37 Hiel's youngest son (1 Kings 16:34)
38 "And ye shall _____ in plenty" (Joel 2:26)
40 "It will be built again, with _____ and moat" (Daniel 9:25 NASB)
43 Isaac's well (Genesis 26:20)
44 Head (obsolete)
45 Son in Aramaic (Matthew 16:17)
46 Where Abraham lived (Genesis 22:19) (2 words)
49 Comedian Caesar
50 Trifle
51 Maacah to Absalom (2 Samuel 3:3)
53 Causes sibling tears (Matthew 7:5)
55 Divorced his foreign wife (Ezra 10:24)

57 "Will cause the sun to go down at _____" (Amos 8:9)
59 "Nor is his _____ satisfied with riches" (Ecclesiastes 4:8 NKJV)
60 "And Arad, and _____" (1 Chronicles 8:15)
61 Where Samson lived (Judges 15:8)
63 What the stone will do (Habakkuk 2:19)
65 Serious (Titus 2:6)
67 Flying saucer's opposite (abbr.)
68 Og's chief city (Deuteronomy 1:4)
69 "For these _____ I weep" (Lamentations 1:16)

DOWN

1 Israel's sheep (Matthew 15:24)
2 "The faith which _____" (Galatians 1:23) (3 words)
3 Frond-producing plant
4 "I will cut off every _____ of Baal" (Zephaniah 1:4 NKJV)
5 "A rod out of the _____ of Jesse" (Isaiah 11:1)
6 Musical priest (Nehemiah 12:36)
7 Ephraim's grandson (Numbers 26:35–36)
8 Earring style (Song of Solomon 1:10 MSG)
9 Luz renamed (Genesis 35:6–7)
10 Reddish-brown and spotted
11 "Gamaliel, a _____ of the law" (Acts 5:34)
12 What God will do to sacred stones (Exodus 34:13 NIV)
17 West Indian fish
21 "How long are you going to _____ over Saul?" (1 Samuel 16:1 MSG)
22 North Star state (abbr.)
26 Married a prostitute on God's command (Hosea 1:2)
27 Southern desert region (Genesis 13:1 AMP notes)
29 Enjoyments (Titus 3:3)
30 "Broke into an _____ of praise" (Luke 2:38 MSG)

by Mary Ann Sherman

33 Tribal leader (Genesis 36:15)
36 "She came to prove him with _____ questions" (1 Kings 10:1)
39 Tree (Isaiah 44:14)
40 Greek philosopher
41 "Though I be _____ the flesh" (Colossians 2:5) (2 words)
42 Where Joram smote the Edomites (2 Kings 8:21)
44 "He is a _____ man" (Habakkuk 2:5)
47 Country code for Cervantes' land
48 "Linen _____ upon their heads" (Ezekiel 44:18) (sing.)
52 Used to cultivate the hills (Isaiah 7:25 NIV)
53 "With what measure ye _____" (Mark 4:24)
54 "Lest he _____ my soul like a lion" (Psalm 7:2)

56 "And the _____ did swim" (2 Kings 6:6)
58 "Then answered _____. . .but I was an herdman, and a gatherer of sycomore fruit" (Amos 7:14)
60 A Gadite (1 Chronicles 5:15)
62 Southwest Asian country (abbr.)
64 Contemporary version of AD (abbr.)
66 Blood type that can be positive or negative

48

ACROSS

1 "Goeth out to Remmon-methoar to
   _____" (Joshua 19:13)
5 Minor prophet
10 "For this _____ is mount Sinai"
   (Galatians 4:25)
14 "And the sons of _____"
   (1 Chronicles 7:39)
15 Range maker
16 Contemptible
17 Uproar
18 "Magpiash, Meshullam, _____"
   (Nehemiah 10:20)
19 Belonging to Hophni's father
20 Devil
22 Slangy denial
23 Confirm
24 "Came unto the valley of _____"
   (Deuteronomy 1:24)
26 "Of the sons of _____, Jonathan"
   (2 Samuel 23:32)
27 Captain _____, Peter Pan's nemesis
29 Reveal
30 Abram's nephew
33 Noxious
35 Brazil, for one
38 Farm females
39 Slug
40 Shaphat's father (Numbers 13:5)
41 Benign cyst
42 "Leave off contention, before it
   be _____ with"
   (Proverbs 17:14)
44 Lade
45 "And straightway they forsook their
   _____" (Mark 1:18)
46 Spume
48 Jehoiada's father (Nehemiah 3:6)
52 "Seven times more than it was wont
   to be _____" (Daniel 3:19)
56 "Then sent I for Eliezer, for _____"
   (Ezra 8:16)
57 Haw's partner
59 Whittle
60 "A colt _____, whereon yet never
   man sat" (Luke 19:30)

61 "Hodiah the sister of _____"
   (1 Chronicles 4:19)
63 Range
64 "Unto the custody of _____"
   (Esther 2:3)
65 Fictional Miss Doolittle
66 Tabernacle, once
67 Cast off
68 "And _____ counsellors against
   them" (Ezra 4:5)
69 Biblical verb

DOWN

1 "Even as a _____ cherisheth her
   children" (1 Thessalonians 2:7)
2 "What the scripture saith of
   _____" (Romans 11:2)
3 "Was in Asher and in _____"
   (1 Kings 4:16)
4 "Again Esther spake unto _____"
   (Esther 4:10)
5 Nope
6 So be it
7 "Wall of Jerusalem, and _____"
   (1 Kings 9:15)
8 Apartment
9 Disfigure
10 "Securely as men _____ from war"
   (Micah 2:8)
11 "And Goshen, and Holon, and
   _____" (Joshua 15:51)
12 Animated
13 "And _____ between Nineveh
   and Calah" (Genesis 10:12)
21 "High _____"
23 Peel
25 "The LORD _____ the prisoners"
   (Psalm 146:7)
26 "And Meshobab, and _____"
   (1 Chronicles 4:34)
28 Types
29 "Smote Job with sore _____"
   (Job 2:7)
30 Actor Ayres
31 "_____ no man any thing"
   (Romans 13:8)

by Tonya Vilhauer

32 "Heaven be likened unto _____ virgins" (Matthew 25:1)
34 Blue
35 "Dwelt in the land of _____" (Genesis 4:16)
36 Bezaleel's father (Exodus 38:22)
37 Gratuity
42 Corn _____
43 Fees
45 "And _____ not that any should testify of man" (John 2:25)
47 "Elkanah, the son of _____" (1 Chronicles 6:35)
48 Trails
49 "King's house, with Argob and _____" (2 Kings 15:25)
50 "The days of the _____ are fulfilled" (Ezekiel 5:2)
51 "Chelub the brother of Shuah begat _____" (1 Chronicles 4:11)

53 "Melech, and _____, and Ahaz" (1 Chronicles 8:35)
54 "That one _____ happeneth to them all" (Ecclesiastes 2:14)
55 "He. . .became obedient unto _____" (Philippians 2:8)
57 Border town in Asher (Joshua 19:25)
58 Confusing layout
61 Old Testament book (abbr.)
62 Irate

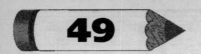

49

ACROSS

2 A town of Benjamin, north of Jerusalem (Joshua 18:25)
7 "According to all the _____ of it" (Numbers 9:3)
13 "The morning _____" (Genesis 19:15)
14 Abraham's old name
15 "Unto him was Carshena, Shethar, _____" (Esther 1:14)
17 Alms
19 "Barley and the _____" (Isaiah 28:25)
20 "Brought _____ unto the man" (Genesis 2:22)
21 "LORD God _____ not caused it to rain" (Genesis 2:5)
22 Duty
23 "Whither thou _____" (Deuteronomy 3:21)
25 Descendants of one of Gad's sons (Numbers 26:16)
27 Not far
28 Lamprey
30 Den
31 Spars
32 Type of satellite (abbr.)
33 "Then shall the people of the Lord go down to the _____" (Judges 5:11)
35 Ulam's brother (1 Chronicles 7:16)
40 Society for women descended from 1776 fighters (abbr.)
43 Sheshan's children (1 Chronicles 2:31)
47 Alternative spelling for Abraham's wife
48 Opposite of WNW
49 "_____ that is above the liver" (Exodus 29:13)
50 Tingles
52 "Should be no _____ in the body" (1 Corinthians 12:25)
54 Begone
55 King of Hamath (2 Samuel 8:9)
56 Before Colossians (abbr.)
57 Dactyl

59 "Not a _____" (1 Timothy 3:3)
61 Factor
63 "_____ are the generations" (Genesis 2:4)
64 "They _____ fields" (Micah 2:2)
65 "The _____ of the LORD" (Exodus 12:41)
66 "_____ white with milk" (Genesis 49:12)

DOWN

1 Piercing
2 Pharaoh
3 Pispah's brother (1 Chronicles 7:38)
4 "They say to their _____" (Lamentations 2:12)
5 "I have eaten _____ like bread" (Psalm 102:9)
6 "And every wise _____ man" (Exodus 36:8)
7 Belonging to Joseph's mother
8 One of David's sons (1 Chronicles 3:6)
9 Swapping
10 "Master shall bore his _____" (Exodus 21:6)
11 "Wherefore _____ thou thy fellow?" (Exodus 2:13)
12 Agate
16 "Great is _____ of the Ephesians" (Acts 19:28)
18 "Touch not; _____ not; handle not" (Colossians 2:21)
24 "They that _____ at meat with him" (Luke 7:49)
26 Pekoe
29 Mononucleosis virus (abbr.)
31 Longitude and latitude, not prime
34 _____ whale
36 "Esar-haddon king of _____" (Ezra 4:2)
37 One of twelve cities (Joshua 19:15)
38 Gad's son (Genesis 46:16)
39 Capes
40 "Fulfilling the _____ of the flesh" (Ephesians 2:3)

by Sarah Lagerquist Simmons

41 "Ye shall be _____ gods"
   (Genesis 3:5)
42 Honor
43 Gain
44 Another form of Ai (Genesis 12:8)
45 "Thy soul _____ after"
   (Deuteronomy 12:15)
46 "_____ with her suburbs"
   (Joshua 21:18)
51 "Whither _____ thou?" (John 16:5)
53 "Which are of the house of _____"
   (1 Corinthians 1:11)
54 "Over the camels also was _____"
   (1 Chronicles 27:30)
58 One of five cities (1 Chronicles 4:32)
60 "_____ hath done this thing"
   (Genesis 21:26)
62 "A lion _____ him by the way"
   (1 Kings 13:24)

And many women were there, beholding afar
which had followed Jesus from Galilee, ministering unto hi

MATTHEW 27:

ACROSS

1 "Hitherto have ye _____ nothing in my name" (John 16:24)
6 Singer Fitzgerald
10 Carpet
13 **WOMAN** of Cenchrea, who went to Rome (Romans 16:1)
14 Advertising gas
15 Used car lot stat. (pl.)
17 Drive back
18 Among
19 "As soon as the sun _____, thou shalt rise early" (Judges 9:33) (2 words)
20 **WOMAN** from Egypt, who went to Kadesh (Numbers 20:1)
22 "And he began again to teach by the _____" (Mark 4:1) (2 words)
24 New Deal org.
26 "Caraway is not threshed with a _____" (Isaiah 28:27 NIV)
27 **WOMAN** of Rome, who went to Ephesus by way of Corinth (Acts 18:1–19)
33 "Guard against all kinds of _____" (Luke 12:15 NIV)
34 Soundtracks
35 Hair "ado"
37 "But ye have not so _____ Christ" (Ephesians 4:20)
39 **WOMAN** of Nahor, who went to Canaan (Genesis 24) (var.)
44 New Mexican pueblo
46 Shady spots
47 Greek goddess
51 **WOMAN** of Judah, whose Nazarene cousin came to visit (Luke 1:36–40) (var.)
53 Negatively charged atoms
55 Lyric poem
56 Crucial

58 **WOMAN** of Jerusalem, who wen to Babylon (Esther 2:5–7)
63 City on the Oka
64 Singer Horne
66 Ratty residence
68 Fern spore cases
69 South African river
70 "Good night" girl of popular song
71 _____ King Cole
72 Resistance units
73 **WOMAN** of Ur, who went to Canaan via Haran (Genesis 11:31)

DOWN

1 Spring month (abbr.)
2 Ark passenger (Genesis 7:13)
3 French military cap
4 Shem's great-grandson (Genesis 10:22–24)
5 It's full of bologna
6 Tooth protector
7 Moon buggy
8 **WOMAN** of Lystra, whose grandson went to Macedonia (2 Timothy 1:5)
9 Chilean range
10 "Then shall stand up in his estate _____ of taxes" (Daniel 11:20)
11 _____ down
12 "_____ not one against another" (James 5:9)
16 Rapidity
21 "If there _____ matter too hard f thee" (Deuteronomy 17:8) (2 word
23 High school subject
25 "In _____ thy ways" (Proverbs 3:
27 Buddy
28 "For ye tithe mint and _____ and all" (Luke 11:42)
29 Mrs. Cantor
30 Dear _____

by David K. Shortess

31 "And his brethren were _____" (Genesis 37:27)
32 "To meet the Lord in the _____" (1 Thessalonians 4:17)
36 Discontinues
38 "Naphtali is a _____ set free" (Genesis 49:21 NIV)
40 Kind of tide
41 Runner Sebastian
42 TV screen, often (abbr.)
43 "And lifts the needy from the _____ heap" (Psalm 113:7 NIV)
45 School zone sign (abbr.)
47 Guitar add-ons
48 "Whose feet they hurt with fetters: he was laid _____" (Psalm 105:18) (2 words)
49 Pitcher Mariano
50 "Pipe down!" (2 words)
52 Standards of excellence

54 Burst of applause
57 **WOMAN** of Haran, who went to Canaan (Genesis 31)
59 Not that
60 Israeli dance
61 At any time
62 California rockfish
65 Site of modern conflict, briefly
67 Oahu wreath

51

ACROSS

1 Rezia's father (1 Chronicles 7:39)
5 "LORD spoke unto Moses and Aaron in mount _____" (Numbers 20:23)
8 Married woman (abbr.)
11 "They _____ to and fro" (Psalm 107:27)
12 "Food for your little ____" (Genesis 47:24)
14 "Bore his ear through with an _____" (Exodus 21:6)
15 Icon
16 Babylonian town from which some Jews returned to Judea with Zerubbabel (Ezra 2:59)
18 Lay
20 "We have borne the image of the _____" (1 Corinthians 15:49)
21 Cut
23 Phares's brother (Matthew 1:3)
24 Micah's son (1 Chronicles 8:35)
25 Viper
26 Yonder
29 Benjamin's son (Genesis 46:21)
30 "Who provideth for the _____ his food?" (Job 38:41)
31 Lod's son (Nehemiah 7:37)
32 Aye
33 Tamar's grandson (Matthew 1:3)
35 Atop
38 Site
39 "The _____ was very fair to look upon" (Genesis 24:16)
42 "He then having received the _____ went immediately out" (John 13:30)
43 "Shama and Jehiel the sons of Hothan the _____" (1 Chronicles 11:44)
46 Krishna
49 Damp
50 Flat
51 Shuthelah's son (Numbers 26:36)
52 Before Habakkuk (abbr.)
53 Drive
54 Assay

DOWN

1 Bezaleel's son (Exodus 31:2)
2 "But God _____ the people about" (Exodus 13:18)
3 "Their horses also are swifter than the _____" (Habakkuk 1:8)
4 Entice
5 Fiery
6 Ace
7 This is to be made at the end of every seven years (Deuteronomy 15:1)
8 Shop
9 Hie
10 Kill
13 "Lest being present I should use _____" (2 Corinthians 13:10)
17 Pispah's brother (1 Chronicles 7:38)
19 Rip
21 Don't go
22 Rabbit
23 Ezer's son (1 Chronicles 1:42)
26 "The _____ stuck fast" (Acts 27:41)
27 Soon
28 _____ wasn't built in a day
34 Twenty years
35 Wear
36 "_____; Thy kingdom is divided" (Daniel 5:28)
37 "In her mouth was an _____ leaf" (Genesis 8:11)
39 "Until the day _____" (2 Peter 1:19)
40 Extent
41 "A garment that is _____ eaten" (Job 13:28)
44 Decade
45 Finish
47 Scar
48 Part

by Sarah Lagerquist Simmons

52

ACROSS

1 "I a _____ of babes" (Romans 2:20)
8 "And Jesus called a little _____ unto him" (Matthew 18:2)
12 Apiece
13 "Have them make a chest of _____ wood" (Exodus 25:10 NIV)
16 Aunt (Sp.)
17 "I went down to the grove of _____ trees" (Song of Solomon 6:11 NIV)
18 Portion of the Bible (abbr.)
19 Zilpah's son by Jacob (Genesis 30:10–11)
20 Pa's partner
21 SMU's state (abbr.)
22 "To know _____ and instruction" (Proverbs 1:2)
24 Grad student, maybe (abbr.)
25 "Wait, I say, _____ the Lord" (Psalm 27:14)
26 Be in poor health
27 Collection of Jewish laws
29 Mend
32 Things to fill in
35 "And one _____ lamb of the first year without blemish" (Leviticus 14:10)
36 Thing to doff
38 "And the Pharisees began to _____ him vehemently" (Luke 11:53)
39 Crimson Tide state (abbr.)
40 The results will _____ the conclusion (2 words)
42 Legume
44 Poetic contraction
45 Abhor
46 _____ de la Cite, en Paris
48 Pox reminder
51 Type of love
52 "He had a firm _____ on the staff of God" (Exodus 4:20 MSG)
53 Break in the action
54 Get on someone's nerves
56 Hospital area (abbr.)
57 One (abbr.)
59 Italian commune in northern Italy
63 Wire measure

65 "And _____ was a keeper of sheep" (Genesis 4:2)
67 Messiah College state (abbr.)
68 "_____ thy way may be known upon earth" (Psalm 67:2)
71 "For God _____ loved the world" (John 3:16)
72 That is (abbr.)
73 Balance due on current debt (abbr.)
74 "My lover is to me a cluster of _____ blossoms" (Song of Solomon 1:14 NIV)
75 Indian rhythmic pattern
76 "He rested on the seventh day from all his _____" (Genesis 2:2)

DOWN

1 "He ran to meet them from the _____ door" (Genesis 18:2)
2 Waters (Fr.)
3 "The _____ of violence is in their hands" (Isaiah 59:6)
4 Part of a book (abbr.)
5 "The person who _____ any of it will be held responsible" (Leviticus 7:18 NIV)
6 _____ Cola
7 Con artist's specialty
8 Pepperdine University state (abbr.)
9 Collegiate racquet org. (abbr.)
10 Where Montauk is (abbr.)
11 "Until the day _____, and the day star arise in your hearts" (2 Peter 1:1)
14 Time past
15 Part of personality
18 What OPEC controls, briefly
20 "He will set up a _____ beside it" (Ezekiel 39:15 NIV)
22 Come out on top
23 "I can _____ all things through Christ which strengtheneth me" (Philippians 4:13)
24 "A nation whose _____ thou shalt not understand" (Deuteronomy 28:49)
25 Exclamation
26 Place

27 Pitch
28 Simile word
29 Young woman entering society, briefly
30 Reverence
31 Belonging to French composer Gabriel
33 Christian of Gentile descent (Philemon 24)
34 "And she made him _____ upon her knees" (Judges 16:9)
36 Iowa college
37 Book section (abbr.)
41 California oak
43 Soiled
45 Israeli dance
47 Fabricate
48 Hercule Poirot, for one
49 "Every _____ in his misbegotten brood" (1 Samuel 25:22 MSG)
50 _____ dente
52 Main body of the United Nations (abbr.)

54 "She bare also. . .Sheva the father of Machbenah, and the father of _____" (1 Chronicles 2:49)
55 Feminine name
58 I _____ (name of God)
59 "But Mordecai found out about the _____ and told Queen Esther" (Esther 2:22 NIV)
60 Colorado ski town
61 "Let their way be _____ and slippery" (Psalm 35:6)
62 "He _____ to meet them from the tent door" (Genesis 18:2)
64 "The Lord _____ my Shepherd" (Psalm 23:1)
66 "Both _____ and high, rich and poor" (Psalm 49:2)
67 Average
69 "_____ taught me also" (Proverbs 4:4)
70 Vanderbilt U. state (abbr.)

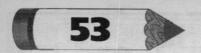

53

Look Beyond the Present

For now we see through a glass, darkly,
but then face to face

1 CORINTHIANS 13:1

ACROSS

1 "She is _____ of life"
   (Proverbs 3:18) (2 words)
6 "Ye have not gone up into the
   _____" (Ezekiel 13:5)
10 Legally impede
15 "Along the _____ man said to him"
   (Luke 9:57 NIV) (2 words)
16 Mine opening
17 Start of **VERSE** (Psalm 126:5 NIV)
18 Ladder parts
19 South American cow catcher
20 Plantain lily
21 Music makers
23 "But the name of the wicked shall
   _____" (Proverbs 10:7)
24 Anesthetic
25 **VERSE**, part 2 (4 words)
28 _____ Four (musical phenomenon)
29 Game piece
30 "Will a man _____ God"
   (Malachi 3:8)
33 Object of casting lots
37 Ancient arsonist
40 City on Lake Michigan
42 Brick ones
44 **VERSE**, part 3
46 "Come unto me, all ye that . . .are
   heavy _____" (Matthew 11:28)
47 Church John was to write
   (Revelation 3:1)
49 Take the bark off
51 "And thou puttest thy _____ in a
   rock" (Numbers 24:21)
52 Main Street pillar
53 _____ *volente* (God willing)
55 _____ chi
57 **VERSE**, part 4 (3 words)
64 Where the humerus meets the ulna
67 "Crib" predecessor (colloq.)
68 Part of R.L.S.

69 Lariat
70 "And thou shalt rule _____ him"
   (Genesis 4:7)
72 City Paul and Silas entered by night
   (Acts 17:10)
73 End of **VERSE** (2 words)
74 "Where thou dwellest, even where
   Satan's _____ is" (Revelation 2:13)
75 "_____ as the east is from the west"
   (Psalm 103:12) (2 words)
76 Roebuck's partner
77 Gaelic
78 Takes five

DOWN

1 Contained in FedEx logo (look
   closely!)
2 "Put forth thine hand. . .and _____
   all that he hath" (Job 1:11)
3 "His sister's son, that he _____
   meet him" (Genesis 29:13) (2 words)
4 "The sharp sword with two _____"
   (Revelation 2:12)
5 "The land of Nod, on the _____
   Eden" (Genesis 4:16) (2 words)
6 Yak
7 "You _____ yourself in vain"
   (Jeremiah 4:30 NIV)
8 "They are steered. . .wherever
   the _____ wants to go"
   (James 3:4 NIV)
9 Pronounced
10 Diaphanous
11 Photos
12 Nonsense, in Nottingham
13 Bony beginning
14 Partridge's tree
22 What ugly duckling became
26 Powerful union (abbr.)
27 "For ye shall speak into the _____"
   (1 Corinthians 14:9)

30 Get a lift
31 Arithmetic column
32 "He hath _____ his bow"
    (Lamentations 3:12)
33 _____ of Sharon
34 Noted office
35 Found along the road
36 "But the _____ is not yet"
    (Matthew 24:6)
38 Tear
39 Corrida cheer
41 "An open door, and no man _____
    shut it" (Revelation 3:8)
43 Laterally
45 Latvian native
48 Dead or Salt
50 Garland's costar in Oz
54 Vie
56 Line on a weather map
57 Helicopter lifter

58 "Yet he did not _____ through
    unbelief" (Romans 4:20 NIV)
59 Thoughts
60 More than portly
61 Squishy toy balls
62 "How _____ Thou Art"
63 "Which. . .and sealeth up the _____"
    (Job 9:7)
64 Statue located in Piccadilly Circus
65 "Narrow is the way, which leadeth
    unto _____" (Matthew 7:14)
66 _____ California
71 66 or 30, e.g.

54

ACROSS

1 Kimono sash
4 Lab _____
6 Ike's initials
9 Stumble
11 Deer, biblically
13 "The governor under _____ the king" (2 Corinthians 11:32)
16 Shamer's son (1 Chronicles 7:34)
18 "Thou shalt _____ covet" (Exodus 20:17)
19 "The vision of _____ the Elkoshite" (Nahum 1:1)
21 "Ye tithe mint and _____ and all manner of herbs" (Luke 11:42)
22 Slay
24 Cave
25 "And will _____ the caul of their heart" (Hosea 13:8)
26 She with the tender eyes (Genesis 29:17)
28 Bard
29 Name of God
30 Salary
31 Pine for
34 Cleanse
37 Radio host Limbaugh
38 "In the month _____, which is the second month" (1 Kings 6:1)
40 Pastures
42 Lubricant
43 Salu's son (Numbers 25:14)
45 He thought Hannah was drunk
46 Saudi Peninsula
48 Ronald Reagan, for one
50 Late afternoon activity, for some
52 Wood
53 Bring in
54 "Eber, Peleg, _____" (1 Chronicles 1:25)
55 "The son of _____, which was the son of Noe" (Luke 3:36)

DOWN

2 Scarab
3 NYC subway (abbr.)
5 Morning (abbr.)
6 Play-_____
7 Bachelor of arts, for example
8 Grade
10 "They _____ in the dry places like a river" (Psalm 105:41)
11 CD-_____
12 Storage building
14 Agitate
15 Gloomy
16 Operate
17 "Thou shalt not approach to his wife: she is thine _____" (Leviticus 18:14)
20 "Who had taken _____ for his daughter" (Esther 2:15)
23 "Cause it to be heard unto _____" (Isaiah 10:30)
25 "Thy servant dwell in the _____ city" (1 Samuel 27:5)
27 Possesses
28 "Delivered me out of the _____ of the lion" (1 Samuel 17:37)
31 Naturalist John
32 "He shall deliver the _____ of the innocent" (Job 22:30)
33 _____ sum, Chinese specialty
35 "Let them _____ the bones of it therein" (Ezekiel 24:5)
36 Angelic glow
37 Path
38 "Jachan, and _____, and Heber, seven" (1 Chronicles 5:13)
39 Backward
41 Dear _____ (pl.)
43 Energy
44 Gershwin brother
47 Evil
49 "They laded their _____ with the corn" (Genesis 42:26) (sing.)
51 Gym class (abbr.)

by Tonya Vilhauer

55

ACROSS
1 Children
5 "Moab shall howl over _____" (Isaiah 15:2)
9 "Set thy face against _____" (Ezekiel 38:2)
12 "A bedstead of _____" (Deuteronomy 3:11)
13 A city of Simeon (1 Chronicles 4:29)
14 Abijam's son (1 Kings 15:8)
15 "In _____ was there a voice heard" (Matthew 2:18)
16 Atoned
18 Caleb's son (1 Chronicles 4:15)
20 Granted
21 Inside
23 "Beyond the tower of _____" (Genesis 35:21)
24 "Neither _____ up the people" (Acts 24:12)
26 "_____ shall be called Woman" (Genesis 2:23)
28 Spanish word for master
29 Abbreviation for last Old Testament book
31 King of Assyria (2 Kings 15:19)
32 "Then began _____ to call" (Genesis 4:26)
33 Descendants of Salma (1 Chronicles 2:54)
35 As
37 Look for
38 Seem to be
41 "Lord God _____ not caused it to rain" (Genesis 2:5)
42 "The _____ cease" (Ecclesiastes 12:3)
45 "_____ thou hast not hated blood" (Ezekiel 35:6)
48 Bani's son (Ezra 10:34)
49 "Who can stand before the children of _____" (Deuteronomy 9:2)
50 "_____, lama sabachthani?" (Mark 15:34)
51 "Mine _____ mourneth" (Psalm 88:9)
52 Abjure
53 Tinted

DOWN
1 "_____ of Moab is laid waste" (Isaiah 15:1)
2 Ikkesh's son (1 Chronicles 11:28)
3 Rule
4 "_____ of death" (2 Samuel 22:6)
5 Abner's father (1 Samuel 14:50)
6 Old Testament prophet (abbr.)
7 Hadad's father (Genesis 36:35)
8 The end
9 Monopoly is one
10 "As he saith also in _____" (Romans 9:25)
11 Sodi's son (Numbers 13:10)
17 Sin
19 "Judgment of _____" (Numbers 27:21)
21 Duke of Edom (Genesis 36:43)
22 Dub
23 "Joshua passed unto _____" (Joshua 10:34)
25 "He shall be called a _____" (Matthew 2:23)
26 Apace
27 Bran
30 Saul's father (1 Samuel 9:3)
34 Ribbed
35 Before eleven
36 "_____ being yet a little child" (1 Kings 11:17)
38 "The burning _____" (Leviticus 26:16)
39 Victim
40 Load
43 "Living creatures _____ and returned" (Ezekiel 1:14)
44 Heavens
46 Part of the foot
47 "Jacob _____ them under the oak" (Genesis 35:4)

by Sarah Lagerquist Simmons

56

ACROSS

1 Moses' sister
6 "And the two sons of _____, Hophni and Phinehas" (1 Samuel 1:3)
8 "The. . .faith. . .which dwelt first in thy grandmother _____" (2 Timothy 1:5)
12 Utah city
13 Ailing
14 Plains state (abbr.)
16 Genetic letters
17 "They will eat their food. . .and _____ their tiny portions of water" (Ezekiel 12:19 NLT)
18 Bend, as in the road (var.)
19 Snake or scarf
21 Borrowed money payable upon request (abbr.)
22 Education (abbr.) _____
23 Cold storage
25 Dash
27 "The rich _____ in low place" (Ecclesiastes 10:6)
29 Where it's _____
30 Bitter (Fr.)
32 Cap
33 Villain
35 Undetonated weapon (abbr.)
36 Article (Ger.)
39 Things to connect
41 Apiece (abbr.)
43 "I have _____ to eat that ye know not of" (John 4:32)
46 David's daughter (2 Samuel 13:1)
48 "With the scab, and with the _____" (Deuteronomy 28:27)
50 Esau (Genesis 25:30)
52 Tokyo, once
53 Ahasuerus's wife (Esther 8:1)
55 "Eat it as a thing offered unto an _____" (1 Corinthians 8:7)
56 Oxidizes
58 Southern state (abbr.)
60 David's wife (2 Samuel 3:3)

65 "Pick up your _____, and walk" (Mark 2:9 NLT)
67 Lazarus's sister
69 Boys' group (abbr.)
70 He died of diseased feet (2 Chronicles 16:12–13)
71 "He went _____ into a mountain apart to pray" (Matthew 14:23)
72 John (Gael.)
73 "A _____ was under the first pair of branches" (Exodus 37:21 NASB)
74 Secret competitor?
76 "There shall be a time of trouble, such as _____ was" (Daniel 12:1)
77 Beverage
78 "Rejoice, O _____ man, in thy youth" (Ecclesiastes 11:9)
79 Alms box
80 "Woe _____ me now" (Jeremiah 4:31)

DOWN

1 Joshua succeeded him (Numbers 27:18–23)
2 Relating to part of the eye
3 Elected official (abbr.)
4 Within (prefix)
5 Coastal city (Acts 20:15)
6 "Even _____. . .is going to have a child in her old age" (Luke 1:36 NIV)
7 Innate
9 Produced when needed (abbr.)
10 Asian country
11 She brought spices to Jesus' tomb (Mark 16:1)
15 "Then said I, What come these to _____" (Zechariah 1:21)
18 Time period
20 Down or from (prefix)
24 Long dash
26 Legal in some states on red (abbr.)
28 Trading center rebuilt by Solomon (1 Kings 9:17–18)

by Marijane G. Troyer

31 "I saw the _____ pushing westward" (Daniel 8:4)

34 Deceased beforehand (abbr.)

37 "_____ thou hast forgotten the law of thy God" (Hosea 4:6)

38 "There is but a _____ between me and death" (1 Samuel 20:3)

40 Very (Fr.)

42 Professional

44 "If any man shall _____ unto these things" (Revelation 22:18)

45 "Shall there arise _____ much contempt" (Esther 1:18)

47 _____ nauseum

48 Belonging, say, to a pet

49 Nationally elected body (abbr.)

51 Metric measure (abbr.)

54 "_____ on your armor and be shattered" (Isaiah 8:9 ESV)

57 "Who can be against _____" (Romans 8:31)

58 Musical note

59 Type of fuel

60 Babylonian town (Ezra 8:15)

61 Deadly poisons (arch.)

62 Adjoins

63 _____ of Patmos

64 Rachel's father

65 First to discover the Resurrection (Matthew 28)

66 Fragrance by Dana

67 Rope-making grass

68 Row

75 "For they shall be _____ ornament of grace" (Proverbs 1:9)

76 Does not pertain (abbr.)

57

Jesus, the I Am

Again the high priest asked him. . .
Art thou the Christ, the Son of the Blessed
And Jesus said, I am. . .

MARK 14:61–6.

ACROSS

1 Word frequently used in Matthew
    1:2–16
6 "And the _____ lying in a manger"
    (Luke 2:16)
10 Wear's cohort
14 "Of Christ, who is the _____ of
    God" (2 Corinthians 4:4)
15 It goes with milk
16 "To speak evil _____ man"
    (Titus 3:2) (2 words)
17 "Encourage the _____, help the
    weak" (1 Thessalonians 5:14 NIV)
18 Eras
19 "And were as swift as the _____
    upon the mountains"
    (1 Chronicles 12:8)
20 British gun
21 Univ. employee
22 "A wholesome tongue is _____ of
    life" (Proverbs 15:4) (2 words)
23 "Then said Jesus unto them. . .I am
    the _____" (John 10:7, 11)
    (2 words)
26 Existed
29 Wrong (prefix)
30 One who excels
31 "In earth, _____ in heaven"
    (Matthew 6:10) (3 words)
33 Course for immigrants (abbr.)
34 "Then Herod called the _____
    secretly" (Matthew 2:7 NIV)
38 "Then spake Jesus again unto
    them, saying, I am the _____"
    (John 8:12) (4 words)
41 "Citizen _____"
42 Gov't. med. research agency
43 Void
44 "_____ the land of the free"
45 Catchall abbreviation
46 Half a donkey bray

47 "Jesus said unto her, I am the
    _____" (John 11:25)
53 Incensed
54 Actor Guinness
55 Parched
59 "That _____ after the dust of the
    earth" (Amos 2:7)
60 Unique individual
61 Theatrical device
62 Italian noble family
63 "Thy god, _____, liveth"
    (Amos 8:14) (2 words)
64 "All ye that labour and are heavy
    _____" (Matthew 11:28)
65 "Ye know that summer is _____"
    (Mark 13:28)
66 Fabled creature
67 Country call

DOWN

1 "Behold, we put _____ in the
    horses' mouths" (James 3:3)
2 Give off
3 "The lazy man does not roast his
    _____" (Proverbs 12:27 NIV)
4 "Senior moment" cause
5 Newsman Baxter, from 70s TV hit
6 Companies' directors
7 Ancient Greek city
8 Corned _____ (breakfast favorite)
    (2 words)
9 Greek goddess of dawn
10 Value
11 Said or thought?
12 Disparaging look
13 Washed, as a deck
21 Murderer, at times
22 Mimic
24 "Command you, do not _____ a
    word" (Jeremiah 26:2 NIV)
25 Unusual

26 Traffic light instruction
27 "Unto the seven churches which are in _____" (Revelation 1:11)
28 "For the Jews require a _____" (1 Corinthians 1:22)
32 "Blessed are _____ meek" (Matthew 5:5)
33 Biblical suffix
34 Calendar abbreviation
35 _____ angel
36 Delight
37 "Every _____ word that men shall speak" (Matthew 12:36)
39 "An offering made by _____ sin offering" (Numbers 15:25 NIV) (3 words)
40 Baylor University locale
44 Mine output
45 Ageless (arch.)
47 Mature

48 Expunge
49 _____ Maria, CA
50 Say
51 "Like unto _____ glass" (Revelation 21:18)
52 Kind of tone
56 Sit in the saddle
57 "The _____ seemed good to me" (Deuteronomy 1:23 NIV)
58 Fender flaw
60 "That is so cool"
61 Priest's robe

by David K. Shortess

ACROSS

1 Jerk
4 "As he saith also in _____"
   (Romans 9:25)
8 Battle
11 Joseph's son (Numbers 13:7)
13 Facial hair
15 Level
16 Tattletale
17 Canaanite king (Numbers 21:1)
18 Shred
19 Borders
21 Naaman was a _____ (2 Kings 5:1)
23 "The children of Keros, the children
   of _____" (Nehemiah 7:47)
24 "From _____ eastward"
   (Joshua 19:12)
25 Argument
29 "Where thou _____, will I die"
   (Ruth 1:17)
30 "Ye _____ men with burdens"
   (Luke 11:46)
31 Before Zephaniah (abbr.)
33 They came from here to live in
   Samaria (2 Kings 17:24)
34 "Which is neither _____ nor sown"
   (Deuteronomy 21:4)
35 Elah's brother (1 Chronicles 4:15)
36 "The people _____ together"
   (Acts 21:30)
37 Shimei's son (1 Chronicles 23:10)
38 Kinds
40 Replies
43 "The _____ wind blew"
   (Acts 27:13)
44 "Hena, and _____" (2 Kings 18:34)
45 Merari's son (1 Chronicles 24:27)
46 "The wall of _____"
   (2 Chronicles 26:6)
49 Yarn
51 "Mine _____ also is dim"
   (Job 17:7)
54 "He called the name of the well
   _____" (Genesis 26:20)
55 "The family of the _____"
   (Numbers 3:27)

58 Become weary
59 "At _____ appointed"
   (Nehemiah 13:31)
60 "Fowl _____ may fly"
   (Genesis 1:20)
61 Assist
62 "And Dishon, and _____"
   (1 Chronicles 1:38)

DOWN

1 Humor
2 Sarai's handmaid (Galatians 4:24)
3 "The _____ received him"
   (John 4:45)
4 Submitted
5 Ocean
6 "Master shall bore his _____"
   (Exodus 21:6)
7 "How long will it be _____ they
   believe me" (Numbers 14:11)
8 "All manner of _____"
   (Nehemiah 13:16)
9 "_____ heart was perfect"
   (1 Kings 15:14)
10 Cherry
12 "Cleanse the _____"
   (Matthew 10:8)
14 This was done to the bullock
   (1 Kings 18:26)
15 Saruch's father (Luke 3:35)
20 Bail
22 Hole
24 The third month (Esther 8:9)
25 Mend
26 Notion
27 After the twenty-ninth
28 "The _____ was without form"
   (Genesis 1:2)
29 Zerah's son (1 Chronicles 2:6)
30 Phalti's father (1 Samuel 25:44)
32 Mass transport
34 "Ethan the _____" (1 Kings 4:31)
38 Sane
39 "Thou art _____ sister"
   (Genesis 24:60)
41 Blinked

by Sarah Lagerquist Simmons

42 "The serpent beguiled _____"
   (2 Corinthians 11:3)
43 He prayed with Paul (Acts 16:25)
46 Ebony
47 "Preach the word in _____"
   (Acts 16:6)
48 Zophah's son (1 Chronicles 7:36)
49 "The troops of _____ looked"
   (Job 6:19)
50 Hushim's father (1 Chronicles 7:12)
52 Affirmative oral vote
53 Old Testament book about a Jewish
   queen (abbr.)
56 "By the cliff of _____"
   (2 Chronicles 20:16)
57 "That which groweth of _____
   own accord" (Leviticus 25:5)

59

Divine Illumination

Then spake Jesus. . .
I am the light of the world: he that followeth me. . .
shall have the light of life.

JOHN 8:12

ACROSS

1 Sail support
5 "And he shall pluck away his _____ with his feathers" (Leviticus 1:16)
9 Pentateuch, at times
14 "But the tongue can no man _____" (James 3:8)
15 Burr's "Perry Mason" costar
16 Relating to the flock?
17 "But such _____ common to man" (1 Corinthians 10:13) (2 words)
18 With, in Paris
19 "Then began _____ call upon the name of the Lord" (Genesis 4:26) (2 words)
20 Start of **QUOTE** (1 John 1:5) (5 words)
23 Cain's land (Genesis 4:16)
24 "Ye shall not _____ of it" (Genesis 3:3)
25 Aswan, for one
28 "They compassed me about like _____" (Psalm 118:12)
31 In the distance
36 "Renew our days _____ old" (Lamentations 5:21) (2 words)
38 Circle segments
40 "Let us get up _____ to the vineyards" (Song of Solomon 7:12)
41 Honda model
43 Tattletale
44 "Am I in God's _____" (Genesis 30:2)
45 City in Egypt or Illinois
46 Thick slice
48 Satisfy fully
49 Weak blooded
51 "She also lieth in wait as for a _____" (Proverbs 23:28)
53 Mal de _____
54 Collar

56 Diving sea bird
58 **QUOTE**, part 2 (4 words)
67 End of **QUOTE** (2 words)
68 "The wringing of the _____ bringeth forth blood" (Proverbs 30:33)
69 Aunt Bee's charge
70 Familiar greeting
71 "To maintain good works for necessary _____" (Titus 3:14)
72 Traveled
73 "But there went up _____ from the earth" (Genesis 2:6) (2 words)
74 Hot _____
75 Loch _____ monster

DOWN

1 "My lover is like a gazelle or a young _____" (Song of Solomon 2:9 NIV)
2 El _____, Texas
3 "God has ascended _____ shouts of joy" (Psalm 47:5 NIV)
4 Tree exudate
5 "And _____ shall be a spoil" (Jeremiah 50:10)
6 Sitarist Shankar
7 Designer Cassini
8 _____ Melba, en Paris
9 Love apples
10 "Our skin was black like an _____" (Lamentations 5:10)
11 Fruit coating
12 Against
13 "But _____ whom it falls will be crushed" (Matthew 21:44 NIV) (2 words)
21 _____ sister
22 _____-Sachs disease
25 Bangladesh capital
26 Flu type
27 Theater offering

by David K. Shortess

29 Makes a mistake
30 Can be flaky
32 King Cole, and namesakes
33 "And, behold, it was a _____" (Genesis 41:7)
34 Bring joy to
35 U-Haul rival
37 "His heart is as _____ as a stone" (Job 41:24)
39 "There fell a great _____ from heaven" (Revelation 8:10)
42 Pay phone feature (2 words)
47 "Thou _____ record of thyself" (John 8:13)
50 "Saying, Who then _____ be saved" (Matthew 19:25)
52 Expression of disgust (var.)
55 More than expected
57 Acquainted
58 "Tee hee"

59 Piece in the paper
60 West African country
61 "Not plagued by human _____" (Psalm 73:5 NIV)
62 Quantity of medicine
63 "There was _____ of glass like unto crystal" (Revelation 4:6) (2 words)
64 Pointless weapon
65 "Though your _____ be as scarlet" (Isaiah 1:18)
66 "The lowly he _____ on high" (Job 5:11 NIV)

60

ACROSS

1 Word in a threat
5 "I will take _____ to my ways" (Psalm 39:1)
9 Blue
12 _____ irae
13 Tear down
14 Digit
15 "Jesus. . .overthrew. . .the _____ of them that sold doves" (Matthew 21:12)
17 Thing (Lat.)
18 Number of Sarah's sons
19 Consumed
21 "Ye have _____ the people of the Lord" (Numbers 16:41)
23 Simulate
27 "Norma _____," Oscar winner
28 "His soul shall dwell at _____" (Psalm 25:13)
29 By dying on the cross, Jesus _____ us
31 Nonmetric measure (abbr.)
33 Needle part
34 "The child was _____ from that very hour" (Matthew 17:18)
35 Exist
36 Letter abbreviation
37 Act like a peacock
38 "All the people said, _____, and praised the LORD" (1 Chronicles 16:36)
39 King (Fr.)
40 What Thomas did
42 Kingdoms
45 Mme (Eng.)
46 Son of (Arabic)
47 Weekday (abbr.)
49 He came with Zerubbabel to Jerusalem (Nehemiah 7:7)
53 Droop
54 Eliphaz's son (1 Chronicles 1:36)
56 "There is _____ of you that is sorry for me" (1 Samuel 22:8)
57 Compass point (abbr.)
58 Word heard in fast-food restaurant
59 Jacob, to Esau

DOWN

1 Sullivan and Wynn
2 Fabrication
3 Salt _____, biblical body
4 "Let the king give her royal _____ unto another" (Esther 1:19)
5 Part of a day (abbr.)
6 "The _____ of the wise seeketh knowledge" (Proverbs 18:15)
7 O.T. book
8 "Whatsoever mine eyes _____ I kept not from them" (Ecclesiastes 2:10)
9 Evening wear, formerly
10 Top quality
11 Board game item
16 Jeanne d'Arc, par exemple (abbr.)
20 "Let him seek peace, and _____ it (1 Peter 3:11)
22 Male friend (Brit.)
23 Heard in the hen house
24 Beams
25 Compass point (abbr.)
26 Threw down the gauntlet
30 "The cruel _____ of asps" (Deuteronomy 32:33)
31 Release
32 "The thoughts of the diligent _____ only to plenteousness" (Proverbs 21:5)
34 "Though they be red like _____" (Isaiah 1:18)
35 Quantity (abbr.)
37 Seasoned elected one
38 "At home in the body, we are _____ from the Lord" (2 Corinthians 5:6)
39 Amana, for one
41 Planter
42 "It shall _____ up wholly like a flood" (Amos 9:5)
43 Israeli diplomat of note

by Evelyn M. Boyington

44 "The _____ came to Jesus by
   night" (John 3:2)
48 Strain
50 "_____ fair is thy love, my sister"
   (Song of Solomon 4:10)
51 One only (comb. form)
52 "They have wandered as blind
   _____ in the streets"
   (Lamentations 4:14)
55 _____ Rev. (abbr.)

61

ACROSS

1 Acts
6 "_____ crieth at the gates" (Proverbs 8:3)
9 Follows Luke (abbr.)
12 The Ashterathite (1 Chronicles 11:44)
13 Lane
14 Dark wood
16 "Yet I _____ not" (Psalm 119:110)
17 Beholden
18 Bane
19 Nethinim whose descendants returned to Jerusalem after Babylonian exile (Nehemiah 7:47)
20 Prowl
22 "Take away all thy _____" (Isaiah 1:25)
23 Colored
24 Own
27 Meshullam's father (Ezra 10:29)
30 Ham's brother (Luke 3:36)
31 Jether's son (1 Chronicles 7:38)
33 Gad's children built this city (Numbers 32:34)
35 Descendants of Kohath (Numbers 3:27)
38 Day before today
39 Vashni's brother (1 Chronicles 6:28)
40 Enhakkore (Judges 15:19)
41 Sick
42 "In _____ sight I shall find grace" (Ruth 2:2)
43 "The Highest gave _____ voice" (Psalm 18:13)
44 "_____ is confounded" (Jeremiah 50:2)
45 City in western half of the tribe of Manasseh (1 Chronicles 6:70)
46 Call
48 Costly
51 "Where _____ seat is" (Revelation 2:13)
54 "Am I in _____ stead" (Genesis 30:2)
55 Club
58 "They shall _____ him" (Deuteronomy 22:19)
59 "It is God that _____ me" (2 Samuel 22:48)
60 One twelfth of a year
61 King of Sodom (Genesis 14:2)
62 Serug's father (Genesis 11:20)
63 "The _____ of the staves" (1 Kings 8:8)
64 "Great _____ the company" (Psalm 68:11)
65 "My gray _____" (Genesis 42:38)

DOWN

1 Fees
2 Chelub's son (1 Chronicles 27:26)
3 Jether's father (1 Chronicles 4:17)
4 Perish
5 Glumly
6 "By thy _____ shalt thou live" (Genesis 27:40)
7 "Doth the _____ fly by thy wisdom" (Job 39:26)
8 "None _____ pitied thee" (Ezekiel 16:5)
9 After Obadiah (abbr.)
10 Hadid's brother (Ezra 2:33)
11 Ode
14 Bad
15 Jaaziah's son (1 Chronicles 24:26)
21 Amram's brother (Ezra 10:34)
22 "The inhabitants of the land of _____ brought water to him" (Isaiah 21:14)
23 "When a man _____ in a tent" (Numbers 19:14)
24 Emerald
25 State
26 Fat
27 Arch
28 Ziphion's brother (Genesis 46:16)
29 Beaks
30 Little
32 Zilpah's son (Genesis 35:26)

by Sarah Lagerquist Simmons

34 Was not with Adonijah
   (1 Kings 1:8)
35 Maasiai's father (1 Chronicles 9:12)
36 Crop
37 One of David's sons
   (1 Chronicles 3:6)
44 Ignoble
46 Barbs
47 Move slowly
48 Pigeons
49 Mahli's brother (1 Chronicles 23:23)
50 This man's children were among the
   Nethinim returning from captivity
   (Ezra 2:50)
51 Ditto
52 Became king in Jerusalem at 22
   (2 Kings 21:19)
53 Keep watch over
54 City of Benjamin (Joshua 18:24)
55 Suah's brother (1 Chronicles 7:36)

56 The children of _____ were among
   the porters (Ezra 2:42)
57 So

62

ACROSS

1 But where is the _____ for a burnt-offering?" (Genesis 22:7)
5 Ceramic fragment, biblically speaking
11 "Thou mayest _____ them for the calling of the assembly" (Numbers 10:2)
12 "From the firstborn of Pharaoh that _____ on his throne" (Exodus 12:29)
13 Russian space station
14 One for your thoughts (abbr.)
15 State official (abbr.)
16 Mature
18 First state (abbr.)
19 British pilots' organization (abbr.)
21 The Commandments, for example
22 Round wooden nail
23 Perky
25 Twosome
26 High navy officer (abbr.)
27 Fastener
30 Carry a load
32 "Shall rule with a _____ of iron" (Revelation 19:15)
33 High standards
36 "Let them shout for joy, and be _____" (Psalm 35:27)
38 Hosp. area
39 Weekday
40 "But his delight _____ in the law of the LORD" (Psalm 1:2)
41 Cable channel (abbr.)
42 "Then they _____ unto the LORD in their trouble" (Psalm 107:19)
44 Born (Fr.)
45 "They were filled with. . .amazement _____ that which had happened" (Acts 3:10)
46 "Wherefore think _____ evil in your hearts?" (Matthew 9:4)
47 Australian marsupial
49 Comforted
53 Witty
54 "_____ I Love You" (Beatles' hit)
55 Sticky substance
57 Great Lake
59 "That in the _____ to come he might show. . .his grace" (Ephesians 2:7)
63 Interjection
65 One of the ten spies (Numbers 13:17)
67 "Let them _____ shout for joy" (Psalm 5:11)
69 Adriatic feeder
70 Certain collegians (abbr.)
72 "He also wrote letters to _____ on the LORD God of Israel" (2 Chronicles 32:17)
73 Addict
75 Indefinitely long periods
76 Small letters (abbr.)
77 "_____ they did eat, and were filled" (Nehemiah 9:25)
78 English singing poet

DOWN

1 "Not greedy of filthy _____" (1 Timothy 3:3)
2 "The Thin Man" pet
3 "But as for _____, I will come into the house" (Psalm 5:7)
4 "And he sent forth a _____" (Genesis 8:7)
6 Hatefully
7 Took to court
8 Printer's measure
9 "And they have caused him to _____ upon the king's mule" (1 Kings 1:44)
10 "Thou hast drunken the _____ of the cup of trembling" (Isaiah 51:17)
12 "Turn Moab into a drunken _____, drunk on the wine of my wrath" (Jeremiah 48:26 MSG)
16 "Mayberry _____," spin-off TV series
17 Arafat's origin (abbr.)
20 "But Jonathan was very _____ of David" (1 Samuel 19:1 NIV)
22 "Then Saul, (who also is called _____), filled with the Holy Ghost" (Acts 13:9)
24 Cannot pertain to (abbr.)
26 "And took thence old cast clouts and old rotten _____" (Jeremiah 38:11)
27 "And failing of eyes, and _____ of mind" (Deuteronomy 28:65)
28 City near Dresden
29 Passover feasts

by Marijane G. Troyer

31 "Then one of them, which was a
_____" (Matthew 22:35)
32 "He is the _____, his work is
perfect" (Deuteronomy 32:4)
34 "For in the day that thou eatest
thereof thou shalt surely _____"
(Genesis 2:17)
35 Ten-step organization (abbr.)
37 "And understood that Saul was come
in very _____" (1 Samuel 26:4)
40 "That which groweth of
_____ own accord of thy harvest"
(Leviticus 25:5)
43 Ready (arch.)
45 "My soul shall be satisfied _____ with
marrow and fatness" (Psalm 63:5)
48 "With anthems of praise to God
using _____ by David"
(2 Chronicles 29:30 MSG)
50 "For thou hast made him a little
lower than the _____" (Psalm 8:5)

51 Ogden's state (abbr.)
52 "Eat not of it _____, nor sodden at
all with water" (Exodus 12:9)
54 "Every several gate was of one
_____" (Revelation 21:21)
56 "And it is a _____ thing that the
king requireth" (Daniel 2:11)
58 One who checks out details (abbr.)
60 Burst of energy (abbr.)
61 D.C. quadrant
62 "O _____, why hast thou made us to
err from thy ways" (Isaiah 63:17)
64 Court
66 Resinous substance
68 "Take some of its blood and _____
it on Aaron's right earlobe"
(Exodus 29:20 MSG)
69 According to
71 Davy Crockett's home state (abbr.)
74 Organization begun by Gen. and
Mrs. Booth (abbr.)

63

ACROSS

1 Chew
5 Canyon
10 "That _____," 60s TV series
14 Unique
15 Medal
16 Solomon's grandson (Matthew 1:7)
17 Tenth part of an ephah (Exodus 16:36)
18 "Moza begat _____" (1 Chronicles 8:37)
19 Zerahiah's father (1 Chronicles 6:6)
20 Hit with, as a snowball
21 Rage
22 Swimmer's lengths
23 High priest in Shiloh
25 Obtain
27 Minor prophet (abbr.)
28 Firearm
30 Plead
32 Hearing
33 Cures
35 Search
36 Gait
37 "In all _____ there is profit" (Proverbs 14:23)
39 "Leave their wealth to _____" (Psalm 49:10)
41 Ziphion's father (Genesis 46:16)
42 Bezaleel's father (Exodus 38:22)
43 Compete
44 And so forth (abbr.)
46 Learning handicap (abbr.)
47 Group
48 Stumble
49 Jether's son (1 Chronicles 7:38)
50 "That lieth before _____ by the way of the wilderness" (2 Samuel 2:24)
52 "Who had taken _____ for his daughter" (Esther 2:15)
54 "Adonijah, Bigvai, _____" (Nehemiah 10:16)
55 Turn up one's nose at
57 Deface
58 Theatrical device
59 Stuffed animal maker
60 "And there was war between _____ and Baasha" (1 Kings 15:16)
61 Adam lived _____ hundred and thirty years (Genesis 5:5)
62 Scandinavian carrier (abbr.)
63 Cooped-up one?
64 License plate

DOWN

1 Fumble around
2 To wit
3 Gad's son (Genesis 46:16)
4 "If thou _____ pure and upright" (Job 8:6)
5 "The men of Ramah and _____" (Nehemiah 7:30)
6 In debt
7 Grasslands
8 Welcome
9 "The tower of _____" (Genesis 35:21)
10 Ancient region of western Europe
11 Judge of Israel (Judges 12:8)
12 Saul's concubine (2 Samuel 3:7)
13 "Cause it to be heard unto _____" (Isaiah 10:30)
24 Harmful
26 Suede, for example
28 Chow
29 Evidence of creation
30 "Then thou shalt _____ thyself" (2 Samuel 5:24)
31 Joy
32 "Lebbaeus, whose surname was _____" (Matthew 10:3)
34 Going from one to another
37 Cargo
38 "Departed from Hazeroth, and pitched in _____" (Numbers 33:18)
39 Invaded
40 Pace
41 Practical jokes
45 Candy _____

by Tonya Vilhauer

51 "The gods of Sepharvaim, _____, and Ivah" (2 Kings 18:34)
53 State of being comfortable
54 "Stayed in _____ for a season" (Acts 19:22)
56 Aves.
58 "Go to the _____, thou sluggard" (Proverbs 6:6)

64

ACROSS
1 Crippled
6 Separated
10 Midianite King slain by the Israelites (Numbers 31:8)
11 Stop
13 One of Berah's sons (1 Chronicles 8:15)
14 Old Testament prophet (abbr.)
15 Before
18 Set
21 Timothy's mother (2 Timothy 1:5)
22 "Save the _____ sort" (2 Kings 24:14)
24 "Be _____ of the Spirit" (Galatians 5:18)
25 Kohath's son (Numbers 3:19)
27 Tint
28 "_____ with her suburbs" (1 Chronicles 6:73)
29 Bang
30 "Become an astonishment, a _____, and a byword" (Deuteronomy 28:37)
33 Hedge
35 "In _____ was there a voice heard" (Matthew 2:18)
36 "He is a _____ of them" (Hebrews 11:6)
39 Chill
40 Zeruiah's son (2 Samuel 2:18)
42 "The children of _____" (Ezra 2:57)
43 "Would they not give _____" (Nehemiah 9:30)
44 Party
45 Mother _____
46 Patmos was one (Revelation 1:9)
47 _____ of Galilee
49 "Barley and the _____" (Isaiah 28:25)
50 Fall
51 Way
52 Roman province in Asia Minor (Acts 27:5)

DOWN
2 The Jairite (2 Samuel 20:26)
3 Cure
4 The Philistines brought the ark from _____ to Ashdod (1 Samuel 5:1)
5 Move quickly
6 Barak's father (Judges 4:6)
7 Parson
8 Jephunneh's brother (1 Chronicles 7:38)
9 "Make them like a _____" (Psalm 83:13)
12 "Moses _____ all the words" (Exodus 24:4)
16 Regret
17 Final
19 After Galatians (abbr.)
20 Ahaz's son (1 Chronicles 8:36)
23 Chief
26 Hug
28 Assyrian king brought inhabitants from here to live in Samaria (2 Kings 17:24)
29 "Called these days Purim after the name of _____" (Esther 9:26)
30 "He was the _____" (Genesis 14:18)
31 A Jewish term of contempt (Matthew 5:22)
32 "Fill an _____ of it" (Exodus 16:32)
33 Loft
34 Beverages
37 One of Benjamin's sons (Genesis 46:21)
38 Vare
40 Elkanah's brother (Exodus 6:24)
41 "The _____ of the feet" (Joshua 3:13)
46 Caleb's son (1 Chronicles 4:15)
48 Bow

by Sarah Lagerquist Simmons

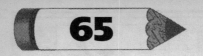

65

Biblical Birds

The spellings of some birds' names differ with some printings of the KJV
The older (Authorized) version is used here

ACROSS

1 "And the _____, because he cheweth the cud" (Leviticus 11:6)
5 Gov't. industrial safety group
9 Editor's mark
14 Enthusiastic
15 _____ dunk
16 Minneapolis suburb
17 **BIRD** (Psalm 55:6)
18 Crow calls
19 Choir boy?
20 Three **BIRDS** (Leviticus 11:13–19)
23 Poetic preposition
24 Type
25 Airport abbr.
26 St. crosser
27 Nick and Nora's dog
29 Noah's son (Genesis 5:32)
32 Hindu mystic
35 Tennis great
36 Little bit
37 Three more **BIRDS** (Leviticus 11:13–19)
40 "It goes through _____ places seeking rest" (Matthew 12:43 NIV)
41 Utah natives
42 Beldam
43 Buttons or Adair
44 "Ye have made it _____ of thieves" (Matthew 21:13) (2 words)
45 Part of many Quebec city names (abbr.)
46 Runner
47 "And I _____ smooth man" (Genesis 27:11) (2 words)
48 **BIRD** (Luke 13:34)
51 Three more **BIRDS** (Leviticus 11:13–19)
57 "Men condemned to die in the _____" (1 Corinthians 4:9 NIV)
58 "Whither have ye made a _____ to day" (1 Samuel 27:10)
59 Persia, today
60 Hog breed
61 "He rolled _____ stone in front" (Matthew 27:60 NIV) (2 words)
62 "The _____ that is in thy brother's eye" (Luke 6:41)
63 **BIRD** (Psalm 104:17)
64 Asherah, for one
65 Adam's grandson (Luke 3:38)

DOWN

1 Biblical verb
2 "And fulfill _____ made to the Lord" (2 Samuel 15:7 NIV) (3 words)
3 David, to Saul
4 First home
5 Sponge's mouth
6 "Let not thine hands be _____" (Zephaniah 3:16)
7 **BIRD** (Job 39:26)
8 "I _____ troubled that I cannot speak" (Psalm 77:4) (2 words)
9 Et _____
10 "He is _____ brother, a faithful minister" (Colossians 4:7 NIV) (2 words)
11 "And the king took off his _____" (Esther 8:2)
12 Organic compound
13 Biblical weed
21 Honda model
22 Living _____ (what Jesus promised)
26 "God has ascended _____ shouts of joy" (Psalm 47:5 NIV)
27 Pale, as a face
28 "_____ the right one for me" (Judges 14:3 NIV)

29 Tramp
30 "Whose breaking cometh suddenly _____ instant" (Isaiah 30:13) (2 words)
31 "Be gathered, every one with her _____" (Isaiah 34:15)
32 Nautical support
33 Existed
34 "Every open container without ___ ___ fastened on it" (Numbers 19:15 NIV) (2 words)
35 Poker prose
36 Memo heading (2 words)
38 Part of multimedia
39 Of eight
44 Have _____ for (2 words)
45 Kind of pot
46 Madrid mister
47 To no _____

48 Part of HOMES
49 Muse believed to inspire poets
50 Endangered Hawaiian birds
51 Units of ionizing radiation
52 Experiencing ennui, with "in" (2 words)
53 _____ Beach, Florida
54 It's a _____ (showbiz talk)
55 Gray wolf
56 "I have sinned this _____" (Exodus 9:27)

by David K. Shortess

66

ACROSS

1 Lax
7 Sow
11 Town in the territory of Ephraim (1 Chronicles 7:28)
12 Ado
14 "_____ have emptied them out" (Nahum 2:2)
16 "At the river of _____" (Ezra 8:21)
17 Coffee holder
18 David and Samuel dwelt here (1 Samuel 19:18)
20 City in the extreme south of Judah (Joshua 15:29)
21 Cad
23 Forswear
24 "Put it on a blue _____" (Exodus 28:37)
25 Senior
27 "They _____ them" (Joshua 7:5)
29 Head
32 Cut
33 "Distributing to the _____ of saints" (Romans 12:13)
34 "I know that thou _____ God" (Genesis 22:12)
36 Town of Canaanites later belonging to Judah (Genesis 38:5)
40 "That the iniquity of _____ house" (1 Samuel 3:14)
41 You
43 Hill
44 Do not lose
46 "These nations shalt thou find no _____" (Deuteronomy 28:65)
48 Angry
49 Ilk
51 Judas's son (Matthew 1:3)
53 After Joshua (abbr.)
54 Urge
55 Precise
56 Before Job (abbr.)
57 "Fill the _____ sacks" (Genesis 44:1)

DOWN

1 Prophet who anointed David as king
2 "The number of them that _____" (Judges 7:6)
3 Craft
4 Abel's murderer
5 Mold
6 "Assaulted the house of _____" (Acts 17:5)
7 Beri's brother (1 Chronicles 7:36)
8 Before Philippians (abbr.)
9 "Was spoken by _____ the prophet" (Matthew 4:14)
10 "He disappointeth the _____" (Job 5:12)
11 Pharaoh _____, king of Egypt (2 Kings 23:29 NKJV)
13 Broken
15 "The wheat and the _____ were not smitten" (Exodus 9:32)
19 "My state shall _____ declare" (Colossians 4:7)
22 "The _____ are cleansed" (Matthew 11:5)
24 Legalist
26 Clan
28 "Ephron dwelt among the children of _____" (Genesis 23:10)
30 Exam
31 Mordecai was _____ cousin (Esther 2:7)
33 Jesus raised the widow's son to life at this city's gate (Luke 7:11)
34 Rare
35 A mighty man of valor from the tribe of Benjamin (2 Chronicles 17:17)
37 Abraham's son (1 Chronicles 1:32)
38 Abraham was _____ father
39 Cot
42 "Perform unto the Lord thine _____" (Matthew 5:33)
45 "Cruel venom of _____" (Deuteronomy 32:33)

by Sarah Lagerquist Simmons

47 A city of Simeon
(1 Chronicles 4:29)

50 Away

52 "Shall the _____ boast itself"
(Isaiah 10:15)

ACROSS

1 "His kingdom was _____ into darkness" (Revelation 16:10 NIV)
7 "Caused it not to rain upon _____ city" (Amos 4:7)
13 Paul imprisoned there (Acts 28:16)
14 "So the men sat down, in _____ about five thousand" (John 6:10)
15 Shimei's father (1 Kings 4:18 NIV)
16 "Wild beasts of the _____" (Isaiah 13:22)
18 Jesus spoke this language
20 "All of God's _____ children" (Hebrews 12:23 CEV)
21 "In those days Israel had _____ king" (Judges 17:6 NLT)
22 In addition
23 Hebrew year's sixth month
24 "_____, we wept" (Psalm 137:1 NKJV)
26 New Zealand bird
27 City where Paul stayed seven days (Acts 21:3–4)
29 "The damsel _____ not dead" (Mark 5:39)
31 How Peter reached Jesus' tomb (Luke 24:12)
32 King of Bashan (Numbers 21:33)
34 "The Jesus whom Paul _____" (Acts 19:13 NKJV)
38 People from here were brought to Samaria (Ezra 4:9–10) (var.)
41 Roman numeral two
42 Harvest (Jeremiah 12:13)
43 "_____ into clay, and tread morter" (Nahum 3:14)
45 "_____ have compassion, making a difference" (Jude 22)
46 "At him they _____ stones" (Mark 12:4)
48 "I will leave _____ men of them" (Ezekiel 12:16) (2 words)
50 Long, fluffy scarf
51 Sermonizing spots
54 "Every _____ from his place" (Zephaniah 2:11)
55 Jane Austen title
57 Reading, 'Riting, and 'Rithmetic: the three _____
58 Early plainsman (Genesis 13:12)
59 About
60 "I am at the point to _____" (Genesis 25:32)
61 "He that loveth _____ shall be a poor man" (Proverbs 21:17)
64 Olympic gymnast _____ Korbut
67 "Who also hath made us _____ ministers" (2 Corinthians 3:6)
69 Satan's minion (Matthew 9:33 NKJV)
70 "He will show you a large upper _____" (Mark 14:15)
71 A _____-do-well (contraction)
72 Wild prairie rose is state flower (abbr.)
73 Extended His mercy to whom? (Ezra 9:9)
74 "Whether they be young ones, or _____" (Deuteronomy 22:6)
75 "None can _____ his hand" (Daniel 4:35)
76 "_____, that great city Babylon" (Revelation 18:10)

DOWN

1 Precedes destruction (Proverbs 16:18 NKJV) (3 words)
2 A worthless person
3 Diacritical mark above vowel
4 Close to
5 "Great unto the _____ of the earth" (Micah 5:4)
6 "Buried in a dry and _____ grave" (Jeremiah 17:13 NLT)
7 Damascus river (2 Kings 5:12)
8 Roman ruler, Paul's contemporary (Acts 25:21 NASB, note)
9 "_____ pro nobis" (Latin) (trans.: "Pray for us")
10 "Apostles, prophets, teachers, miracle workers, _____" (1 Corinthians 12:28 MSG)
11 Shaphat's son (1 Kings 19:19)

by Mary Ann Sherman

12 Masked mammal (var.)
17 Yankeedom (abbr.)
19 "On their way to _____ out the land" (Joshua 18:8 NIV)
25 "_____ they believe me" (Numbers 14:11)
28 Biblical pleasure-seekers (Acts 17:18)
29 "Out of whose womb came the _____?" (Job 38:29)
30 Tibetan sheep
33 "I clothed Lebanon with _____" (Ezekiel 31:15 NIV)
35 Iranian currency (pl.)
36 What Jonathan gave his lad (1 Samuel 20:40)
37 Government watchdog (abbr.)
39 Town in Judah (Joshua 15:26)
40 "Have mercy on _____" (Matthew 15:22)

43 "Uphold me by your _____ spirit" (Psalm 51:12 NKJV)
44 "_____ no man any thing" (Romans 13:8)
47 Without issue (Latin) (abbr.)
49 "As far as Appii _____" (Acts 28:15)
52 Part of the foot
53 Telescopic surveying method for elevation
56 "Even over them that had not sinned after. . ._____ transgression" (Romans 5:14) (possessive)
61 Guilty or not guilty
62 "Shut up the words, and _____ the book" (Daniel 12:4)
63 Lowest-ranking naval officer (abbr.)
65 Measure of oil (Leviticus 14:10)
66 "I am against thee, O _____" (Ezekiel 38:3)
68 Wager

ACROSS

1 Kind of exam
4 Flight to the fjords (abbr.)
7 "And the _____ God said, It is not good that the man should be alone" (Genesis 2:18)
12 Cape Town's country (abbr.)
13 High jinks
15 Balmoral Castle's river
16 "God shall send forth his _____ and his truth" (Psalm 57:3)
18 "Thus saith the LORD, I have _____ these waters" (2 Kings 2:21)
21 Its capital is Pierre (abbr.)
22 Town in northeastern Pennsylvania
24 "That he should still _____ for ever" (Psalm 49:9)
25 Meadow
26 Mode of transportation (abbr.)
27 Make lace
29 Compete
30 "The mouth of the righteous man _____ wisdom" (Psalm 37:30 NIV)
34 State for newlyweds (abbr.)
35 Tree or street
36 Indian currency (abbr.)
38 Hawaiian bird
39 Title Paul gave to other Christians (abbr.)
40 "Why did we _____ leave Egypt" (Numbers 11:20 NIV)
42 "To offer unto the LORD the _____ sacrifice, and his vow" (1 Samuel 1:21)
44 Own (Scot.)
46 "And thou shalt _____ up the tabernacle according to the fashion" (Exodus 26:30)
48 "Thou trustest in the staff of this broken _____" (Isaiah 36:6)
49 _____ mode
50 Calling or greeting
51 Classic car
52 Model Cheryl

53 "And saveth such _____ be of a contrite spirit" (Psalm 34:18)
55 "But if the LORD make a _____ thing" (Numbers 16:30)
58 Certain parchment scroll (var.)
60 Emergency crew (abbr.)
61 "And ten asses _____ with the good things of Egypt" (Genesis 45:23)
64 "And _____ of Rehoboth by the river reigned in his stead" (Genesis 36:37)
66 Cornhusker state (abbr.)
67 Jacob _____ Israel (abbr.)
68 Pharaoh name
70 Sal of songdom was one
72 "Locks with the _____ of the night" (Song of Solomon 5:2 NASB)
74 "The same came for a witness, _____ bear witness of the Light" (John 1:7)
76 What Santa says
77 Name of God
78 "Let us build us a city and a _____" (Genesis 11:4)

DOWN

1 Bone
2 "Behold behind him a _____ caught in a thicket" (Genesis 22:13)
3 "You got fat, became obese, a tub of _____" (Deuteronomy 32:15 MSG)
4 Pig's home
5 City in Canaan
6 "It is only a _____ from the burn" (Leviticus 13:28 NIV)
8 Paean
9 "For my flesh is _____ food" (John 6:55 NIV)
10 "The LORD is my rock, and my fortress, and my _____" (2 Samuel 22:2)
11 "For I know that my _____ liveth" (Job 19:25)
14 Billy Graham's home state (abbr.)
17 Rebekah's son

by Marijane G. Troyer

18 "And God called the firmament
    _____" (Genesis 1:8)
19 "Some _____ beast hath devoured
    him" (Genesis 37:20)
20 "Tabernacle shall be sanctified by
    my _____" (Exodus 29:43)
22 "He who hurries his footsteps
    _____" (Proverbs 19:2 NASB)
23 European country (abbr.)
26 Property (abbr.)
28 Hebrew letter
31 "Then Joshua _____ his clothes
    and fell facedown" (Joshua 7:6 NIV)
32 "And the servant _____ Isaac all
    things that he had done"
    (Genesis 24:66)
33 Trite
37 Dried up
41 "_____ abode at Corinth"
    (2 Timothy 4:20)
43 Time period (var.)

45 "Othello" role
47 Twelfth month of the Jewish year
49 Irish nobleman
51 "Which shall be cities of _____"
    (Numbers 35:14)
54 "Praise be to my Rock! Exalted be
    God my _____" (Psalm 18:46 NIV)
56 Certain railway, familiarly
57 Famed pianist Landowska
59 Spanish cheer
62 "And the _____ beast shall be his"
    (Exodus 21:34)
63 _____ Valley, California
64 "Moses _____ to judge the people"
    (Exodus 18:13)
65 Golfer Ernie
69 "Pull me out of _____ net"
    (Psalm 31:4)
71 Selma's state (abbr.)
73 One who heals (abbr.)
75 First part of the Bible (abbr.)

69

A Proverbial Facelift

LORD, lift thou up the light of thy countenance upon us
Thou hast put gladness in my heart.

PSALM 4:6–7

ACROSS

1 "In _____ was there a voice heard"
   (Matthew 2:18)
5 Lupino, and others
9 Group of jurors
14 "Ahira the son of _____"
   (Numbers 1:15)
15 ICBM hangar
16 "That I _____ not my power in the
   gospel" (1 Corinthians 9:18)
17 Big Island city
18 "And she shall bring forth _____"
   (Matthew 1:21) (2 words)
19 Oscar de la _____
20 Start of **QUOTE** (Proverbs 15:13)
   (3 words)
23 Sew
24 Class of dog
25 _____ relief
28 _____ for Humanity
32 "If I wash thee not, thou hast no
   _____ with me" (John 13:8)
33 Commercials
36 Zhivago's love
37 "The _____ of the mountains is his
   pasture" (Job 39:8)
38 **QUOTE**, part 2 (3 words)
42 "They of _____ salute you"
   (Hebrews 13:24)
43 Brain wave records (abbr.)
44 Amount owed
45 "But only one _____ the prize"
   (1 Corinthians 9:24 NIV)
46 Motown
49 Sugary finish?
50 Big _____, California
51 Grain for grinding
55 End of **QUOTE**
59 Expunge
63 Thunderclap

64 Tribe
65 Violinist's aid
66 Scarlett's home
67 Architect Saarinen
68 Wince
69 "There is no _____ in thee"
   (Song of Solomon 4:7)
70 End of road?

DOWN

1 Substance abuse treatment, briefly
2 Soul, according to psychologist Jung
3 Gender members
4 "As _____ wind brings rain"
   (Proverbs 25:23 NIV) (2 words)
5 "_____ unto thee, Arise"
   (Mark 2:11) (2 words)
6 Gossip (colloq.)
7 Medicinal plant
8 Beethoven's "Moonlight _____"
9 Political group
10 "Honest" one
11 Joshua's father (Joshua 1:1)
12 Winter time in PA
13 Meadow
21 Property for sale
22 "But the name of the wicked shall
   _____" (Proverbs 10:7)
25 National park west of Calgary
26 "Will you _____ the case for God"
   (Job 13:8 NIV)
27 Stone marker
29 Scrooge's syllable
30 "And _____ also the Jairite was
   a chief ruler about David"
   (2 Samuel 20:26)
31 Musically silent
32 Average
33 Juan's buddy

by David K. Shortess

34 "Times and _____ we do not need"
   (1 Thessalonians 5:1 NIV)
35 Stingray
37 Call it quits
39 Golfer Ernie
40 Not his
41 Part of psyche
46 Pair
47 Bursts forth
48 Copies
50 "Yet through the _____ of water it
   will bud" (Job 14:9)
52 Water strip
53 Frighten
54 "And we told him according to the
   _____ of these words"
   (Genesis 43:7)
56 Tide type

57 Poi source
58 Red Sea port
59 Sounds of hesitation
60 Permanent CD
61 Righteous king of Judah
   (1 Kings 15:11)
62 _____ Walter Scott

70

ACROSS

1 "Get thee up into this mountain
_____" (Deuteronomy 32:49)
7 "_____, why do ye these things?"
(Acts 14:15)
11 "Three days _____ I fell sick"
(1 Samuel 30:13)
12 "I will _____ off from the top"
(Ezekiel 17:22)
14 "The _____ owl also shall rest
there" (Isaiah 34:14)
16 Ancestral head of one of the
subdivisions of porters of the temple
(Ezra 2:42)
18 Type of tree
19 Head vermin
21 Hangout
22 Big cat
24 Duke of Edom (Genesis 36:43)
25 "Make a mercy _____ of pure gold"
(Exodus 25:17)
26 Flag
28 Back
30 Even
31 "What am I _____" (Job 16:6)
32 "The wicked is _____"
(Psalm 9:16)
35 Skill
36 "Bread to the _____" (Isaiah 55:10)
38 Method
42 "_____, against my sanctuary"
(Ezekiel 25:3)
43 Mask
45 "My heart standeth in _____"
(Psalm 119:161)
46 "A third part shall be at the gate of
_____" (2 Kings 11:6)
47 Moses was _____ brother
49 Zephaniah's son (Zechariah 6:14)
50 Damp
52 "Riotous _____ of flesh"
(Proverbs 23:20)
54 Joyce Kilmer wrote about one
55 Gape
56 On this day Abraham saw the far-
off place (Genesis 22:4)
57 "Like a _____ of scarlet"
(Song of Solomon 4:3)

DOWN

2 Head of one of the families of the
Nethinims who returned from the
exile with Zerubbabel (Ezra 2:53)
3 Eon
4 A kind of deer or hart
5 "Hearts _____ to follow"
(Judges 9:3)
6 Eshton's father (1 Chronicles 4:11)
7 Plan
8 Ikkesh's son (1 Chronicles 11:28)
9 "Tree that will not _____"
(Isaiah 40:20)
10 "Whose trust shall be a _____ web"
(Job 8:14)
13 "My heart _____" (Isaiah 21:4)
14 "The _____ of thy foot"
(Deuteronomy 28:35)
15 Eve's son
17 Pick on
20 Vehicle
23 "As vinegar upon _____, so is he"
(Proverbs 25:20)
25 "The chief _____ in the
synagogue" (Matthew 23:6)
27 "Pelican, and the _____ eagle"
(Deuteronomy 14:17)
29 "It was _____ good" (Genesis 1:31)
32 "Abundance of the _____, and of
treasures" (Deuteronomy 33:19)
33 Follows Micah
34 City on the border of Ephraim
(Joshua 16:2)
35 Daughter of the priest of On
(Genesis 41:45)
37 Mr.
39 Melech's brother (1 Chronicles 9:41)
40 "Following the _____ great with
young" (Psalm 78:71)
41 "When _____ began to multiply"
(Genesis 6:1)
43 Despised
44 "Thou _____ well" (Genesis 4:7)

by Sarah Lagerquist Simmons

47 "Of the tribe of _____ were sealed twelve thousand" (Revelation 7:6)
48 Ace
51 Uzziel's brother (1 Chronicles 7:7)
53 Rather

71

ACROSS

1 "Paul, an apostle of Jesus Christ and _____ our brother" (2 Corinthians 1:1)
7 Japanese coin
9 Held up arms of Moses (Exodus 17:12)
12 Biblical region (Genesis 35:21)
13 "And it is a _____ thing that the king requireth" (Daniel 2:11)
15 "In the twentieth year of Jeroboam king of Israel reigned _____ over Judah" (1 Kings 15:9)
16 Mid-twentieth-century failed car
18 "Tracks of a wild donkey in _____" (Jeremiah 2:24 MSG)
19 "If a maiden _____ out to draw water" (Genesis 24:43 NIV)
20 "For they were _____ strong for me" (Psalm 18:17)
21 Type of response system (abbr.)
23 "For they shall _____ an ornament of grace unto thy head" (Proverbs 1:9)
24 Aurora or dawn
25 Yes for Juan
26 "They'll cover every square _____ of ground" (Exodus 10:5 MSG)
29 "Which are blackish by reason of the _____" (Job 6:16)
30 "The name of it [is] called _____; because the LORD did there confound the language of all the earth" (Genesis 11:9)
32 Short laugh
33 Archie Bunker's wife
35 Accepted standard
36 "When you _____ at them with drawn bow" (Psalm 21:12 NIV)
37 Not
38 Persian coin
40 Sunshine state (abbr.)
41 South American country
43 "_____ shall I keep thy law continually" (Psalm 119:44)
44 Meadow
46 "Jacob took him rods. . .of the _____ and chesnut tree" (Genesis 30:37)
47 Bronze Chinese coin
49 Actress Amanda _____

50 "They fled before the men of _____" (Joshua 7:4)
52 "For _____ have I seen righteous before me in this generation" (Genesis 7:1)
54 "And, _____, I am with you always" (Matthew 28:20)
56 "Again, _____ made seven of his sons to pass before Samuel" (1 Samuel 16:10)
58 Rejects
60 A Catholic woman who dedicates her life to Christ
62 Fuegan Indian
63 Rodent
65 "Go to the _____, thou sluggard; consider her ways" (Proverbs 6:6)
66 "So the officials took Jeremiah and lowered him into an empty cistern in the prison _____" (Jeremiah 38:6 NLT)
68 "It is vain for you to rise up early, to sit up _____" (Psalm 127:2)
70 Sounds an owl makes
71 Opposite of oohs
72 "They're already at Hazazon Tamar, the _____ of En Gedi" (2 Chronicles 20:2 MSG)

DOWN

1 "The flesh was still between their _____" (Numbers 11:33)
2 A leader of the tribe of Manasseh (1 Chronicles 27:21)
3 Stone worker
4 Raw mineral
5 Sixty minutes makes one (abbr.)
6 "She shops around for the best _____ and cottons" (Proverbs 31:13 MSG)
7 Prepare flax
8 "Then Abraham. . .picked out a _____ plump calf" (Genesis 18:7 MSG)
9 "_____ came to the banquet with Esther" (Esther 7:1)
10 "_____ hospitality one to another" (1 Peter 4:9)
11 Tablets discovered in Syria (2 words)
14 Eurasian country (abbr.)
17 Horseleach (Proverbs 30:15 NIV)
22 Fish eggs

by Marijane G. Troyer

23 Worn to protect baby's clothes
25 Clothes worn by Indian women (pl.)
26 State of Chicago (abbr.)
27 Greek letter
28 Hebrew name for God, translated "Lord" (Preface NIV)
29 "_____ waxeth old because of all mine enemies" (Psalm 6:7)
30 "And shut and _____ the gates" (Nehemiah 7:3 MSG)
31 President's command (abbr.)
33 Printer's measure
34 Rural Midwestern state bordering Ohio (abbr.)
35 "_____, a servant of Jesus Christ, called to be an apostle" (Romans 1:1)
36 Words to praise God (Revelation 19:1) (pl.)
38 One who heals (abbr.)
39 Firm (abbr.)
41 "Can you make a _____ of him like a bird?" (Job 41:5 NIV)
42 Aboveground trains (abbr.)
45 Collar

46 Samuel's mother (1 Samuel 1:20)
48 "That which groweth of _____ own accord" (Leviticus 25:5)
49 "Found this man a real _____" (Acts 24:5 NASB)
51 Girl's name
53 "Then Joseph _____ husband, being a just man" (Matthew 1:19)
55 "For _____ you is born this day. . .a Saviour" (Luke 2:11)
56 "Oh, the _____ of those who trust in him" (Psalm 34:8 NLT)
57 "Through faith also _____. . .conceived strength to conceive seed" (Hebrews 11:11)
59 "When he _____ how good is his resting place" (Genesis 49:15 NIV)
61 Colorful card game
64 "For then I would fly away, and be _____ rest" (Psalm 55:6)
67 Person who bats in place of the pitcher (abbr.)
68 New Orleans state (abbr.)
69 Seventh note of a musical scale

72

ACROSS

1 "Be clean, and change _____ garments" (Genesis 35:2)
5 "_____, let God be true" (Romans 3:4)
8 "Dwelled between Kadesh and _____" (Genesis 20:1)
12 "Woe to them that are at _____ in Zion" (Amos 6:1)
13 Antique
14 Employ
15 "The righteous shall flourish like the palm _____" (Psalm 92:12)
16 "Carried the people of it captive to _____" (2 Kings 16:9)
17 Rim
18 "Then I will give you rain in _____ season" (Leviticus 26:4)
20 "And Rekem, and _____, and Taralah" (Joshua 18:27)
22 "He that findeth his life shall _____ it" (Matthew 10:39)
24 "Waters bring forth. . .the. . .creature that _____ life" (Genesis 1:20)
25 _____ money
26 Sleeping dogs do this
28 Belonging to slugger Sammy
32 Gem shape
34 "They passed through the Red sea as by _____ land" (Hebrews 11:29)
35 "And Abimelech took an _____ in his hand" (Judges 9:48)
36 "Put on the new man, which is _____ in knowledge" (Colossians 3:10)
38 "I will make thee _____ over many things" (Matthew 25:21)
40 Esther's king
42 "He lieth under the _____ trees" (Job 40:21)
45 "_____ not the poor" (Proverbs 22:22)
46 "Straightway the spirit _____ him" (Mark 9:20)
47 Fire starter?
49 Jezebel's "better" half

53 Sadoc's father (Matthew 1:15)
54 "And Adam called his wife's name _____" (Genesis 3:20)
55 Letter
56 Cincinnati team
57 Pop
58 Perfect place

DOWN

1 "_____ they shall flee away" (Nahum 2:8)
2 Row
3 Employ
4 "The _____ and flags shall wither" (Isaiah 19:6)
5 "The _____ of my transgressions" (Lamentations 1:14)
6 "Samuel arose and went to _____" (1 Samuel 3:6)
7 "We were driven up and down in _____" (Acts 27:27)
8 "Ebal, _____, and Onam" (Genesis 36:23)
9 Conceal
10 "Pharisees began to _____ him vehemently" (Luke 11:53)
11 "They _____ to and fro" (Psalm 107:27)
19 Bani's son (Ezra 10:34)
21 Football positions (abbr.)
22 Not taped
23 Judah's son with Shuah (Genesis 38:4)
24 "The firstlings of our _____" (Nehemiah 10:36)
25 _____ favor, amigo
27 Thought
29 Zimri's father (Numbers 25:14)
30 "Come against her with _____" (Jeremiah 46:22)
31 Sunday speech (abbr.)
33 "They be blind _____ of the blind" (Matthew 15:14)
37 "_____ hast thou forsaken me" (Psalm 22:1)
38 Antique auto

by Tonya Vilhauer

39 Suave
41 Pleaded
42 "When they saw the _____, they rejoiced" (Matthew 2:10)
43 Confusion
44 Nickname of baseball standout Alex
47 "Thou in thy mercy hast _____ forth the people" (Exodus 15:13)
48 Eggs
50 "Bezer, and _____, and Shamma" (1 Chronicles 7:37)
51 "I _____ no pleasant bread" (Daniel 10:3)
52 David _____-Gurion

73

ACROSS

1 Sihon and Israel fought here (Deuteronomy 2:32)
6 Isaac's grandfather (Genesis 11:26)
11 Equal
12 "Beyond the tower of _____" (Genesis 35:21)
14 A bunch of this was dipped in blood (Exodus 12:22)
16 Amateur
18 Peleg's son (Genesis 11:18)
20 King of Moab (2 Kings 3:4)
21 "Under oaks and poplars and _____" (Hosea 4:13)
23 "_____ hath done this thing" (Genesis 21:26)
25 Amos's father (Luke 3:25)
26 "According to the _____ of grace" (Romans 11:5)
28 "Purge away our _____" (Psalm 79:9)
29 Spoiled
31 Leah's son (Genesis 29:33)
34 Below
38 Aware of
39 Samson was buried between _____ and Zorah (Judges 16:30–31)
42 "That which groweth of _____ own accord" (Leviticus 25:5)
43 "As he saith also in _____" (Romans 9:25)
44 "I _____ not" (Luke 17:9)
46 "Swift as the _____ upon the mountains" (1 Chronicles 12:8)
48 City on the coast of Syria (Acts 13:4)
50 Ready
51 Old Testament prophet
52 Sales is one type
53 Frock

DOWN

2 Feign
3 "The Sovereign LORD _____ sworn" (Amos 6:8 NIV)
4 Old Testament prophet
5 Before Haggai (abbr.)
6 After nine
7 Another name for Esau (Genesis 25:30)
8 "The _____ brought him bread" (1 Kings 17:6)
9 "Parmashta, and _____, and Aridai" (Esther 9:9)
10 Trey
13 "Row of cedar _____" (1 Kings 6:36)
15 Scream
17 One of the cities of Hadarezer (1 Chronicles 18:8)
19 Fired a gun
22 Turn
23 "Of whom it is _____ that he liveth" (Hebrews 7:8)
24 Each
27 Besides
30 Almond
31 "I spread my _____ over thee" (Ezekiel 16:8)
32 "From thence it was parted, and became _____ four heads" (Genesis 2:10)
33 Aaron died and was buried here (Deuteronomy 10:6)
35 "Partakers of the divine _____" (2 Peter 1:4)
36 Tabitha (Acts 9:36)
37 "_____, lama sabachthani?" (Mark 15:34)
40 Look
41 Baanah's son (1 Chronicles 11:30)
45 Combat
47 After five
49 Follows 2 Chronicles (abbr.)

by Sarah Lagerquist Simmons

74

Slices of the Bread of Life—the Scriptures

Search the scriptures; for in them. . .
ye have eternal life.

JOHN 5:39

ACROSS
1 Kind of door
5 "And I will _____ sign among them" (Isaiah 66:19) (2 words)
9 **Small slice**
13 "The LORD shall _____ over you" (Judges 8:23)
14 **Small slice**
15 "The wife of _____ the Hittite" (2 Samuel 11:3)
17 Elevator man
18 One under Columbus
19 St. _____, Paris suburb
20 **Large slice** (3 words)
23 "Just a _____"
24 _____ polloi
25 Snug place
28 Kind of code
31 **Medium slice**
36 Hessian house
38 What a wheel rotates on
40 Spunk
41 Fungal spore sacs
42 **Whole loaf**
44 "Thou shalt not _____" (Exodus 20:13)
45 Coach Amos Alonzo _____
47 "I may _____ all my bones" (Psalm 22:17)
48 Thailand, once
49 **Small slice**
51 "And parted them to all men, as every man had _____" (Acts 2:45)
53 Title or occupation (suffix)
54 Refusals
56 Bill's partner
58 **Large slice** (3 words)
67 Seeps
68 Choir member
69 Fencing need
70 Limbless bodies (var.)
71 "Let the sea _____, and the fulness thereof" (Psalm 98:7)
72 Essence
73 Bridge response
74 Makes a lap
75 **Small slice**

DOWN
1 Pony gait
2 **Small slice**
3 "Who changed the truth of God into _____" (Romans 1:25) (2 words)
4 Mexican moola (pl.)
5 Beach crustacean (2 words)
6 Give off
7 Atmosphere
8 "A woven tunic, a turban and _____" (Exodus 28:4 NIV) (2 words)
9 Reform or Conservative
10 Utah city
11 "_____ Kleine Nachtmusik"
12 "He had _____ in the grave four days already" (John 11:17)
16 FDR follower
21 Meadow
22 Big _____ (circus tent)
25 Moon appearance
26 Kilns
27 Old European coin
29 Way out
30 Harry's vice president
32 Affirmations from space
33 VII x IX=_____
34 La Scala locale
35 Alabama civil rights town
37 Sound of regret
39 Fashion magazine
43 Registered voters
46 **Medium slice**
50 Tiff

by David K. Shortess

52 Accident fatality, often (abbr.)

55 "When the morning _____ sang together" (Job 38:7)

57 "I am Alpha and _____" (Revelation 21:6)

58 Small child

59 Hula-_____

60 **Small slice**

61 "The Untouchables" role

62 "_____, lama sabachthani" (Mark 15:34)

63 Immediately, in a hospital

64 Heroic tale

65 "I shall die in my _____" (Job 29:18)

66 Asian holidays

75

ACROSS

1 "And which had not worshipped the _____" (Revelation 20:4)
6 "They bring thee a red _____ without spot" (Numbers 19:2)
11 Baseball player who only bats (abbr.)
13 Boredom
14 Large amount
15 Mediocre grade
16 African antelope
18 Army volunteer (abbr.)
19 La _____ tar pits
20 American Indian
22 Church in Revelation
25 "_____ no more so exceeding proudly" (1 Samuel 2:3)
27 Amazon tributary
28 One who rents
29 "Abram passed through the land unto the place of _____, unto the plain of Moreh" (Genesis 12:6)
30 Person in early 20s (abbr.)
32 Biblical language (abbr.)
34 Place of the seal (Lat.)
37 "And behold a great red _____" Revelation 12:3)
39 Sinai wanderer (abbr.)
41 "I will give unto thee the _____ of the kingdom of heaven" (Matthew 16:19)
44 President's command (abbr.)
45 Mid-Atlantic state (abbr.)
47 "Shall tribulation, or distress, or persecution. . .or _____, or sword" (Romans 8:35)
49 Early Christian pulpit or lectern
51 "The _____ of Jesus Christ, which God gave unto him, to shew unto his servants" (Revelation 1:1)
54 "One to his _____, another to his merchandise" (Matthew 22:5)
55 "And the LORD _____ me of thee" (1 Samuel 24:12)
56 Home of the von Trapp family (abbr.)
57 _____ Peng, Chinese prime minister
58 "_____ waxeth old because of all mine enemies" (Psalm 6:7)
59 Jet (abbr.)

60 "For the _____ is touching the whole multitude thereof" (Ezekiel 7:13)
63 American _____, coll. course
66 Cooling system (abbr.)
68 Church to whom Paul wrote (abbr.)
69 Major network (abbr.)
71 Revelation was written to _____ (2 words)

DOWN

1 "That I may dwell in the house of th LORD. . .to behold the _____ of the LORD" (Psalm 27:4)
2 Printer's short measure
3 "For he shall give his _____ charge over thee" (Psalm 91:11)
4 "And unto the great sea toward the go ing down of the _____" (Joshua 1:4)
5 Germanic god
7 Einsteinium (abbr.)
8 Nailed (colloq.)
9 "Of whom the whole _____ in heaven and earth is named" (Ephesians 3:15)
10 Mr. Sullivan
11 North Sea feeder
12 "In the beginning God created the _____ and the earth" (Genesis 1:1)
15 "Better a dry _____ with peace and quiet than a house full of feasting" (Proverbs 17:1 NIV)
17 "And rejoiceth as a strong man to ru a _____" (Psalm 19:5)
21 Instructor's helper (abbr.)
22 "And Israel sent messengers unto _____" (Numbers 21:21)
23 "A voice is heard in _____" (Matthew 2:18 NIV)
24 "When he had opened the fourth _____" (Revelation 6:7)
26 "So Saul took the _____ over Israel (1 Samuel 14:47)
31 "An _____ pleasing to the Lord" (Leviticus 2:9 NIV)
33 "Wherefore I abhor myself, and _____ in dust and ashes" (Job 42:6

by Marijane Troyer

35 Amateur play
36 "In Thee, O Lord, do I put _____ trust" (Psalm 31:1)
37 "And they bring unto him one that was _____" (Mark 7:32)
38 Precursor to modern language (abbr.)
40 EU country (abbr.)
42 "One for Moses, and one for _____" (Matthew 17:4)
43 "And I, even I, will chastise you seven times for your _____" (Leviticus 26:28)
46 Book of laws (abbr.)
48 "Facts of Life" actress Charlotte
50 Siblings (abbr.)
51 "For the Lord God had not caused it to _____ upon the earth" (Genesis 2:5)
52 "And the _____ of the temple was rent in twain from the top to the bottom" (Mark 15:38)

53 "He sendeth _____ his word" (Psalm 147:18)
57 "_____, I am with you alway" (Matthew 28:20)
59 Elm, for one (abbr.)
60 "And when one came to the wine _____ to draw fifty measures" (Haggai 2:16 NASB)
61 Connected wiring (abbr.)
62 Eisenhower's nickname
63 Gehrig of baseball
64 Not normal (abbr.)
65 "I will saddle me with an _____" (2 Samuel 19:26)
67 Without name (Lat.)
68 Abram, originally (abbr.)
69 Trials occur here (abbr.)
70 Exist

76

ACROSS

2 Mattathias's son (Luke 3:26)
5 Pet
8 "Israel mine _____" (Isaiah 45:4)
10 Asher's son (1 Chronicles 7:30)
12 "No man that _____ entangleth himself" (2 Timothy 2:4)
14 Not false
15 Pass away
16 "Riotous _____ of flesh" (Proverbs 23:20)
18 "A spider's _____" (Job 8:14)
19 Name
20 "The borders of _____ on the west" (Joshua 11:2)
22 Abdiel's son (1 Chronicles 5:15)
24 "_____, I am warm" (Isaiah 44:16)
27 Reuben's son (Joshua 18:17)
29 "Sailed into Syria, and _____ at Tyre" (Acts 21:3)
31 "Upon all the _____ of Bashan" (Isaiah 2:13)
32 "The children of _____" (Nehemiah 7:23)
33 Pispah's brother (1 Chronicles 7:38)
34 One of Simeon's descendants (1 Chronicles 4:36)
37 Slip
38 Guy
40 Shobal's son (1 Chronicles 1:40)
43 "He left nothing _____" (Joshua 11:15)
46 Belonging to Isaac's son
47 "Give a distinction in the _____" (1 Corinthians 14:7)
48 "_____ art thou wroth?" (Genesis 4:6)
49 Jonathan's son (Ezra 8:6)

DOWN

1 Morning moisture
2 Place where the Israelites murmured for want of water (Deuteronomy 32:51)
3 "As it were a half _____ of land" (1 Samuel 14:14)
4 "_____ the sacrifices of the dead" (Psalm 106:28)
5 Dry mud
6 Variant of Hosea (Romans 9:25)
7 Watch over
9 Load
11 More
13 "Brought _____ unto the man" (Genesis 2:22)
17 Eliphaz's son (Genesis 36:12)
19 "The iron, the _____, and the lead" (Numbers 31:22)
21 Free
23 "The Sovereign LORD _____ sworn" (Amos 6:8 NIV)
25 Pildash's brother (Genesis 22:22)
26 Town in the southern part of Judah (Joshua 11:21)
27 "There came other _____" (John 6:23)
28 Blade
30 "With the point of a _____" (Jeremiah 17:1)
32 Exclude
34 Hanani's son (1 Kings 16:1)
35 Get up
36 "He put forth his _____" (Genesis 3:22)
39 Bird's home
41 Gash
42 Wage
43 Utilize
44 "The priests that were in _____" (2 Samuel 22:11)
45 "Rain in _____ season" (Leviticus 26:4)

by Sarah Lagerquist Simmons

77

How Great a Love

Greater love hath no man than thi
that a man lay down his life for his friend

JOHN 15:1

ACROSS

1 Goose or thistle
7 "Out of the _____ of Jesse" (Isaiah 11:1)
11 Company agent (abbr.)
14 "An ephod, a robe, _____ tunic" (Exodus 28:4 NIV) (2 words)
15 _____ dweller
16 "_____ Town," Wilder play
17 Start of **VERSE** (from 1 John 3:1)
18 Locale
19 Exist
20 **VERSE**, part 2 (3 words)
23 Pacific _____
26 Inhabitant of (suffix)
27 Incline
28 What came out of Lazarus's tomb
30 What Alice's cookie said (2 words)
34 "A certain man. . .went into _____ country" (Mark 12:1) (2 words)
35 A root of evil
37 Scorches
39 **VERSE**, part 3 (3 words)
44 "Which I have _____ will declare" (Job 15:17) (2 words)
45 "Do not be _____ together with unbelievers" (2 Corinthians 6:14 NIV)
47 Soft drink, to a New Yorker
51 Groups of three
53 "For the sake of _____ will not destroy it" (Genesis 18:32 NIV) (2 words)
54 What Jesus did on Easter
56 H.S. student's hurdle (abbr.)
58 "_____, thy sins be forgiven thee" (Mark 2:5)
59 **VERSE**, part 4 (2 words)
64 Esquire (abbr., var.)
65 Tenth of an homer (Ezekiel 45:14)
66 End of **VERSE** (2 words)
70 Louis XV, *par exemple*

71 Hairy one
72 "The stones of the _____ carcase trodden under feet" (Isaiah 14:19) (3 words)
73 Is
74 Actress Susan and family
75 Unfired bricks of the Southwest

DOWN

1 Thing to hail
2 "Stand in _____, and sin not" (Psalm 4:4)
3 Formal Japanese drama
4 "We have four men which have _____ on them" (Acts 21:23) (2 words)
5 City on the Jumna
6 "I took the little book out of the angel's hand, _____ it up" (Revelation 10:10) (2 words)
7 Swindler's game
8 O'Hara estate
9 Tied
10 Wherewithal
11 "Listen to the _____ the lions" (Zechariah 11:3 NIV) (2 words)
12 Jupiter's moon
13 "If I _____ not Jerusalem above m chief joy" (Psalm 137:6)
21 "Thou art a _____ come from God" (John 3:2)
22 Shimei's dad (1 Kings 4:18 NIV)
23 N.T. book
24 Baal, for one
25 Not stereo
29 Gun a motor
31 "_____ said unto you, Dread not" (Deuteronomy 1:29) (2 words)
32 Member of the mob
33 Notable period
36 Affirmative

by David K. Shortess

38 Pig's place
40 Lunar New Year, in Vietnam
41 "My heart was _____ within me" (Psalm 39:3)
42 Scrimps, with "out"
43 Nevada city
46 "He will silence her noisy _____" (Jeremiah 51:55 NIV)
47 African desert
48 Tertullus, for one (Acts 24:1)
49 Feminine nickname
50 _____ Wednesday
52 _____ tree (make firewood or lumber) (3 words)
55 Slipped away
57 Lukewarm
60 At _____
61 "Or who can _____ the bottles of heaven" (Job 38:37)
62 Therefore

63 "What profit shall this birthright _____ me" (Genesis 25:32) (2 words)
67 Catch a crook
68 "_____ not vain repetitions" (Matthew 6:7)
69 Airline to Oslo (abbr.)

78

ACROSS

1 The Nethinims dwelt here (Nehemiah 3:26)
6 A lawyer (Titus 3:13)
11 Eleventh month of the Jewish year (Zechariah 1:7)
13 "Lot lifted up his _____" (Genesis 13:10)
15 "He _____ on my hand" (2 Kings 5:18)
17 A range of mountains (Song of Solomon 2:17)
19 Unwell
20 Opined
22 Sack
23 Song, "_____ and Circumstance"
25 "As a _____ is shaken" (1 Kings 14:15)
26 In time
27 Ishuah's brother (Genesis 46:17)
29 "_____, Jesus Christ maketh thee whole" (Acts 9:34)
32 "Appointed barley and the _____" (Isaiah 28:25)
34 Rip
35 Grave
38 "A third part shall be at the gate of _____" (2 Kings 11:6)
40 "And I will punish _____ in Babylon" (Jeremiah 51:44)
41 Be gone
44 Not less
46 "Solomon made a _____ of ships" (1 Kings 9:26)
47 "She is not afraid of the _____" (Proverbs 31:21)
49 Tear down
51 Herod's brother (Luke 3:1)
53 Add
54 "The _____ of your faith" (1 Peter 1:7)
57 "A people great and _____" (Deuteronomy 9:2)
58 "For God took _____" (Genesis 5:24)
59 "God is _____ judge" (Psalm 75:7)
60 "Master shall bore his _____" (Exodus 21:6)
61 Continent
62 Old Testament book about a Jewish queen (abbr.)
63 "We will go with _____ young" (Exodus 10:9)

DOWN

2 Hymns
3 Rooster's mate
4 Gaal's father (Judges 9:26)
5 After
6 John and James were _____ sons (Matthew 4:21)
7 "Saul _____ David from that day and forward" (1 Samuel 18:9)
8 Gain
9 "The house of _____" (1 Chronicles 4:21)
10 Skid
12 "So be it done unto _____" (Matthew 8:13)
14 Coax
16 "_____, lama sabachthani?" (Mark 15:34)
18 "_____ to hear" (Deuteronomy 29:4)
21 "It shall be for _____" (Genesis 1:29)
24 "_____ purge away thy dross" (Isaiah 1:25)
28 "They departed from _____" (Numbers 33:45)
30 Esli's son (Luke 3:25)
31 Mistake
33 "Adam, Sheth, _____" (1 Chronicles 1:1)
36 Old Testament prophet (abbr.)
37 After Exodus (abbr.)
39 "Of _____" (Numbers 26:44)
42 Come together
43 Phuvah's brother (Genesis 46:13)
45 Hasty
46 "_____ of checker work" (1 Kings 7:17)

by Sarah Lagerquist Simmons

48 "Vex you with their _____"
   (Numbers 25:18)
50 Abraham purchased a sepulcher
   from the children of _____
   (Acts 7:16)
51 Prayer
52 "Cast him into the _____ of
   ground" (2 Kings 9:26)
55 Possessive pronoun
56 Rohgah's brother
   (1 Chronicles 7:34)

79

ACROSS

1 Alaskan city
4 "My heart _____ for Moab like a harp" (Isaiah 16:11 NIV)
9 "Which we have heard. . .and our fathers have told _____" (Psalm 78:3)
11 High priest, to Samuel
12 Two _____ in one month equals a blue one
13 Tell Legend site
14 "And I will make thy seed to multiply as the stars of _____" (Genesis 26:4)
16 Hawaiian dish
17 Hair _____
18 Sea arm of the Mediterranean between Greece and Turkey
20 "That I should not _____ down to the pit" (Psalm 30:3)
21 Chief federal law officer (abbr.)
22 "But God _____ it for good" (Genesis 50:20)
24 "_____ panteth my soul after thee" (Psalm 42:1)
25 Greek letter
26 "I will both lay me down _____ peace, and sleep" (Psalm 4:8)
27 Jewish homeland
31 Minor prophet (abbr.)
33 Love (Lat.)
34 "And out of the midst thereof as the colour of _____" (Ezekiel 1:4)
35 Loud noise
37 Popular greeting
38 "_____the good shepherd" (John 10:11) (2 words)
39 Engineer (abbr.)
40 Nevada city
41 "_____ LORD is my strength and my shield" (Psalm 28:7)
43 More infused with rosy hues
47 Certain votes
48 Cool drink
49 Common navy man (abbr.)

50 "Four days _____ I was fasting until this hour" (Acts 10:30 NKJV)
52 Fads
54 Door part
55 "The hand of God has turned the _____" (Psalm 118:15 MSG)
58 Afterward
59 International organization for peace (abbr.)
60 "And he made the waters to stand as _____ heap" (Psalm 78:13)
61 Mallards' flight
62 Giant
65 Organization aiding in disasters (abbr.)
66 "Be quiet"
68 Alert
70 "More to be desired are they than gold, yea, than much _____ gold" (Psalm 19:10)
71 "David took _____ of gold that were on the servants" (2 Samuel 8:7)
72 "Likewise, ye _____, be in subjection to your own husbands" (1 Peter 3:1)

DOWN

1 He rebuilt the temple walls
2 Heard at bullfight
3 Not accounted for in war (abbr.)
4 "How _____ shall the wicked. . . triumph" (Psalm 94:3)
5 Money ledger belonging to (abbr.)
6 Midwestern state (abbr.)
7 Cable sports channel
8 Triangular-shaped musical instrument (Daniel 3:5–10 NASB)
9 Bathsheba's husband
10 "The time of the _____ of birds is come" (Song of Solomon 2:12)
12 "When my brother Esau _____ you and asks, To whom do you belong" (Genesis 32:17 NIV)
13 "I will lift _____ my hands in thy name" (Psalm 63:4)

15 "Vanity of _____, saith the
   Preacher" (Ecclesiastes 1:2)
19 City in Judah (Joshua 15:34)
23 "And I will put _____ between
   thee and the woman" (Genesis 3:15)
25 Promised land (var.)
28 "Consider well her _____, view her
   citadels" (Psalm 48:13 NIV)
29 "The Philistines took the ark of
   God, and brought it from _____
   unto Ashdod" (1 Samuel 5:1)
30 Onion relative
32 Presidential nickname
36 "Because there is _____ light in
   them" (Isaiah 8:20)
40 Freight transportation (abbr.) (pl.)
42 "Christ is the _____ of the church"
   (Ephesians 5:23)
44 Baking potatoes (var.)
45 Greek goddess

46 Unruly crowd
47 Sacred places
51 City of refuge (Deuteronomy 4:43)
53 "He shall surely _____ her to be
   his wife" (Exodus 22:16)
54 "And he took the fire in his hand,
   and a _____; and they went. . .
   together" (Genesis 22:6)
56 "They'll cover every square _____
   of ground" (Exodus 10:5 MSG)
57 Word in a threat
59 Mormon state (abbr.)
63 Poetic contraction
64 "Behold, I make all things _____"
   (Revelation 21:5)
67 Parliament chamber (abbr.)
69 Nation's revenue (abbr.)

80

ACROSS

1 "Salvation thereof as a _____ that burneth" (Isaiah 62:1)
4 Flow
8 Esau dwelt in this mount (Genesis 36:8)
10 To
12 "_____ thou hast not hated blood" (Ezekiel 35:6)
14 Aaron was one (Exodus 4:14)
16 Manahath's brother (Genesis 36:23)
18 A lawyer (Titus 3:13)
19 "Jael went out to meet _____" (Judges 4:18)
20 "Be _____ upon her knees" (Isaiah 66:12)
22 "Took the little book out of the angel's hand, and _____ it up" (Revelation 10:10)
24 Yep
26 Eyot
29 "My lips should _____ your grief" (Job 16:5)
32 "Cast him _____ this pit" (Genesis 37:22)
34 "Like the _____ of a calf's foot" (Ezekiel 1:7)
35 "Rushed with one accord into the _____" (Acts 19:29)
37 Before Song of Solomon (abbr.) (var.)
39 "He that _____ me before men" (Luke 12:9)
42 After Micah (abbr.)
43 Old Testament prophet (abbr.)
44 Ill
47 King of Hamath (1 Chronicles 18:9)
48 Defy
50 Guni's grandson (1 Chronicles 5:15)
51 Corrode
53 Bustle
54 Aaron and _____ held up Moses' hands (Exodus 17:12)
55 Shammah's father (2 Samuel 23:11)
56 After Galatians (abbr.)

DOWN

1 Claim
2 Island whose inhabitants are associated with Tyre (Ezekiel 27:8)
3 Set down
4 "God, the _____ of heaven and earth" (Genesis 14:22)
5 "Good works for necessary _____" (Titus 3:14)
6 Mature
7 "All the Chaldeans, Pekod, and _____" (Ezekiel 23:23)
9 "For the _____ sake" (Matthew 24:22)
11 Poor
13 Mob
15 Before Jeremiah (abbr.)
17 "With thy _____ treasure" (Psalm 17:14)
21 "I am the _____ in my father's house" (Judges 6:15)
22 "What _____ thee" (Psalm 114:5)
23 "_____ marked her mouth" (1 Samuel 1:12)
25 "_____ no man any thing" (Romans 13:8)
27 "He will be _____" (Jeremiah 20:10)
28 "_____ have said" (Acts 17:28)
30 "The LORD _____ him" (Genesis 38:7)
31 Per
33 "I am _____ root" (Revelation 22:16)
36 Ahitub's son (1 Samuel 14:3)
37 Ample
38 Make happen
40 Before Daniel (abbr.)
41 Zeruah's son (1 Kings 11:26)
45 One of the cities of Hadarezer (1 Chronicles 18:8)
46 "Syria shall go into captivity unto _____" (Amos 1:5)
47 Net
48 "They _____ the ship aground" (Acts 27:41)

by Sarah Lagerquist Simmons

49 One of three cities built by Elpaal's
sons (1 Chronicles 8:12)
52 Before eleven

81

ACROSS

1 "_____, though I walk through the valley" (Psalm 23:4)
4 "Thy _____ shall return upon thine own head" (Obadiah 1:15)
10 Holler
14 Row
15 "Arisai, and _____, and Vajezatha" (Esther 9:9)
16 "_____, lama sabachthani?" (Mark 15:34)
17 Try out
18 Hana Mandlikova's game
19 Rescue
20 Bring up
22 "Let them praise his name in the _____" (Psalm 149:3)
24 "As a _____ doth gather her brood" (Luke 13:34)
25 Corp.'s cousin
28 North Carolina Tar_____
30 Actress Shirley, and others
33 "Thou _____ up mighty rivers" (Psalm 74:15)
37 Harsh
38 "Thou art my _____ and my deliverer" (Psalm 40:17)
40 "Tekoa had two wives, Helah and _____" (1 Chronicles 4:5)
41 Scraped by, with "out"
43 Distort
45 Onesimus, for one
46 "And from _____, and from Berothai" (2 Samuel 8:8)
48 Banner, for one
50 Level
51 "And Jiphtah, and _____, and Nezib" (Joshua 15:43)
53 "For as ye have _____ your members" (Romans 6:19)
55 "That at the name of Jesus every ____ should bow" (Philippians 2:10)
57 "Wheat and _____ were not smitten" (Exodus 9:32)
58 "_____ they shall flee away" (Nahum 2:8)

61 Soil
63 Dense
68 Like a track
70 Grind
73 "By the river of _____" (Daniel 8:2)
74 _____ avis
75 "Shall move out of their _____ like worms" (Micah 7:17)
76 "There is a sound of abundance of _____" (1 Kings 18:41)
77 "I _____ that thou art a gracious God" (Jonah 4:2)
78 Cure
79 "Thy land shall be divided by _____" (Amos 7:17)

DOWN

1 "Be clean, and change _____ garments" (Genesis 35:2)
2 "Woe to them that are at _____ in Zion" (Amos 6:1)
3 _____ code
4 Rodent
5 Poetic contraction
6 "He caused an east _____ to blow in the heaven" (Psalm 78:26)
7 "Captains of thousands; _____ the chief" (2 Chronicles 17:14)
8 "And had _____ down manna upon them to eat" (Psalm 78:24)
9 "I could not _____ the form thereof" (Job 4:16)
10 Positive response
11 "Whom thou slewest in the valley of _____" (1 Samuel 21:9)
12 "They shall prosper that _____ thee" (Psalm 122:6)
13 "Though ye have _____ among the pots" (Psalm 68:13)
21 _____ Grande
23 "What the scripture saith of _____" (Romans 11:2)
26 _____ degree
27 Masticate
29 "Ye are _____ unto the day of redemption" (Ephesians 4:30)

by Tonya Vilhauer

30 Makes cookies, say
31 "If he hath wronged thee, or _____ thee" (Philemon 1:18)
32 "Surely thou wilt _____ the wicked" (Psalm 139:19)
34 "And he _____ them from the judgment seat" (Acts 18:16)
35 Rescued
36 Next
37 "And _____, which were dukes" (Joshua 13:21)
39 Victim
42 Marred by mildew
44 Couple
47 "The night is far spent, the day is at _____" (Romans 13:12)
49 "And _____, and the mighty men" (1 Kings 1:8)
52 Stature
54 Allow

56 Mistake
58 Duke of _____
59 Apparel maker _____ Picone
60 "Straightway the spirit _____ him" (Mark 9:20)
62 "They gave them in full _____ to the king" (1 Samuel 18:27)
64 Pitch
65 "_____ the Ahohite" (1 Chronicles 11:29)
66 "They have gone in the way of _____" (Jude 11)
67 "Hear this word, ye _____ of Bashan" (Amos 4:1)
69 Mosaic _____
71 Pekoe, for one
72 Agency (abbr.)

82

ACROSS

1 Not back
5 Mesha's son (1 Chronicles 2:42)
8 Banes
10 "_____ lieth at the door" (Genesis 4:7)
12 A town of Judah (Nehemiah 11:29)
14 Aria
17 "It is _____ for a camel" (Luke 18:25)
18 Before Proverbs (abbr.)
20 City of David (2 Samuel 5:7)
22 "Sorrows of _____ compassed me" (2 Samuel 22:6)
23 King before David
24 Jamin's brother (1 Chronicles 2:27)
26 Free
28 Raamah's son (Genesis 10:7)
30 "Under oaks and poplars and _____" (Hosea 4:13)
31 It's rude to do this
32 One of the cities of Zebulon (Joshua 19:15)
34 "By his _____ a light doth shine" (Job 41:18)
36 Japheth's son (Genesis 10:2)
38 Vow
39 Pile
41 Mary's father-in-law (Luke 3:23)
42 "He planteth an _____" (Isaiah 44:14)
43 Belonging to Abigail's husband (1 Samuel 25:14)
45 Ham's brother (Luke 3:36)
46 Make fun of
48 Manahath's brother (1 Chronicles 1:40)
49 Stir
50 "He that is dead is _____ from sin" (Romans 6:7)
51 Elizabeth Barrett Browning was one

DOWN

2 Beholden
3 Nary
4 Sarah's father-in-law (Genesis 11:31)
5 Town in the mountain district of Judah (Joshua 15:54)
6 Hostel
7 David's great-grandfather (1 Chronicles 2:12–15)
9 This man was killed by a woman (Judges 5:26)
10 "LORD _____ a sweet savor" (Genesis 8:21)
11 Colt
13 5,280 feet
15 City in the extreme south of Judah (Joshua 15:29)
16 "He _____ roast and is satisfied" (Isaiah 44:16)
18 "Cry from the _____" (Jeremiah 22:20)
19 Take to civil court
21 An Ammonite (1 Samuel 11:1)
23 Fifth in line of the ancient kings of Edom (Genesis 36:36–37)
25 Mattithiah's brother (1 Chronicles 25:3)
27 Shem's son (Genesis 10:22)
29 King of Syria (1 Kings 20:1)
31 "Thou shalt be broken by the _____" (Ezekiel 27:34)
32 Abraham's son
33 Pit
34 Belonging to Ham, Shem, and Japheth's father
35 City in Benjamin (Isaiah 10:31)
37 A town captured by the Philistines in the reign of Ahaz (2 Chronicles 28:18)
40 Purple or red fruit
43 Adam lived _____ hundred and thirty years (Genesis 5:5)
44 Trip
46 "Deliver thyself as a _____" (Proverbs 6:5)
47 After Genesis (abbr.)

by Sarah Lagerquist Simmons

83

ACROSS

1 "When he _____ the lamps" (Exodus 30:7 NASB)
6 Summit of Mt. Pisgah
10 "Saw no _____ come to him" (Acts 28:6)
14 Forbidden
15 Right away (abbr.)
16 Choir member
17 "My sister just _____ here" (Luke 10:40 NLT)
18 Radar target
19 "Even _____ the tongue is a little member" (James 3:5)
20 List of government deceased beneficiaries (abbr.)
21 One who suits to please?
23 "_____ hospitality one to another" (1 Peter 4:9)
25 "Guilded with silver _____" (Jeremiah 10:9 MSG)
26 "Unto the angel of the church in _____ write; these things saieth he" (Revelation 3:1)
28 "A shameful wife _____ his strength" (Proverbs 12:4 NLT)
30 "Arba, a great _____ of the Anakites" (Joshua 14:15 NLT)
31 Doctors' group (abbr.)
32 "Give us our food for _____" (Matthew 6:11 NLT)
35 "Thou hast made heaven. . .the _____, and all things that are therein" (Nehemiah 9:6)
38 Netherlands Antilles Island
40 Highest navy rank (abbr.)
41 "Naphtali is a _____ let loose" (Genesis 49:21 NASB)
42 Something not to drop
43 "_____ the man" Musial
45 "Coated it with _____ and pitch" (Exodus 2:3 NIV)
47 Anesthetic
49 The *New York Times*, and others
51 "The ways of Zion _____ mourn" (Lamentations 1:4)
53 Former Princess of Wales, familiarly
54 "A sword is upon the liars; and they shall _____" (Jeremiah 50:36)
55 "Prophets that make my people _____" (Micah 3:5)
57 Cush's son (1 Chronicles 1:10)
61 San Francisco, for one
65 "Who lay on a bed _____ noon" (2 Samuel 4:5)
67 Bright sign
68 Television diva
69 Major prophet
70 "Have you not put _____ around him and his household" (Job 1:10 NIV) (2 words)
71 So be it
72 Above
73 Man's title
74 D.C. quadrant (abbr.)

DOWN

1 Puts words on a machine (abbr.)
2 Ancient Canaanite city Ugarit, today (2 words)
3 In the same place (abbr.)
4 Dominant themes
5 "Help!"
6 Abigail's first husband
7 Christ's ancestor (Luke 3:25)
8 "After they had posted _____" (Acts 17:9 NLT)
9 "Instructing those that _____ themselves" (2 Timothy 2:25)
10 "The leech _____ two daughters" (Proverbs 30:15 NASB)
11 "Cry _____ at Beth-Aven" (Hosea 5:8)
12 Way to veer (abbr.)
13 Zipporah's husband (Exodus 2:21)
21 Former European dictator
22 "A _____ thing that the king requireth" (Daniel 2:11)
24 Seventh tone of diatonic scale
27 "Whither have ye made a _____ today?" (1 Samuel 27:10)
28 Swedish import

by Marijane G. Troyer

29 Missionary with Silas

30 "They had sung an _____" (Mark 14:26)

32 Grad student, maybe (abbr.)

33 "It is now out of _____" (Hebrews 8:13 NLT)

34 "Went up to _____, and fetched a compass to Karkaa" (Joshua 15:3)

36 Memorization using repetition

37 "And _____ their claws in pieces" (Zechariah 11:16)

39 Jesus _____ and died for me

43 "Be quiet"

44 "I _____ down under his shadow" (Song of Solomon 2:3)

46 Indian currency (abbr.)

48 "With silver, iron, _____, and lead" (Ezekiel 27:12)

49 Pea holder

50 Salt's companion

51 Erase (abbr.)

52 "Whether therefore ye eat, _____ drink" (1 Corinthians 10:31)

54 Put on

56 "Remember. . .against the sons of Edom. . .who said. . ._____ it to its very foundation" (Psalm 137:7 NASB)

58 Amazon cetacean genus

59 "And it was not _____ for us to see" (Ezra 4:14)

60 Candy bar

62 Former California military base

63 "All our righteousnesses are as filthy _____" (Isaiah 64:6)

64 Biblical "you"

66 "And he wrote. . .the words of the covenant, the _____ commandments" (Exodus 34:28)

68 Unit of electrical resistance

69 Dorothy's Auntie _____

84

ACROSS

1 "The body by _____ and bands" (Colossians 2:19)
6 Amasai's son (2 Chronicles 29:12)
11 "When he came unto _____" (Judges 15:14)
12 Yes
14 "Should I have _____ still" (Job 3:13)
15 Group of cows
16 Type of tree
19 "I gave ear to your _____" (Job 32:11)
21 Dampen
23 "When ye _____ the harvest" (Leviticus 19:9)
25 "Every plant of the _____" (Genesis 2:5)
26 "If his offering be a _____" (Leviticus 3:12)
27 Jephunneh's son (Numbers 26:65)
29 It's beside Ezion-geber (1 Kings 9:26)
30 "I have in a figure _____ to myself" (1 Corinthians 4:6)
35 "Let him go _____" (Exodus 21:26)
36 Alternative spelling for Abraham's wife
38 "Godliness with _____ is great gain" (1 Timothy 6:6)
42 "I have seen thy _____" (2 Kings 20:5)
44 A city of Lycaonia (Acts 14:6)
46 Mar
47 Bukki's father (Numbers 34:22)
51 Certificate of land ownership
52 Skill
53 Noah's son
55 "_____ blessed Elkanah and his wife" (1 Samuel 2:20)
56 Jeroham's grandfather (1 Chronicles 6:34)
57 Colorado ski resort
59 "Their border was Helkath, and _____" (Joshua 19:25)
60 If not
61 Kohath's son (Numbers 3:19)
62 "There sat a certain man at _____" (Acts 14:8)

DOWN

2 Bad
3 Close
4 Crook
5 "Came to the Desert of _____" (Exodus 19:2 NIV)
6 Heman's father (1 Kings 4:31)
7 Alter
8 "If the firstborn son be _____" (Deuteronomy 21:15)
9 Plus
10 Hunt
13 "Elam, _____, Bani" (Nehemiah 10:14)
17 "Joseph gathered corn as the sand of the _____" (Genesis 41:49)
18 Stop
20 I
21 Log
22 Sup
24 "I will _____ the oath" (Genesis 26:3)
26 "So she _____ in the field" (Ruth 2:17)
28 "So shall thy _____ be filled" (Proverbs 3:10)
29 "They also that _____ in spirit" (Isaiah 29:24)
31 Mesh
32 Eye
33 Before Job (abbr.)
34 Bump into
37 City in Judah where David sent the spoil of his enemies (1 Samuel 30:30)
38 Dray
39 "Time drew _____ that Israel must die" (Genesis 47:29)
40 Maple is one
41 Mean

by Sarah Lagerquist Simmons

43 "Give _____ to his
   commandments" (Exodus 15:26)
45 "_____ boweth down" (Isaiah 46:1)
47 Solomon's servant (Ezra 2:56)
48 "Brought gold from _____"
   (1 King 10:11)
49 Straighten
50 Aquila and Priscilla came from here
   (Acts 18:2)
53 Asaph's son (2 Kings 18:18)
54 Snake sound
56 "All _____ counsel of God"
   (Acts 20:27)
58 "_____ there be light"
   (Genesis 1:3)

85

ACROSS

1 "As thou _____ to do unto those that love thy name" (Psalm 119:132)
6 Appendage
10 Israeli leader Golda
14 End of many Psalms
15 "Kish the son of _____" (2 Chronicles 29:12)
16 River in Italy
17 Make amends
18 Seek
19 "Whosoever shall say to his brother, _____" (Matthew 5:22)
20 Hard to locate merchandise (pl.)
21 Stubborn one
22 Peter, for one (var.)
23 "John also was baptizing in _____" (John 3:23)
25 "And he said, _____; but I will die here" (1 Kings 2:30)
27 "And Hadoram, and _____, and Diklah" (Genesis 10:27)
30 Terminate
31 "The king will _____ him with great riches" (1 Samuel 17:25)
35 "His _____ come to honour" (Job 14:21)
36 Effortless
38 Glamorous accessory
39 "Bezaleel the son of _____" (2 Chronicles 1:5)
40 "Cast all their sins into the _____ of the sea" (Micah 7:19)
42 "Dishon, and _____, and Dishan" (1 Chronicles 1:38)
43 Level (Brit.)
45 "And when he came unto _____" (Judges 15:14)
46 Demean
47 "I commend unto you _____ our sister" (Romans 16:1)
49 Terms of duty
50 Rodent
51 Nun's son (Numbers 13:8)
53 "And the coast reacheth to _____" (Joshua 19:22)

56 "The righteous shall flourish like the palm _____" (Psalm 92:12)
57 Window part
61 Middle East gulf
62 "Shall come forth a vessel for the _____" (Proverbs 25:4)
63 "Stayed in _____ for a season" (Acts 19:22)
64 "Call me not Naomi, call me _____" (Ruth 1:20)
65 "Absalom made _____ captain of the host" (2 Samuel 17:25)
66 Annoying person (colloq.)
67 Shechaniah's father (Nehemiah 6:18)
68 "Abraham gave a _____ part of all" (Hebrews 7:2)
69 Former game show host Monte

DOWN

1 Academy in CO (abbr.)
2 Egyptian king
3 College in North Carolina
4 "The thongs of whose _____ I am not worthy" (John 1:27 NIV)
5 "_____ are the generations of Noah" (Genesis 6:9)
6 "The porters, Akkub, _____" (Nehemiah 11:19)
7 "Consolation also _____ by Christ" (2 Corinthians 1:5)
8 Baal, for one
9 Effigy
10 "Antipas was my faithful _____" (Revelation 2:13)
11 Ages
12 Peruvian tribe
13 Lion's lament
24 "The north side of Bethemek, and _____" (Joshua 19:27)
26 Some
27 "Nor to _____ authority over the man" (1 Timothy 2:12)
28 "The coast of their inheritance was _____" (Joshua 19:41)
29 Dill seed

by Tonya Vilhauer

32 Judge of Israel (Judges 12:8)
33 Something that may be clear
34 Speedy mammals
37 Aram's brother (1 Chronicles 7:34)
41 Pin down
42 "Elkanah his son, and _____ his son" (1 Chronicles 6:23)
44 "From Jotbathah, and encamped at _____" (Numbers 33:34)
46 Dined
48 Give _____ to
49 "And his daughter was _____" (1 Chronicles 7:24)
51 "The threshingfloor of _____ the Jebusite" (2 Chronicles 3:1)
52 "_____ thou a man diligent in his business" (Proverbs 22:29)
53 Iowa town on U.S. 30
54 "On the thirteenth day of the month _____" (Esther 9:17)

55 "That these made war with _____" (Genesis 14:2)
56 Again's partner
58 _____ Minor
59 Place for a flowerpot
60 Corridor
62 Obese

ACROSS

1 "The plowman shall overtake the
  _____" (Amos 9:13)
6 "Beauty is a _____ flower"
  (Isaiah 28:1)
11 "There was no _____"
  (Judges 18:28)
13 Drop
14 New Testament prophetess
15 Mr. and _____
18 The Netophathite
  (1 Chronicles 27:13)
20 To and _____
22 Tree juice
23 Fancy
24 Atmosphere
25 Shade of red
27 After nine
28 Mute
30 "Joseph is without doubt _____ in
  pieces" (Genesis 37:33)
31 "I shall die in my _____" (Job 29:18)
32 "_____ the sacrifices of the dead"
  (Psalm 106:28)
35 Bar
37 Criticize
41 "Sweet _____ unto the God"
  (Ezra 6:10)
45 Arodi's brother (Genesis 46:16)
46 Discharge
48 Slap
49 Cure
50 Walker
51 After Amos (abbr.)
52 "Written not with _____"
  (2 Corinthians 3:3)
53 Joseph's nephew (Genesis 46:21)
54 Abner's father (1 Samuel 14:50)
55 Prepare for crops
57 "Whether it be fat or _____"
  (Numbers 13:20)
60 Variant of Hosea (Romans 9:25)
61 Besides
62 "_____, and sacrificeth unto the
  Lord" (Malachi 1:14)
63 Uz's father (Genesis 36:28)

DOWN

2 Put together
3 Let
4 Bathsheba's father (2 Samuel 11:3)
5 Gomer's son (Genesis 10:3)
6 "_____ the wrath of the king"
  (Hebrews 11:27)
7 A descendant of David (1
  Chronicles 3:21)
8 "I _____ him not" (1 Kings 20:7)
9 The Jairite (2 Samuel 20:26)
10 "Blast with the _____ horn"
  (Joshua 6:5)
12 "Sin lieth at the _____"
  (Genesis 4:7)
16 Odd
17 "Whose heart stirred them up in
  wisdom _____ goats' hair"
  (Exodus 35:26)
19 Ripen
20 "His _____ was noised"
  (Joshua 6:27)
21 "He took one of his _____"
  (Genesis 2:21)
26 Sun
29 Open
33 Emyd
34 Always
35 Ruin
36 "They _____ the deeds of the
  wicked" (Jeremiah 5:28)
37 "_____ ye from him" (2 Samuel
  11:15)
38 Shuthelah's son (Numbers 26:36)
39 Baby girl color
40 City built by Reuben's children
  (Numbers 32:37)
41 "They _____ him" (1 Kings 13:27)
42 On
43 Toga
44 "As the _____ fly upward"
  (Job 5:7)
47 "Let thine _____ now be attentive"
  (Nehemiah 1:6)
55 "Strong shall be as _____"
  (Isaiah 1:31)

by Sarah Lagerquist Simmons

56 Allow
58 Priest who raised Samuel
   (1 Samuel 1:25)
59 Before Esther (abbr.)

Biblical Siblings

*Say of your brothers,
"My people," and of your sisters,
"My loved one."*

HOSEA 2:1 NIV

ACROSS

1 Thailand, once
5 "And broke the _____ that were in their hands" (Judges 7:19 NIV)
9 Martha's **SISTER**
13 Author Ferber
14 Speak pompously
16 He had an Irish Rose
17 High school student, usually
18 "Each man _____ a sword to his side" (Exodus 32:27 NIV)
19 "And the Lord _____ mark upon Cain" (Genesis 4:15) (2 words)
20 Formerly Sandwich Islands
22 Biblical suffix
23 Blind part
24 Eastern European
26 New York Indian
28 American Beauty fruit
31 Peter's **BROTHER**
35 **BROTHER** of 50 Down (see Exodus 7:1)
36 "I've got a _____ Kalamazoo" (2 words)
38 "See, I told you!" (var.)
39 Foot part?
40 King of Tyre and an admirer of David (1 Kings 5:1)
41 "Tsk, tsk" (2 words)
42 Pill passer (abbr.)
43 Faithful spy (Numbers 13:30)
44 John's **BROTHER**
45 Previous
47 Flag-waving fetes
49 "_____ La Douce"
51 "That at the _____ of Jesus" (Philippians 2:10)
52 Banned apple spray
55 Ivory, for one
57 Awoke (2 words)

61 "And _____ am not alone, because the Father is with me" (John 16:32) (2 words)
62 Bathsheba's Hittite husband
64 "Do ye to them _____ good in your eyes" (Genesis 19:8) (2 words)
65 "In _____ was there a voice heard" (Matthew 2:18)
66 "As _____ Lord, and not to men" (Ephesians 6:7) (2 words)
67 Neck part
68 Ham's **BROTHER**
69 Actress Patricia
70 Site of Xerxes' palace (Esther 1:2 NIV)

DOWN

1 **BROTHER** of 10 Down (See Genesis 4:25)
2 Creative concept
3 "O sing unto the LORD _____ song" (Psalm 96:1) (2 words)
4 **BROTHER** of 15 Down (See Genesis 41:51–52)
5 Good king of Judah (2 Chronicles 34:33)
6 "Where _____ thou" (Genesis 3:9)
7 Valuable
8 "I have learned, in whatsoever _____ I am" (Philippians 4:11)
9 Gathered together
10 Cain's **BROTHER**
11 Actress Hayworth
12 "Why marvel _____ this" (Acts 3:12) (2 words)
15 **BROTHER** of 4 Down
21 French islands
25 Purposeful watch
27 "There was no room for them in the _____" (Luke 2:7)
28 Musical composition

by David K. Shortess

29 Movie award
30 Dept. of Energy 80s ecology project (abbr.)
32 Poem, often
33 Modern furniture designer
34 Wherefores' mate
35 Offend
37 Rebekah's **BROTHER**
40 "Do him no _____ do unto him" (Jeremiah 39:12) (2 words)
41 "Who hath _____ mouth" (Exodus 4:11) (2 words)
43 Wax (comb. form, var.)
44 M.D.'s journal
46 **SISTER** of 50 Down (See Exodus 15:20)
48 **SISTER** of 53 Down (See Genesis 29:16)
50 **BROTHER** of 46 Down and 35 Across

52 River and town in southern Scotland (pl.)
53 **SISTER** of 48 Down
54 "Are ye angry _____" (John 7:23) (2 words)
56 Ceremony
58 Jacob's **BROTHER**
59 Suggestions
60 "Why was it _____ that you fled" (Psalm 114:5 NIV) (2 words)
63 Detective's exclamation

88

ACROSS

1 Irritation
3 Elihu's father (Job 32:2)
8 "_____ eyes shall be opened" (Genesis 3:5)
10 A kind of deer or hart
12 City in the northern part of Judah (Micah 1:12)
14 "Is the seed yet in the _____?" (Haggai 2:19)
15 Dusk
18 "Sluices and _____ for fish" (Isaiah 19:10)
19 Vermin
20 "Destroy the _____ also" (2 Samuel 14:7)
21 "_____ on the east" (Genesis 12:8)
22 "I will requite thee in this _____" (2 Kings 9:26)
24 Letter
27 Pay
29 Old Testament prophet (abbr.)
30 Earl Grey
31 Jehu's father (1 Kings 19:16)
33 See
35 Jephthah fled to this land (Judges 11:3)
38 Greek letter
39 Zeruiah's son (1 Samuel 26:6)
41 "Fine linen, of the house of _____" (1 Chronicles 4:21)
45 "Thou shalt no more be _____ Forsaken" (Isaiah 62:4)
46 Take to court
47 Make a mistake
48 Ahinadab's father (1 Kings 4:14)
49 "Neither be ye _____, as were some of them" (1 Corinthians 10:7)
52 Song
53 "These _____ the generations" (Genesis 2:4)
54 A duke of Edom (1 Chronicles 1:51)
55 Leah's son (Genesis 30:11)

DOWN

1 Rendition
2 Sacred song
3 Covered from view
4 One of Gad's sons (Genesis 46:16)
5 Ember
6 "Family of the _____" (Numbers 26:36)
7 "The _____ our God is one" (Deuteronomy 6:4)
9 Curse
11 Follow
13 A would-be assassin (Esther 2:21)
14 "The wicked _____ of his heart's desire" (Psalm 10:3)
16 Dale
17 One of five cities (1 Chronicles 4:32)
18 Twenty-first letter of the Greek alphabet
23 "Take away all thy _____" (Isaiah 1:25)
25 A town in Edom where Hadad reigned (1 Chronicles 1:50)
26 Leg of a race
28 "Thou shalt truly _____ all the increase" (Deuteronomy 14:22)
29 Ishuah's brother (Genesis 46:17)
32 A priest who returned from Babylon (Nehemiah 12:5)
34 "For days, and _____" (Genesis 1:14)
36 Boaz's son (Ruth 4:22)
37 "Can a _____ fall in a snare" (Amos 3:5)
40 "The _____ of the country went up" (Genesis 19:28)
41 "Bore his ear through with an _____" (Exodus 21:6)
42 Dead is one
43 Zopha's son (1 Chronicles 7:37)
44 "Yet I _____ not" (Psalm 119:110)
46 Kind
50 Expire
51 Tab

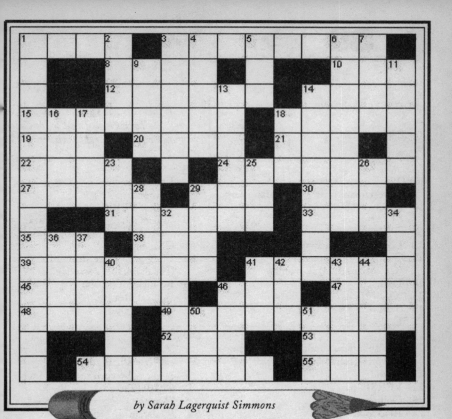

by Sarah Lagerquist Simmons

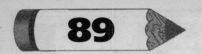

89

Our Obligatior

What does the LORD require of you
To act justly and to love merc
and to walk humbly with your Go

MICAH 6:8 N.

ACROSS

1 "A testament is of _____ after men are dead" (Hebrews 9:17)
6 "The sun to _____ by day" (Psalm 136:8)
10 Learning handicap (abbr.)
13 "For _____ him record" (Colossians 4:13) (2 words)
14 Dash
15 XXI ÷ III = _____
16 Start of **VERSE** (taken from Ecclesiastes 12:13) (4 words)
19 Kind
20 "Oh that thou wouldest _____ the heavens" (Isaiah 64:1)
21 Magic _____
22 **VERSE**, part 2
23 Golf peg
24 1040 folks
25 **VERSE**, part 3
31 "Let it become _____" (Psalm 69:22) (2 words)
34 Dancer Montez
35 King of Judah
36 Part of ASAP
37 "Let the righteous _____ me" (Psalm 141:5)
39 "But _____ I have hated" (Romans 9:13)
40 "And God said unto him _____ dream" (Genesis 20:6) (2 words)
41 "His own parents will _____ him" (Zechariah 13:3 NIV)
42 Growl menacingly
43 **VERSE**, part 4 (4 words)
47 Biblical mount (Numbers 20:22)
48 "And copper is smelted from _____" (Job 28:2 NIV)
49 New York, for one (abbr.)
52 "Joshua made _____ long time" (Joshua 11:18) (2 words)

54 Land measure
56 Low area (poet.)
57 End of **VERSE** (4 words)
60 "There am _____ the midst of them" (Matthew 18:20) (2 words)
61 Challenge
62 "_____ of these shall fail" (Isaiah 34:16) (2 words)
63 Resident of (suffix)
64 Biblical measure
65 Cash, for one

DOWN

1 "And in the _____ year shall ye eat" (Leviticus 19:25)
2 "_____ beseech thee" (Jeremiah 38:20) (2 words)
3 "A man _____ what he sows" (Galatians 6:7 NIV)
4 Part of TLC
5 Work unit
6 "In famine he shall _____ thee" (Job 5:20)
7 _____ Bator
8 Alight
9 _____ times
10 "As men _____ from war" (Micah 2:8)
11 Atkins, for one
12 "Who _____ bread into the bowl" (Mark 14:20 NIV)
17 City north of Provo, Utah
18 Hindu destiny
23 Box _____ (what to send in)
24 Devil's workshop hands?
25 "Who _____ hear it" (John 6:60)
26 Excuse
27 "Thou shalt _____ kill" (Matthew 5:21)
28 Shuttle group (abbr.)
29 Romanoff ruler

by David K. Shortess

30 Kish's son (1 Samuel 9:1–2)
31 "Yeah, right" (colloq.) (2 words)
32 "Do violence _____ man" (Luke 3:14) (2 words)
33 "Let the sea _____" (Psalm 98:7)
37 "That ye _____ not up, nor awake my love" (Song of Solomon 8:4)
38 More (Sp.)
39 Chemical suffix
41 Sandbar
42 Not he
44 "Upon the _____ of David" (Isaiah 9:7)
45 Organizer
46 Die with three pips
49 Port of call for Paul (Acts 20:15)
50 Geometrical surface
51 Principle
52 DDE's conflict
53 SRO show (2 words)

54 "For as in _____ all die" (1 Corinthians 15:22)
55 Heal
56 Radio transmitter tuners (abbr.)
58 Tokyo, once
59 _____ roll (2 words)

90

ACROSS

1 "Be ye not unequally _____"
   (2 Corinthians 6:14)
5 Bat
9 Also
10 "When a man _____ in a tent"
   (Numbers 19:14)
11 "My beloved is like a _____"
   (Song of Solomon 2:9)
13 Mehir's son (1 Chronicles 4:11)
14 He was sick with palsy for eight
   years (Acts 9:33)
15 Dwelling place of Abraham, near
   Hebron (Genesis 23:17)
17 Raw
20 Shade of color
21 Don't go
23 Nagge's son (Luke 3:25)
25 "Pelican, and the _____ eagle"
   (Deuteronomy 14:17)
26 Dressed
27 "Thirty milch camels with their
   _____" (Genesis 32:15)
29 Jeroboam's father (1 Kings 11:26)
32 Aholibamah's father (Genesis 36:2)
33 Taxi
35 Hebrew for where Ten
   Commandments were given
   (Acts 7:38)
36 "Balaam, who taught _____ to
   cast" (Revelation 2:14)
38 Favor
40 "David took the _____ of Zion"
   (1 Chronicles 11:5)
42 Succumb
43 "In _____, and in high places"
   (1 Samuel 13:6)
44 Follows the book of Daniel (abbr.)
45 "Cherub, _____, and Immer"
   (Ezra 2:59)
46 "Am I in God's _____"
   (Genesis 30:2)

DOWN

1 Yup
2 "_____ daubed it with untempered
   mortar" (Ezekiel 13:10)
3 Bela reigned in this land
   (Genesis 36:32)
4 Leah's daughter (Genesis 30:21)
5 Gawk
6 "So be it done unto _____"
   (Matthew 8:13)
7 "_____ in me a clean heart"
   (Psalm 51:10)
8 Probably the Kuti, who lived north
   of Babylon (Ezekiel 23:23)
9 Three hundred and sixty-five days
   equals one
12 Spot
16 Melodic
18 "John also was baptizing in _____"
   (John 3:23)
19 King Azariah built and restored this
   city to Judah (2 Kings 14:22)
21 "Rings by the _____ of the ark"
   (Exodus 25:14)
22 A descendant of David
   (1 Chronicles 3:21)
24 "That which groweth of _____
   own accord" (Leviticus 25:5)
25 Abbreviation for first book of the
   Bible
27 "No man _____ for my soul"
   (Psalm 142:4)
28 "Seven days, while their feast _____"
   (Judges 14:17)
30 One of seven eunuchs of King
   Xerxes (Esther 1:10)
31 Fables
33 Jair was buried here (Judges 10:5)
34 "Turn their _____ unto thee"
   (Exodus 23:27)
36 King of Sodom (Genesis 14:2)
37 "_____ out this bondwoman"
   (Genesis 21:10)

by Sarah Lagerquist Simmons

39 One of the Nethinim whose
    descendants returned with
    Zerubbabel (Nehemiah 7:47)
41 One of three cities built by Elpaal's
    sons (1 Chronicles 8:12)

91

ACROSS

1 Atarah's son (1 Chronicles 2:26)
5 Noah's son (Genesis 5:32)
9 "Libnah, and Ether, and _____" (Joshua 15:42)
14 Heart
15 "The gods of Sepharvaim, _____, and Ivah" (2 Kings 18:34)
16 Platform
17 Uproar
18 Open
19 Tendon
20 Concur
22 "Traps unto you, and _____ in your sides" (Joshua 23:13)
24 "Have to give to him that _____" (Ephesians 4:28)
26 "Ben-_____"
27 Devotion
28 "Husham of the land of _____" (Genesis 36:34)
33 Alms
37 "O ye travelling companies of _____" (Isaiah 21:13)
38 "And the sons of his wife _____" (1 Chronicles 4:19)
39 "That these made _____ with Bera king of Sodom" (Genesis 14:2)
40 "As the trees of _____ aloes" (Numbers 24:6)
41 "And Zelah, _____, and Jebusi" (Joshua 18:28)
42 _____ of God (Jesus)
43 King of Moab (2 Kings 3:4)
44 Wax's mate
45 "Restore unto me _____ joy" (Psalm 51:12)
46 "She _____ also while it is yet night" (Proverbs 31:15)
47 Scottish denial
48 Corn, for one
49 Savings account (abbr.)
52 "Clean the _____ of the cup" (Luke 11:39)
54 "But if _____ bear a maid child" (Leviticus 12:5)

57 Regurgitate
59 Aram's son (Genesis 10:23)
60 "The _____ of Ethiopia" (Job 28:19)
62 Swiftly
63 "By grace ye _____ saved" (Ephesians 2:5)
64 "_____ my heart to fear thy name" (Psalm 86:11)
65 Baanah's son (1 Chronicles 11:30)
66 Embarrassed
67 _____ reader

DOWN

1 Pagiel's father (Numbers 10:26)
2 "Make a joyful _____ unto the LORD" (Psalm 100:1)
3 "Esther _____, and stood before the king" (Esther 8:4)
4 "A nation _____ out and trodden down" (Isaiah 18:2)
5 "And _____ his eyes from seeing evil" (Isaiah 33:15)
6 Fowl for stewpot
7 "So is thy praise unto the _____ of the earth" (Psalm 48:10)
8 King of Gath (1 Samuel 27:2)
9 "I will give you _____ peace" (Jeremiah 14:13)
10 "Who shall _____ him up" (Numbers 24:9)
11 _____ ten
12 Playwright James
13 CBS, for one
21 "The children of _____" (Nehemiah 7:56)
23 _____ Banks of North Carolina
25 Fodder
29 "And slew all the _____" (Genesis 34:25)
30 Dill seed
31 "On that _____ could not the king sleep" (Esther 6:1)
32 Asher's son (1 Chronicles 7:30)
33 Masticate
34 "Greetings" (Sp.)

by Tonya Vilhauer

35 Former British Middle East colony
36 Mature
37 "Thy god, O _____, liveth" (Amos 8:14)
39 "_____ is me for my hurt" (Jeremiah 10:19)
42 "And the next unto him was Carshena, _____" (Esther 1:14)
43 "Trophimus have I left at _____ sick" (2 Timothy 4:20)
45 Greek letter
46 Disencumber
47 "Which is _____ in the scripture of truth" (Daniel 10:21)
48 "One cake of _____ bread" (Exodus 29:23)
49 "City of Sepharvaim, of Hena, and _____" (2 Kings 19:13)
50 Cord
51 Helem's son (1 Chronicles 7:35)

53 Confident
54 Roasting tool
55 "If the world _____ you" (John 15:18)
56 Son of the ruler of Mizpah (Nehemiah 3:19)
58 Pack or box
61 "Thou believest that there is _____ God" (James 2:19)

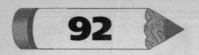

92

From the Psalms

ACROSS

1 Uriah _____ Hittite
   (2 Samuel 11:17)
4 "The _____ of hosts" (Isaiah 31:4)
7 "That dippeth with me in the
   _____" (Mark 14:20)
10 "The Lord is my _____"
   (Psalm 23:1)
12 "Go and _____ thou likewise"
   (Luke 10:37)
13 Crow's call
15 Old salt's okay (var.)
16 "It was from the _____ of God"
   (Ecclesiastes 2:24)
17 Bowls over
19 "Have pity upon _____"
   (Job 19:21)
20 Either _____
21 Present, for one
22 Appendage
24 "Seinfeld" character
26 Pertaining to Swiss mountains
28 "_____ in and possess the land"
   (Deuteronomy 8:1)
29 Author Fleming
31 "The lot is cast into the _____"
   (Proverbs 16:33)
32 Asian currency (abbr., pl.)
34 "Rejoice not when thine _____
   falleth" (Proverbs 24:17)
35 "Thou art neither cold nor _____"
   (Revelation 3:15)
37 Concorde, for one (abbr.)
38 Revelation, for one (abbr.)
39 "Thy rod and thy staff, they _____
   me" (Psalm 23:4)
40 Yes (Sp.)
41 "Alice" role
43 Prerequisite for most colleges (abbr.)
44 Rehoboam's father-in-law
   (2 Chronicles 13:2)
46 Weight measure (abbr.)
48 Jacques, to Jeanne (Fr.)
50 Singing syllable
51 Hirt or Jolson

52 Rat, for one
55 Town of Reuben (Numbers 32:3)
57 Sweater neck
58 Light boat
59 Undergrad's deg.
61 Great Britain (abbr.)
62 Enthusiasm
64 Biblical mount
66 City conquered after Jericho
67 Energy
69 "The harvest truly _____ great"
   (Luke 10:2)
70 "Surely _____ and mercy shall
   follow me" (Psalm 23:6)
72 "Shall call on the _____ of the
   LORD" (Joel 2:32)
73 Trivial quarrel
74 Mischievous child

DOWN

1 "Hallowed be _____ name"
   (Matthew 6:9)
2 "_____ was but a youth"
   (1 Samuel 17:42)
3 Joseph's second son (Genesis 41:52)
4 Season starting in February
5 "Put his household in _____"
   (2 Samuel 17:23)
6 Hospital employee (abbr.)
7 "Naphtali is a _____ let loose"
   (Genesis 49:21 NASB)
8 Columbia is its capital (abbr.)
9 "How is the _____ of the whole
   earth cut asunder" (Jeremiah 50:23)
10 Utter
11 "He saith among the trumpets,
   _____" (Job 39:25)
12 "I will _____ in the house of the
   LORD" (Psalm 23:6)
14 "What a _____ we weave"
17 Third king of Judah (1 Kings 15:9)
18 Goofs
20 Hospital area (abbr.)
23 Kind of box
24 Tire, with "out" (colloq.)

by Marijane Troyer

5 "That the waters _____ again upon the Egyptians" (Exodus 14:26) (2 words)

7 "He. . .shall go in and out, and find _____" (John 10:9)

8 Phoenician seaport (Psalm 83:7)

0 "Why art thou _____ from helping me" (Psalm 22:1) (2 words)

3 "He leadeth me beside the _____ waters" (Psalm 23:2)

5 "_____ Pinafore"

6 Small child

0 "Now the coat was without _____" (John 19:23)

2 Spoon soup

5 What Mary Magdalene once called Jesus

7 "The scripture cannot be _____" (John 10:35)

49 Ancient Peruvians

50 "Dwell in the land which I shall tell _____" (Genesis 26:2) (2 words)

53 Ouch's cousin

54 Salon offering

55 What "Ibn" means (2 words)

56 Support group (abbr.)

57 "My _____ runneth over" (Psalm 23:5)

60 "For _____ name's sake they went forth" (3 John 7)

63 "_____ down in green pastures" (Psalm 23:2)

65 Education group (abbr.)

66 "Shall play on the hole of the _____" (Isaiah 11:8)

68 Dad, to some

70 Anatomical tract (abbr.)

71 Long dash, to editors

93

ACROSS

1 _____ of Righteousness
6 Cattle thief (1 Chronicles 7:21)
11 "A day of _____ and desolation" (Zephaniah 1:15)
13 Baby Jesus was laid here
15 Input
16 "Beasts that _____ not clean" (Genesis 7:8)
17 "At the brook of _____" (Psalm 83:9)
19 "Jacob _____ them under the oak" (Genesis 35:4)
21 Sift through
23 Animal's hand
24 Cut
25 "The son of _____, in Aruboth" (1 Kings 4:10)
27 Paralysis
28 Bunk
29 Before Acts (abbr.)
30 "It came to pass in the month _____" (Nehemiah 2:1)
33 Uzai's son (Nehemiah 3:25)
36 Strong desire
37 Asphalt
39 Meshullam's father (Ezra 10:29)
40 Abbreviation for Old Testament book of prophecy
41 Hiel's son (1 Kings 16:34)
43 Frost a cake
44 "As he saith also in _____" (Romans 9:25)
46 Head
48 "Anoint themselves with the chief _____" (Amos 6:6)
49 King Azariah built and restored this city to Judah (2 Kings 14:22)
50 "Whosoever _____ any work" (Exodus 31:14)

DOWN

2 Possessors
3 Satchel
4 "He called the name of the well _____" (Genesis 26:20)
5 Type of mall
6 "He shall surely _____ her to be his wife" (Exodus 22:16)
7 Bony
8 Old Testament book about Mordecai's cousin (abbr.)
9 Zeruiah's son (2 Samuel 2:18)
10 Hit
12 Rosy
14 "Shama and Jehiel the sons of Hothan the _____" (1 Chronicles 11:44)
18 Speak
20 Episode
22 Reumah's son (Genesis 22:24)
24 David's great-great grandmother (Matthew 1:5–6) (var.)
26 Lion's home
27 Soda
30 "In the _____ year of Hoshea" (2 Kings 17:6)
31 Fish travel in one
32 Children's game
34 "Thou _____ not down" (var.) (Luke 19:21)
35 "Their _____ in wait" (Joshua 8:13)
37 Molars
38 "Days when the judges _____" (Ruth 1:1)
41 "He _____ forth the dove" (Genesis 8:10)
42 Shoham's brother (1 Chronicles 24:27)
45 "The children of Keros, the children of _____" (Nehemiah 7:47)
47 "Took the little book out of the angel's hand, and _____ it up" (Revelation 10:10)

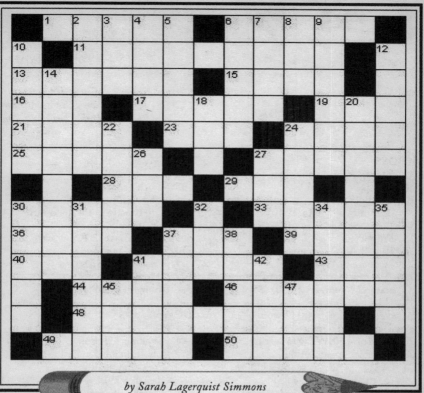

by Sarah Lagerquist Simmons

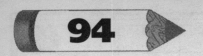

94

What Do You Know?

For the which cause I also suffer these things
nevertheless I am not ashamed
for I know whom I have believed. . .

2 TIMOTHY 1:12

ACROSS

1 Zhivago's love, and others
6 Compact one?
10 "Bring of the _____ which ye have now caught" (John 21:10)
14 Leave via ladder, once
15 Prophetess
16 Part of Alaska occupied by the Japanese in WWII
17 "We saw in _____ men of a great stature" (Numbers 13:32) (2 words)
18 "Make haste, and _____ I have done" (Judges 9:48) (2 words)
19 Twins, for example
20 Start of **ANSWER** (5 words)
23 Regulus's constellation
24 "A _____ that is set on a hill" (Matthew 5:14)
25 Jether's son (1 Chronicles 7:38)
28 Kind of wheel
31 "And he was _____ at that saying" (Mark 10:22)
34 Ecce _____ (Behold, the man)
36 Cry of triumph (var.)
37 Spanish porch
39 Morphine source
41 Speaker of **ANSWER**
43 More unusual
44 Harass
46 "And if any man will _____ thee" (Matthew 5:40)
48 Kind of worm
49 Superlative ending
50 "Will he _____ his anger" (Jeremiah 3:5)
53 "Groweth of _____ own accord" (Leviticus 25:5)
54 North Sea feeder
55 Powerful union (abbr.)
57 Conclusion of **ANSWER** (2 words)

64 "My strength and my _____" (Isaiah 12:2)
65 Cattle (arch.)
66 John Philip _____
67 Off-Broadway theater award
68 Up above
69 King of Tyre (1 Kings 5:1)
70 Takes a spouse
71 Pianist Dame Myra
72 "How right they are to _____ you" (Song of Solomon 1:4 NIV)

DOWN

1 Explorer Ericsson
2 Choir member
3 "Yea, they shall _____" (Isaiah 5:29)
4 March follower?
5 Looker
6 Pedestal part
7 "What have _____ done" (1 Samuel 17:29) (2 words)
8 "And he shall _____ on the right hand" (Isaiah 9:20)
9 Money changer?
10 Arbuckle of early films
11 One of a series
12 _____ the course
13 Make music, in a way
21 "But saved _____ the eighth person" (2 Peter 2:5)
22 Fragrant rose oil
25 "Since we have such _____" (2 Corinthians 3:12 NIV) (2 words)
26 On the _____ (in a bad position)
27 "There fell on him _____ and a darkness" (Acts 13:11) (2 words)
29 _____ Mahal
30 Opted for

by David K. Shortess

31 "But _____ was barren"
   (Genesis 11:30)
32 Highly skilled
33 "Who _____ to rouse him"
   (Genesis 49:9 NIV)
35 "Get _____!"
38 "Pick up your _____ and walk"
   (John 5:8 NIV)
40 Singer Haggard
42 Chestnut covering
45 She loved Jacob
47 "Deliver us from _____"
   (Matthew 6:13)
51 Descendant of Shem, literally
52 Elijah's companion
54 Wins narrowly
56 "But _____ foolish questions"
   (Titus 3:9)
57 Item won by casting lots

58 Oklahoma city
59 Cainan's father (Genesis 5:9)
60 House members, for short
61 Continental currency
62 Old Russian despot
63 Harness part
64 Farm doyenne

95

ACROSS

1 Make a point
6 "No man also _____ a piece of new cloth" (Mark 2:21)
12 Judah's son (Numbers 26:19)
13 Not dead
15 "Of Benjamin, and of _____ men" (2 Samuel 2:31)
17 Protection
19 Angry
20 Continent
22 Drop
23 Ishuah's brother (Genesis 46:17)
25 All
26 "Unto the tower of _____" (Nehemiah 3:1)
27 Din
29 Wet
30 Door
31 Tola's father (Genesis 46:13)
33 "John also was baptizing in _____" (John 3:23)
34 After Wednesday (abbr.) (var.)
35 "Their _____ were backward" (Genesis 9:23)
38 Canaan's firstborn (Genesis 10:15)
42 Joktan's son (Genesis 10:28)
43 Lean
46 One of the five Kings of Midian (Numbers 31:8)
47 Irony
48 "God created great _____" (Genesis 1:21)
50 Sleeping place
51 "Nor the _____ of their shoes be broken" (Isaiah 5:27)
53 A mighty man of valor from the tribe of Benjamin (2 Chronicles 17:17)
55 Free
56 Dust
57 "Thou shalt no more be _____ Forsaken" (Isaiah 62:4)
58 "As it _____ out the nations that were before you" (Leviticus 18:28)

DOWN

2 "The _____ of the upper pool" (2 Kings 18:17)
3 Alone
4 Level of meat doneness
5 Happen
6 Azor's son (Matthew 1:14)
7 A city of the inheritance of Benjamin (Joshua 18:28)
8 Mrs.
9 Adam's wife
10 "Labor of the righteous _____ to life" (Proverbs 10:16)
11 "There was a _____ in the land" (Genesis 12:10)
14 Zelophehad's father (Numbers 26:33)
16 "Poureth water into a _____" (John 13:5)
18 Nethinim whose descendants returned to Jerusalem (Ezra 2:44)
21 Wireless
24 Homeland of the Jews
26 Joseph's grandson (Genesis 50:23)
28 "Noah found grace in the _____ of the LORD" (Genesis 6:8)
29 "To the moles and to the _____" (Isaiah 2:20)
32 "As a _____ which melteth" (Psalm 58:8)
35 "The _____ of the air" (Genesis 6:7)
36 Rehoboam's son (1 Chronicles 3:10)
37 "Adam gave names to all _____" (Genesis 2:20)
39 Argue
40 Rahab's grandson (Matthew 1:5)
41 Aaron's son (Exodus 6:23)
43 "_____ were the sons of Joktan" (Genesis 10:29)
44 "And Esau _____ Jacob" (Genesis 27:41)
45 "He will _____ be a judge" (Genesis 19:9)
48 "The man _____ he had formed" (Genesis 2:8)

by Sarah Lagerquist Simmons

49 Error
52 Before Galatians (abbr.)
54 Elah's brother (1 Chronicles 4:15)

96

ACROSS

1 Addition column
5 Idols, to Ahab
10 Beriah's son (1 Chronicles 8:16)
14 "Be not _____ with thy mouth" (Ecclesiastes 5:2)
15 "Captains of thousands; _____ the chief" (2 Chronicles 17:14)
16 Utah city
17 Noodle
18 "From Allon to Zaanannim, and _____" (Joshua 19:33)
19 Store sign
20 Aminadab's father (Matthew 1:4)
21 Boundaries
22 "The children of _____ of Hezekiah" (Ezra 2:16)
23 "For every one that doeth evil _____ the light" (John 3:20)
25 Eli's grandson (1 Samuel 4:21)
27 "An _____ of the Hebrews" (Philippians 3:5)
29 "Achbor died, and _____ reigned in his stead" (Genesis 36:39)
30 "The third to Harim, the fourth to _____" (1 Chronicles 24:8)
31 "Yet thou never gavest me a _____" (Luke 15:29)
34 "Seven trumpets of _____ horns" (Joshua 6:13)
36 Arrow's ally
38 Fashionable, on 60s Carnaby Street
40 Soaked
42 Shimei's father (1 Kings 2:8)
43 "Make their nobles like _____" (Psalm 83:11)
45 Midday
46 "With horses and horsemen and _____" (Ezekiel 27:14)
47 Detach
49 "Whose mouths _____ be stopped" (Titus 1:11)
51 Profusion, say, of flowers
52 "When ye see a cloud. . .There cometh a _____" (Luke 12:54)
54 Balaam's father (Micah 6:5)
56 "And Adam called his wife's name _____" (Genesis 3:20)
57 "Set a king in the midst. . .even the son of _____" (Isaiah 7:6)
59 Depart
61 "Yet will I _____ them" (Hosea 9:12)
62 Ner's son (1 Samuel 14:50)
63 "_____ and Medad do prophesy in the camp" (Numbers 11:27)
64 "That I might rest in the _____ of trouble" (Habakkuk 3:16)

DOWN

1 Naomi's daughter-in-law
2 "Tekoa had two wives, Helah and _____" (1 Chronicles 4:5)
3 "I will settle you after your old _____" (Ezekiel 36:11)
4 "And _____ king of Zeboiim" (Genesis 14:2)
5 "From Bashan unto _____ and Senir" (1 Chronicles 5:23)
6 "Melchi, which was the son of _____" (Luke 3:28)
7 "Johanan, and Dalaiah, and _____" (1 Chronicles 3:24)
8 Noah's father (Genesis 5:30)
9 "That _____ king of Egypt came up against Jerusalem" (1 Kings 14:25)
10 "And _____ the Gederathite" (1 Chronicles 12:4)
11 Accomplished speaker
12 Baanah's son (1 Chronicles 11:30)
13 USA (abbr.)
24 "These going before tarried for us at _____" (Acts 20:5)
26 "Adonijah, Bigvai, _____" (Nehemiah 10:16)
28 Knowledge
32 "_____ the dogs came and licked his sores" (Luke 16:21)
33 Plain of _____, at the end of Canaan
35 Feel in one's bones

by Tonya Vilhauer

36 "Repent ye, and _____ the gospel" (Mark 1:15)
37 Wear away
38 Growth on rocks
39 Consecrate
41 "The dream was _____ unto Pharaoh" (Genesis 41:32)
42 "The going up to _____, which is by Ibleam" (2 Kings 9:27)
44 Be on guard
48 Mutineer
50 "At Bilhah, and at Ezem, and at _____" (1 Chronicles 4:29)
53 Construe
55 WB sitcom
58 Actress Gardner
60 Some

97

ACROSS

1 "Now _____ was straitly shut up because of the children of Israel" (Joshua 6:1)

7 "Doth his _____ fail for evermore?" (Psalm 77:8)

14 Enthusiastic spirit (Fr.)

15 Filmstar Gardner

17 Used a telephone's rotary disk

18 "The heart also of the _____ shall understand knowledge" (Isaiah 32:4)

19 "So he _____ during the harvest and has nothing" (Proverbs 20:4 NASB)

21 Land surrounded by water east of New York City (abbr.)

22 High office command (abbr.)

23 Hesitation syllable

24 Middle East governor

26 Process for metals and ores

28 "But the name of the wicked shall _____" (Proverbs 10:7)

29 "And Moses said, I will now turn _____, and see this great sight" (Exodus 3:3)

31 "Timotheus my workfellow, and _____, and Jason" (Romans 16:21)

34 "For if any be a hearer of the word, and not a _____" (James 1:23)

36 "The vultures also be gathered, every one with her _____" (Isaiah 34:15)

37 "But _____ rose up to flee unto Tarshish from the presence of the LORD" (Jonah 1:3)

39 Dormitory adviser (abbr.)

40 Market of Christian books (abbr.)

41 "Let's beat up some old man, _____ some old woman" (Proverbs 1:11 MSG)

42 "Provide things _____ in the sight of all men" (Romans 12:17)

46 "_____ and saffron, calamus and cinnamon" (Song of Solomon 4:14 NIV)

49 "Come unto me, all ye that _____ and are heavy laden" (Matthew 11:28) (var.)

50 "Bind. . .the ephod with _____ of blue" (Exodus 28:28) (2 words)

52 Pig's home

54 Thirteenth letter of the Greek alphabet

55 "There shall _____ strange god be in thee" (Psalm 81:9)

56 Great Lake

57 "You can tame a _____" (James 3:7 MSG)

59 "Upon the thumb of his right hand, and upon the great _____ of his right foot" (Leviticus 14:28)

61 Fifth note on the scale

63 Knocked out of the ballpark (abbr.)

64 "Plucked _____ by the roots" (Jude 1:12)

65 "Behold, there was a swarm of _____" (Judges 14:8)

67 Evil Roman emperor (Acts 25:21 NASB, note)

70 "Does he not. . .plant. . ._____ within its area?" (Isaiah 28:25 NASB)

72 Includes the Pentateuch (abbr.)

74 "For there is no _____ of persons with God" (Romans 2:11)

77 Roman Christian (Romans 16:11)

78 Greek with Paul (Galatians 2:3)

DOWN

1 "Before the wilderness of _____" (2 Chronicles 20:16)

2 Shem's son (Genesis 10:22)

3 Belonging to the Egyptian sun god

4 "The land shall be divided for an _____ according to the number of names" (Numbers 26:53)

5 "Slack _____ and sloppy work are as bad as vandalism" (Proverbs 18:9 MSG)

6 "And to rule _____ the day" (Genesis 1:18)

8 Nutrition professional (abbr.)

9 "Of bread, and one cake of _____ bread" (Exodus 29:23)

10 Posted

11 White Sox are there (abbr.)

12 "Taste and _____ that the LORD is good" (Psalm 34:8)

13 "Now these are the generations of Esau, who is _____" (Genesis 36:1)

by Marijane G. Troyer

16 Farming (abbr.)
20 Army draft (abbr.)
25 A pout (Fr.)
27 "There was a man of mount Ephraim, whose name was _____" (Judges 17:1)
29 "The whole earth was _____, gaping at the Beast" (Revelation 13:3 MSG)
30 "Should he _____ with unprofitable talk?" (Job 15:3)
32 Wesley's denomination today (abbr.)
33 Trucker sits here
35 A rock east of Jordan (Isaiah 10:26)
37 Book after Joshua
38 "She was found with child of the _____" (Matthew 1:18) (2 words)
41 Title of courtesy to a man (abbr.)
43 South America's opposite (abbr.)
44 "The priests, did blow with the _____" (1 Chronicles 15:24)
45 "Give me your _____ and compass" (Psalm 43:3 MSG)

47 Hightop bird's nest
48 "So _____ maids and her chamberlains" (Esther 4:4)
51 British water closet
53 Asian plant or shrub
58 Fast first-aid spot (abbr.)
60 Shem's great-grandson (Genesis 10:21)
62 Reubenite leader rebelled against Moses (Numbers 16:1)
66 Emergency call
68 Second tone of a musical scale
69 "And God _____ Balaam" (Numbers 23:4)
71 Person coming of age (abbr.)
73 Poet Eliot
75 Mathematical 3.142
76 Symbol for element with atomic number 29

98

ACROSS

1 Eshek's son (1 Chronicles 8:39)
7 "_____ with fire" (Exodus 12:8)
12 "Fathers found no _____" (Acts 7:11)
14 David's son (2 Samuel 3:5)
16 One of the king's chamberlains (Esther 4:5)
18 Cease to live
19 Hushim's father (Genesis 46:23)
20 Likewise
21 "_____, my lord" (Numbers 12:11)
23 Village in the lowlands of Judah (Joshua 15:34)
25 _____ and now
26 "Bread and pottage of _____" (Genesis 25:34)
28 "The _____ of the door" (Ezekiel 41:2)
29 No matter which
30 Chapter (abbr.) (var.)
33 Belonging to Jezebel's husband
37 Sacred
39 Jahdai's son (1 Chronicles 2:47)
40 Shammah's father (2 Samuel 23:11)
41 Levi's son (Genesis 46:11)
42 Crash into
43 Enlighten
46 Jewish divorce
47 Covetous
49 Gibeonite (1 Chronicles 12:4)
52 "I will make my covenant between me and _____" (Genesis 17:2)
53 Ogre
54 "Naphtali is a _____ let loose" (Genesis 49:21)
55 Seasoned

DOWN

2 Village in the mountains of Judah (Joshua 15:52)
3 Aaron and _____ held up Moses' hands (Exodus 17:12)
4 Take advantage of
5 Grand
6 Margin
7 Shema's son (1 Chronicles 2:44)
8 Er's brother (Numbers 26:19)
9 "The _____ of violence is in their hands" (Isaiah 59:6)
10 "In a portion of the lawgiver, was he _____" (Deuteronomy 33:21)
11 Type of wave
13 "Put off thy _____ from off thy feet" (Exodus 3:5)
15 "Take thee a _____" (Ezekiel 4:1)
17 Center
19 Smashed
22 Paper attacher
24 Clear
25 "He was _____ than any of the people" (1 Samuel 9:2)
27 "Breathed _____ his nostrils" (Genesis 2:7)
28 "It will surely be a _____ unto thee" (Exodus 23:33)
30 "He gave him a _____" (Genesis 28:6)
31 Ishmael's mother
32 Jehoadah's son (1 Chronicles 8:36)
34 Hammedatha was one (Esther 3:1)
35 Sopater was from here (Acts 20:4)
36 "All the craftsmen and _____" (2 Kings 24:14)
38 "_____ blessed Elkanah and his wife" (1 Samuel 2:20)
41 "They passing by _____" (Acts 16:8)
43 Paradise
44 Stained
45 "Take a lump of _____" (2 Kings 20:7)
48 Naaman's brother (Genesis 46:21)
50 Abbreviation for last Old Testament book
51 Insect

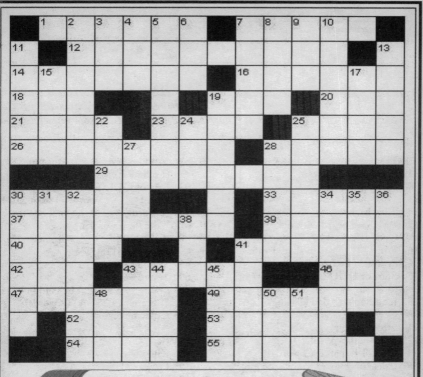

by Sarah Lagerquist Simmons

99

Why Worry

*Do not be anxious about anything,
but in everything, by prayer and petition,
with thanksgiving, present your requests to God.*

PHILIPPIANS 4:6 NIV

ACROSS

1 Speak pompously
6 Lampoon
11 _____ culpa
14 Turn back
15 "We have heard with our _____ God" (Psalm 44:1) (2 words)
16 "Your _____ men shall dream dreams" (Joel 2:28)
17 Start of **QUOTE** (1 Peter 5:7 NIV) (3 words)
19 Jehoshaphat's dad (1 Kings 22:41)
20 Copycat
21 Street shader
22 Body makeup? (pl.)
24 **QUOTE**, part 2 (2 words)
28 Uncle of note
31 "Lights _____"
32 Entourage
36 Renders harmless
38 Make a lap
39 Not specific (abbr.)
40 "Forgetteth what manner of _____ was" (James 1:24) (2 words)
41 **QUOTE**, part 3
42 "_____ me great works" (Ecclesiastes 2:4) (2 words)
43 "Service, _____ the Lord" (Ephesians 6:7) (2 words)
44 "Unto us a _____ is given" (Isaiah 9:6)
45 "Have seen his _____ the east" (Matthew 2:2) (2 words)
46 Beveled edge
48 Old N.R.C.
49 Dictator Amin
50 **QUOTE**, part 4 (2 words)
53 "And many shall fall down _____" (Daniel 11:26)
56 Apres-_____
57 Lady's man

61 "And he gave _____ unto me" (Psalm 77:1)
62 End of **QUOTE** (3 words)
66 "But I _____ worm" (Psalm 22:6) (2 words)
67 "The flesh was yet between their teeth, _____ was chewed" (Numbers 11:33)
68 Wading bird
69 Young man
70 "Were _____ that he could not see" (1 Samuel 4:15 NIV) (2 words)
71 Cubic meter

DOWN

1 Killer whale
2 Gather
3 Church area
4 Neon _____ , tropical fish
5 "Shimei son of _____, in Benjamin" (1 Kings 4:18 NIV)
6 "Buy the truth, and _____ not" (Proverbs 23:23) (2 words)
7 "_____ that thou owest" (Matthew 18:28) (2 words)
8 Granada gold
9 Corvallis college (abbr.)
10 Had a "senior moment"
11 Be in pain
12 Word in a threat
13 Feminine name (pl.)
18 Luxury car model
23 Conundrum
25 Alaska port
26 Fit
27 "_____ ye have not, because ye ask not" (James 4:2)
28 Poison ivy kin
29 "He planteth _____, and the rain doth nourish" (Isaiah 44:14) (2 words)

by David K. Shortess

30 Devilfish
33 "Jacob, Come _____ pray thee" (Genesis 27:21) (2 words)
34 Annulled
35 Nicholas Gage book
37 Equilateral parallelograms (var.)
38 What we all do, since Adam
41 Israeli dance
42 "With the scab, and with the _____" (Deuteronomy 28:27)
44 "Just a _____"
45 "And _____ there be any wicked way in me" (Psalm 139:24) (2 words)
47 Receives stolen property
48 Seeks permission (2 words)
51 "Of what _____ money in the hand of a fool" (Proverbs 17:16 NIV) (2 words)
52 White heron

53 "Set me as a _____ upon thine heart" (Song of Solomon 8:6)
54 "Eli, Eli, _____ sabachthani" (Matthew 27:46)
55 "And when king _____ the Canaanite" (Numbers 21:1)
58 Brontë's Jane
59 Jordan's Queen _____
60 Something to carry
63 "Blessed _____ the pure in heart" (Matthew 5:8)
64 Not working (abbr.)
65 Words of surprise

100

ACROSS

1 Offspring
5 Harm
10 Joshua's father
11 Shuthelah's son (Numbers 26:36)
13 Littlest
14 "Who can stand before the children of _____" (Deuteronomy 9:2)
17 Deed
19 Baruch's father (Jeremiah 32:12)
20 Not a Jew
22 Shobal's son (Genesis 36:23)
23 Before Philippians (abbr.)
25 "All that dwelt at Lydda and _____" (Acts 9:35)
26 "As an oak whose leaf _____" (Isaiah 1:30)
29 Hodesh's son (1 Chronicles 8:9–10)
31 A city of the inheritance of Benjamin (Joshua 18:28)
34 Type of blade or skate
36 Abner's son (1 Chronicles 27:21)
38 "That which groweth of _____ own accord" (Leviticus 25:5)
39 Levi's son (Genesis 46:11)
40 Before Proverbs (abbr.)
41 "Heshbon, and Elealeh, and _____" (Numbers 32:3)
43 "The LORD that _____ thee" (Exodus 15:26)
45 "_____, she is broken" (Ezekiel 26:2)
46 Melchi's father (Luke 3:28)
47 "There came a man from _____" (2 Kings 4:42)

DOWN

2 "Every one that useth milk is _____" (Hebrews 5:13)
3 Before Deuteronomy (abbr.)
4 "They _____ upon me" (Psalm 35:16)
5 "The LORD _____ in us" (Numbers 14:8)
6 "These _____ the generations" (Genesis 2:4)
7 "Carpenters, and _____" (2 Samuel 5:11)
8 "Go to the _____, thou sluggard" (Proverbs 6:6)
9 "Like a _____ or a swallow" (Isaiah 38:14)
12 "Hast thou _____ of the tree" (Genesis 3:11)
15 Ishamael's firstborn (Genesis 25:13)
16 Jephunneh's brother (1 Chronicles 7:38)
17 Tune
18 "Though thou _____ thyself with crimson" (Jeremiah 4:30)
21 Weeds
24 Via
27 A town of Judah near Shochoh (1 Samuel 17:1)
28 "As an oven _____ by the baker" (Hosea 7:4)
30 As well
32 Jahath's son (1 Chronicles 4:2)
33 "A _____, and a harp" (1 Samuel 10:5)
34 "Jesus was _____" (Mark 16:9)
35 "The _____ shall come" (John 11:48)
36 "Kedemoth, Mephaath" (Joshua 13:18 NKJV)
37 The brother of Goliath the Gittite (1 Chronicles 20:5)
42 "The valley of _____" (Psalm 84:6)
44 "Should thy _____ make men" (Job 11:3)

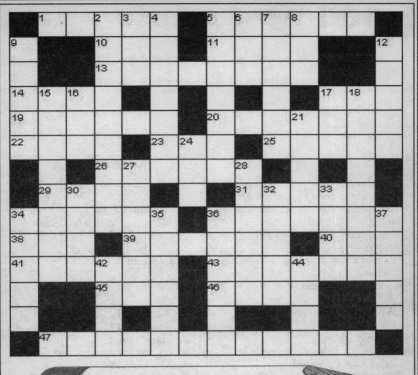

by *Sarah Lagerquist Simmons*

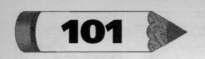

101

Some Parables of Jesus

And with many such parables spake he the word unto them,
as they were able to hear it.

MARK 4:33

ACROSS

1 "Beau _____"
6 Part of centerpiece
10 Belonging to good king of Judah
14 Top story?
15 Smidgen
16 Where Jesus met the Samaritan woman
17 "So that a bow of _____ is broken" (2 Samuel 22:35)
18 Care facility workers (abbr.)
19 _____ bellum
20 **PARABLE** (Luke 18:2–8) (2 words)
23 Architect I.M. _____
24 "For _____ stiffnecked people" (Exodus 34:9) (3 words)
25 **PARABLE** (Luke 10:30–37) (2 words)
32 Money, biblically
33 Radio host Limbaugh
34 Test for some seniors (abbr.)
37 Tolkien's bad guys
38 Queen of _____, Solomon's guest
40 "And fashioned it with a graving _____" (Exodus 32:4)
41 "Be prepared" organization (abbr.)
42 Chow _____
43 "How _____ that day will be" (Jeremiah 30:7 NIV)
44 **PARABLE** (Matthew 25:31–46) (3 words)
48 "_____ sending you out like lambs" (Luke 10:3 NIV) (3 words)
50 Keats product
51 Start of **PARABLE** (Matthew 13:3–9) (4 words)
59 Left _____, in Paris
60 Despise
61 "How right they are to _____ you" (Song of Solomon 1:4 NIV)
62 S-shaped molding
63 Sea eagle
64 "That the aged men be _____" (Titus 2:2)
65 Comedian Foxx
66 "As _____ man who casteth firebrands" (Proverbs 26:18) (2 words)
67 Cornered

DOWN

1 "I cry out, I _____ and pant" (Isaiah 42:14 NIV)
2 Major ending
3 Follower of young or old alike
4 Bow and ascot
5 Solar, for one
6 "Then you will become their _____" (Habakkuk 2:7 NIV)
7 Top drawer
8 Funny man Laurel, familiarly
9 "On the _____ of Eden" (Genesis 4:16)
10 "And we eagerly _____ Savior" (Philippians 3:20 NIV) (2 words)
11 "Is the _____ message by the hand of a fool" (Proverbs 26:6 NIV) (3 words)
12 Choir members
13 "And they _____ bullock" (1 Samuel 1:25) (2 words)
21 Salt _____, biblical body
22 Away or back (comb. form)
25 Shapeless mass
26 Belonging to you and me
27 "I have _____ the death of all the persons of thy father's house" (1 Samuel 22:22)
28 Doctors (abbr.)
29 "Condemned to die in the _____"

by David K. Shortess

(1 Corinthians 4:9 NIV)
30 "There's the _____"
31 O.T. book
35 Lopsided win
36 Building additions
38 Understand
39 With it
40 "And she threw in _____ mites"
(Mark 12:42)
42 Same, in Strasbourg
43 Get older rapidly (2 words)
45 Peddled
46 "I have _____ of you"
(1 Corinthians 12:21 NKJV)
(2 words)
47 Banned insecticide (abbr.)
48 Eva of "Green Acres"
49 Missouri river
52 Flightless bird

53 Cozy
54 Sicilian spewer
55 "By this time there is a bad _____"
(John 11:39 NIV)
56 "And put on him a scarlet _____"
(Matthew 27:28)
57 "Hast thou eaten of the _____"
(Genesis 3:11)
58 "Into the _____ of swine"
(Matthew 8:31)

Puzzle 1

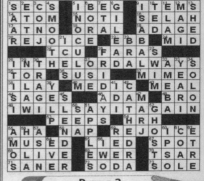

Puzzle 2

Puzzle 3

Puzzle 4

Puzzle 5

Puzzle 6

Puzzle 7

Puzzle 8

Puzzle 9

Puzzle 10

Puzzle 11

Puzzle 12

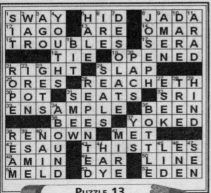

PUZZLE 13

PUZZLE 14

PUZZLE 15

PUZZLE 16

PUZZLE 17

PUZZLE 18

PUZZLE 19

PUZZLE 20

PUZZLE 21

PUZZLE 22

PUZZLE 23

PUZZLE 24

Puzzle 25

Puzzle 26

Puzzle 27

Puzzle 28

Puzzle 29

Puzzle 30

Puzzle 31

| N E O N | | C O D S | | P A S T A |

```
N E O N ■ C O D S ■ P A S T A
O G R E ■ A V O W ■ O L L A S
E R A S ■ V E N A ■ P L A C E
L E T T H E R E B E L I G H T
S T E ■ E R I E ■ V A N ■ ■ ■
■ P A N T ■ H E R ■ F O E ■ ■
A M O L D ■ D A N ■ A I R Y ■
J E S U S S A I D I A M T H E
A M O S ■ A W N ■ G A S E S ■
R O N ■ B Y E ■ T A N S ■ ■ ■
■ ■ T E T ■ S O R E ■ C P A ■
L I G H T O F T H E W O R L D
I N N E R ■ L E A N ■ R O A D
S N A F U ■ A N N A ■ M A T E
T O R T E ■ T O G S ■ E K E D
```

PUZZLE 31

Puzzle 32

```
L A M A ■ D E B T ■ I B S E N
E B E R ■ E V E R ■ S E E T O
A D A R ■ P I N E ■ A S N E R
P I T I F U L ■ T R A I T S ■
■ ■ V A T S ■ ■ ■ I C E ■ ■ ■
M I S E R Y ■ B A D ■ G A A L
A S I D E ■ J U D E ■ E S L I
S U E ■ L O R D S ■ S O N ■ ■
S A V E ■ A N N S ■ S T O N E
A H E R ■ S A T ■ P U R S E S
■ ■ ■ E S T ■ ■ ■ L A C E ■ ■
A C C E S S ■ A S H A M E D ■
A G A T E ■ O A R S ■ D A R A
S E V E R ■ U R G E ■ E D A R
S E E D S ■ L I E D ■ R E N T
```

PUZZLE 32

Puzzle 33

```
J A S H E N ■ V I L E S T ■ ■
■ H E A V E ■ A L I V E ■ ■ ■
■ F O W L E R ■ L I F E R S ■
M A L ■ T R I ■ L E E ■ P H I
E L I S ■ A G E ■ P E O R ■ ■
A S A P H ■ H A Y ■ M A N N A
H E B R E W ■ L ■ R E S T E D
■ ■ I D O L A T E R S ■ ■ ■ ■
C H A N G E ■ ■ D E E M E D ■
R A N G E ■ B I T ■ S T O R E
A L A S ■ E A R ■ H A R T ■ ■
F A N ■ A R A ■ I T S ■ B E E
T H I T H E R ■ E Y E L I D S
Y ■ A H E A D ■ T R E A T ■ T
■ S H E R D S ■ H E R M E S ■
```

PUZZLE 33

Puzzle 34

```
M A O ■ E N S ■ A ■ A M B E R
O ■ S A S ■ T E M P L E ■ U ■
S ■ U M P I R E ■ L A ■ A C E
E L ■ M Y R A ■ C A S T L E ■
S E M I ■ P L A Y ■ A T O P ■
A P E D ■ A L A ■ M A ■ E ■ ■
A V ■ L E N T I L ■ B E R E A
■ E G ■ F E A R E D ■ S S ■ ■
S N O W Y ■ B ■ D A R E ■ T I
H ■ S O ■ B L T ■ R A M ■ H ■
E C H O ■ S E A M ■ M E E K ■
E E L S ■ T ■ O ■ S A ■ R I ■
T O N ■ O N ■ J O S H U A ■ N
E R ■ N O M A D ■ E S P ■ G ■
A L O E S ■ A ■ Y O D ■ P P S
```

PUZZLE 34

Puzzle 35

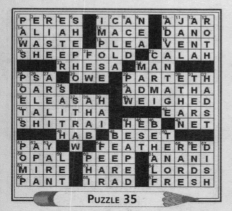

```
P E R E S ■ I C A N ■ A J A R
A L I A H ■ M A C E ■ D A N O
W A S T E ■ P L E A ■ V E N T
S H E E P F O L D ■ C A L A H
■ ■ ■ R H E S A ■ M A N ■ ■ ■
P S A ■ O W E ■ P A R T E T H
O A R S ■ A D M A T H A ■ ■ ■
E L E A S A H ■ W E I G H E D
■ ■ T A L I T H A ■ E A R S ■
S H I T R A I ■ H E B ■ N E T
■ ■ H A B ■ B E S E T ■ ■ ■ ■
P A Y ■ W ■ F E A T H E R E D
O P A L ■ P E E P ■ A N A N I
M I R E ■ H A R E ■ L O R D S
P A N T ■ I R A D ■ F R E S H
```

PUZZLE 35

Puzzle 36

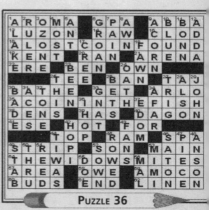

```
A R O M A ■ G P A ■ A B B A
L U Z O N ■ R A W ■ C L O D
A L O S T C O I N F O U N D
K E N T ■ R A N ■ A R E N A
E R E ■ B E N ■ O W N ■ ■ ■
■ ■ ■ T E E ■ B A N ■ T A J
B A T H E ■ G E T ■ A R L O
A C O I N I N T H E F I S H
D E N S ■ H A S ■ D A G O N
E S E ■ H O T ■ F O R ■ ■ ■
■ ■ ■ T O P ■ R A M ■ S P A
S T R I P ■ S O N ■ M A I N
T H E W I D O W S M I T E S
A R E A ■ O W E ■ A M O C O
B U D S ■ E N D ■ L I N E N
```

PUZZLE 36

Puzzle 37

Puzzle 38

Puzzle 39

Puzzle 40

Puzzle 41

Puzzle 42

Puzzle 43

```
K I N D S . H O S T . A B B A
I S A A C . E V E R . B O I L
S H U N A M M I T E . I D E A
H I M . R E A D . A D D E R S
. . S E A M . A S I A . . .
A R T I S T . B L U E N E S S
S H O R T . G O U R D . L I E
N E T S . C H O S E . H E L M
A S A . C L O T H . B A A L E
H A L O H E S H . H E L D A I
. . P E A T . S E A L . . .
M O D E R N . R E E L . G A T
O N A N . S W A L L O W E T H
A C R E . E A S E . T H R E E
B E N D . D Y E D . H O A R Y
```

Puzzle 44

```
T O A D . S O D . S A F E
O L L A . E V E . A B E D
I D O L . M A W . L O V E
L E N A S . L . R I V E N
. R E I N S . G O M E R .
. . A H L A B . . . . .
. R E P E A T E T H . . .
Z E N . T H E . H A B . .
B E L A . H A S . E V E N
E R E C T . I . P R I C E
S E A T . I R I . E L O I
E S S E . N O N . T A M E
T H E E . K I N . O H E L
```

Puzzle 45

```
. G R A C E . M S . D E B T
G N O M E . N E E D . Y E A S
O A H U . R A R E . M E . B C
D T . S T E M . T A . F L O
S . E . J E S U . D O . E N
J E S S O . U R N . L U T E
O V A . W I M P . A G E . S S
Y O R E . C A P S . S O O .
. T N . S E E L . A . R R
Y E . S O . Y E S . R E E F
O R A C L E . T A R . B F A
D . M . A W E D . I V Y . I
E I N . R E C O R D . O A S T
L . O N . S H E D . M U . T H
. S N O W . O R . M E R C Y
```

Puzzle 46

```
B U T . S W I M S . H I R E D
A S H . T O S I T . A M A N A
L E E . A R E N A . R A N D Y
A S F O R M E A N D M Y . .
K A T E . S K I . K U R D
. R A N T . M E N N O W
W H O . N A O M I . N O B L E
H O U S E H O L D W E W I L L
I S T A Y . I S I A M . D A T
L E A V E N . D R Y S . .
E A S E . O A R . E S T A
. S E R V E T H E L O R D .
I S G O D . A S S I T . R O O
A N A M E . I T A R E . E A R
S O M E N . N A R E S . S S N
```

Puzzle 47

```
L O F T Y . S H E P H E R D S
O N E R . S T A R E . L O O M
S C R A B . E N A N . B A C A
T E N C O M M A N D M E N T S
H . E G O . N . A N T . O H
E N . A P P I A N . H E R .
O D E D . E L . N T . E . H
S E G U B . E A T . P L A Z A
E S E K . P A S H . L . B A R
A T B E E R S H E B A . S I D
R . S O U . M O T H E R . A
M O T E . U R I . N O O N . A
E Y E . A D E R . N . E T A M
T E A C H . S O B E R . I F O
E D R E I . N . T H I N G S
```

Puzzle 48

```
N E A H . N A H U M . A G A R
U L L A . A M A N A . V I L E
R I O T . H E Z I R . E L I S
S A T A N . N O T . P R O V E
E S H C O L . R . J A S H E N
. H O O K . B A R E .
L O T . N O I S O M E . N U T
E W E S . S N A I L . H O R I
W E N . M E D D L E D . D I P
. N E T S . S C U M .
P A S E A H . M . H E A T E D
A R I E L . H E M . S H A V E
T I E D . N A H A M . A R E A
H E G E . E L I Z A . T E N T
S H E D . H I R E D . H A T H
```

PUZZLE 49

PUZZLE 50

PUZZLE 51

PUZZLE 52

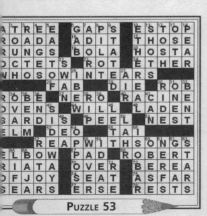

PUZZLE 53

PUZZLE 54

Puzzle 55

Puzzle 56

Puzzle 57

Puzzle 58

Puzzle 59

Puzzle 60

Puzzle 61

```
D E E D S . S H E . . . J O H
U Z Z I A . W A Y . E B O N Y
E R R E D . O W E . V E N O M
S I A . L U R K . T I N . N .
. D Y E D . . B E L O N G . .
B A N I . L . S E M . A R A .
A R O E R . A M R A M I T E S
Y E S T E R D A Y . A B I A H
. L E H I . I L L . W H O S E
H I S . B E L . . A N E R . .
. . D I A L . D E A R . . . .
S A T A N S . G O D S . B A T
A M E R C E . A V E N G E T H
M O N T H . B E R A . R E U .
E N D S . . W A S . H A I R S
```

PUZZLE 61

Puzzle 62

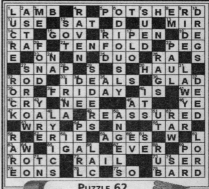

```
L A M B . R . P O T S H E R D
U S E . S A T . D . U . M I R
C T . G O V . R I P E N . D E
R A F . T E N F O L D . P E G
E . O N . N . D U O . R A S .
. S N A P . S . S . H A U L .
R O D . I D E A L S . G L A D
O R . F R I D A Y . I S . W E
C R Y . N E E . A T . Y E . .
K O A L A . R E A S S U R E D
. W R Y . P S . N . T A R . .
R . E R I E . A G E S . W . L
A W . I G A L . E V E R . P O
R O T C . R A I L . U S E R .
E O N S . L C . S O . B A R D
```

PUZZLE 62

Puzzle 63

```
G N A W . G O R G E . G I R L
R A R E . A W A R D . A B I A
O M E R . B I N E A . U Z Z I
P E L T . A N G E R . L A P S
E L I . R . G E T . L . N A H
. Y . G U N S . B E G . H . .
. T R I A L . H E A L S . . .
. H U N T . . S T E P . . . .
. L A B O U R . O T H E R S .
G A D . U R I . V I E . E T C
A D D . S E T . E R R . A R A
G I A H . H E R . A D I N . .
S N E E R . M A R . A S I D E
. G U N D . A S A . N I N E .
. S A S . H E N . T A G . . .
```

PUZZLE 63

Puzzle 64

```
. M A I M E D . A P A R T . .
W . R E B A . B A R . . . . W
H . . A D E R . I S A . . . R
E R E . I N T E N T . J . O .
E U N I C E . P O O R E S T .
L E D . I Z E H A R . H U E .
. A N E M . M . P O P . . . .
P R O V E R B . G U A R D . .
R A M A . R E W A R D E R . .
I C E . A S A H E L . A M I .
E A R . S O C I A L . H E N .
S . I S L E . S E A . . K . .
T . R I E . E R R . . . S . .
C O U R S E . L Y C I A . . .
```

PUZZLE 64

Puzzle 65

```
H A R E . O S H A . C A R E T
A V I D . S L A M . E D I N A
D O V E . C A W S . T E N O R
S W A N C U C K O W E A G L E
T I L . I L K . A R R . . . .
. . A V E . A S T A . H A M .
S W A M I . A S H E . I O T A
P E L I C A N H E R O N B A T
A R I D . U T E S . C R O N E
R E D . A D E N . S T E . . .
. . S K I . A M A . H E N . .
R A V E N O W L V U L T U R E
A R E N A . R O A D . I R A N
D U R O C . A B I G . M O T E
S T O R K . P O L E . E N O S
```

PUZZLE 65

Puzzle 66

```
. S L A C K . J . S E E D .
N A A R A N . A . U P S E T .
E M P T I E R S . A H A V A .
C U P . N A I O T H . I I M .
H E E L . D E N Y . L A C E .
O L D E R . . . C H A S E D .
. . . P A T E . H E W . S . .
. . N E C E S S I T Y . . . .
F E A R E S T . C H E Z I B .
E L I S . T H O U . R I S E .
W I N . A . E A S E . M A D .
. A . S O R T . Z A R A . . .
J D G . P U S H . E X A C T .
A . E S T . S . M E N S . . .
```

PUZZLE 66

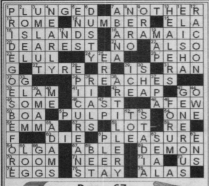

PUZZLE 67

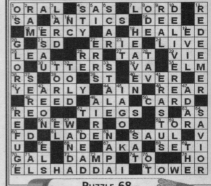

PUZZLE 68

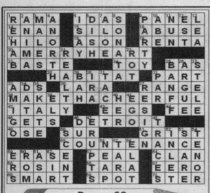

PUZZLE 69

PUZZLE 70

PUZZLE 71

PUZZLE 72

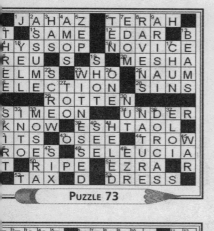

Puzzle 73

Puzzle 74

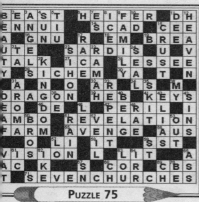

Puzzle 75

Puzzle 76

Puzzle 77

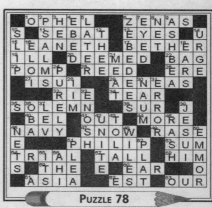

Puzzle 78

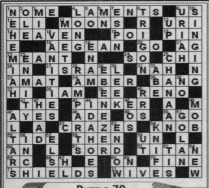

PUZZLE 79

PUZZLE 80

PUZZLE 81

PUZZLE 82

PUZZLE 83

PUZZLE 84

PUZZLE 85

PUZZLE 86

PUZZLE 87

PUZZLE 88

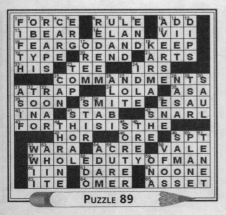

PUZZLE 89

PUZZLE 90

PUZZLE 91

O N A M		S H E M		A S H A N

ONAM SHEM ASHAN
CORE HENA STAGE
RIOT UNDO SINEW
ASSENT SCOURGES
NEEDETH HUR
ZEAL TEMANI
CHARITY DEDANIM
HODIAH WAR LIGN
ELEPH SON MESHA
WANE THE RISETH
NAE OIL
IRA OUTSIDE SHE
VOMIT HUL TOPAZ
APACE ARE UNITE
HELED RED METER

PUZZLE 92

THE LORD DISH
SHEPHERD DO CAW
AY HAND AWES ME
Y OR TENSE LIMB
KRAMER ALPINE
GO IAN S LAP RS
ENEMY HOT SST T
BK COMFORT SI
A FLO SAT URIEL
LB AMI R TRA AL
RODENT SHEBAM
COWL CANOE BA H
UK ELAN NEBO AI
PEP IS GOODNESS
NAME MIFF IMP

PUZZLE 93

ROBES ELEAD
S WASTENESS R
MANGER DATA U
ARE KISON HID
SORT PAW REND
HESED Y PALSY
R BED JOH T
NISAN T PALAL
ITCH TAR BANI
NEH SEGUB ICE
T OSEE LEADER S
OINTMENTS
ELATH DOETH

PUZZLE 94

LARAS DISC FISH
ELOPE ANNA ATTU
ITARE DOAS TEAM
FORIKNOWTHATMY
LEO CITY
ARA RATCHET SAD
HOMO HAH RAMADA
OPIUM JOB RARER
PESTER SUE TAPE
EST RESERVE ITS
ELBE ILA
REDEEMERLIVETH
SONG KINE SOUSA
OBIE ATOP HIRAM
WEDS HESS ADORE

PUZZLE 95

SCORE SEWETH
F ONAN ALIVE H
ABNERS DEFENSE
MAD EUROPE DIP
ISUI EACH MEAH
NOISE D BATHE
ENTRY ISSACHAR
AENON TH
FACES A SIDON
OBAL THIN REBA
WIT WHALES BED
LATCHET ELIADA
S LOOSE DIRT B
TERMED SPUED

PUZZLE 96

ONES BAALS JOHA
RASH ADNAH OREM
PATE ADAMI SALE
ARAM LINES ATER
HATETH ICHABOD
HEBREW HADAR
SEORIM KID M
M RAMS S N BOW
MOD SODDEN GERA
OREB NOON MULES
SEVER MUST RIOT
SHOWER BEOR EVE
TABEAL LEAVE
BEREAVE ABNER
ELDAD DAY

Puzzle 97

```
J E R I C H O   P R O M I S E
E L A N   A V A   D I A L E D
R A S H   B E G S   L I   E O
U M   E M I R   S M E L T   M
E   R O T   A S I D E   R
L U C I U S   G   C   D O E R
  M A T E   J O N A H   R A
C B A   M U G   H O N E S T
L   N A R D   E   L A B O R
A L A C E   G   S T Y   N U
N O   E R I E   T I G E R   M
T O E   I   S O H   H R   U P
E   B E E S   N E R O   M   E
R Y E   O T   R E S P E C T
N A R C I S S U S   T I T U S
```

Puzzle 98

```
  J E H U S H   R O A S T
T   S U S T E N A N C E   S
I   T H R E A M   H A T A C H
D I E   T   D A N   T O O
A L A S   E N A M   H E R E
L E N T I L E S   S I D E S
    A N Y T H I N G
C H A P T   E   A H A B S
H A L L O W E D   R E G E M
A G E E   L   M E R A R I
R A M   E D I F Y   G E T
G R E E D Y   I S M A I A H
E   T H E E   G I A N T S
  H I N D   S A L T E D
```

Puzzle 99

```
O R A T E   S P O O F   M E A
R E P E L   E A R S O   O L D
C A S T A L L Y O U R   A S A
A P E R   E L M   G E N E S
    A N X I E T Y O N
S A M   O U T   R E T I N U E
U N A R M S   S I T   G E N L
M A N H E   H I M   I M A D E
A S T O   S O N   S T A R I N
C H A M F E R   A E C   I D I
    B E C A U S E H E
S L A I N   S K I   G E N T
E A R   C A R E S F O R Y O U
A M A   E R E I T   H E R O N
L A D   S E T S O   S T E R E
```

Puzzle 100

```
  Y O U N G   D A M A G E
C   N U N   E R A N     E
R   S M A L L E S T     A
A N A K   S   I   O   A C T
N E R I A H   G E N T I L E
E B A L   E P H   S A R O N
  A   F A D E T H   R   T
  J E U Z   R   E L E P H
R O L L E R   J A A S I E L
I T S   K O H A T H   P S A
S H E B A M   H E A L E T H
E   A H A   A D D I   M
N   C   N   Z   E   I
  B A A L S H A L I S H A
```

Puzzle 101

```
G E S T E   V A S E   A S A S
A T T I C   I O T A   W E L L
S T E E L   C N A S   A N T E
P E R S I S T E N T W I D O W
    P E I     I T I S A
G O O D S A M A R I T A N
L U C R E   R U S H   G R E
O R C S   S H E B A   T O O L
B S A   M E I N   A W F U L
  S H E E P A N D G O A T S
G O I A M     O D E
A S O W E R W E N T F O R T H
B A N K   H A T E   A D O R E
O G E E   E R N E   S O B E R
R E D D   A M A D   T R E E D
```